The Art of
Turkish Cooking

From Spanish salsas to Russian pirogi, from Israeli delicacies to Hungarian pastries, **HIPPOCRENE INTERNATIONAL COOKBOOK CLASSICS** provide an array of tantalizing recipes from across the globe.

ALL ALONG THE DANUBE
by Marina Polvay
0491 ISBN 0-7818-0098-6 $11.95pb

A BELGIAN COOKBOOK
by Juliette Elkon
0535 ISBN 0-7818-0461-2 $14.95pb

THE ART OF BRAZILIAN COOKERY
by Dolores Botafogo
0250 ISBN 0-7818-0130-3 $9.95pb

THE JOY OF CHINESE COOKING
by Doreen Yen Hung Feng
0288 ISBN 0-7818-0097-8 $8.95pb

THE BEST OF FINNISH COOKING
by Taimi Previdi
0354 ISBN 0-7818-0284-9 $19.95hc

THE HONEY COOKBOOK
by Maria Lo Pinto
0283 ISBN 0-7818-0149-4 $8.95pb

THE ART OF HUNGARIAN COOKING
by P. Pogany Bennett & V. Clark
0165 ISBN 0-7818-0202-4 $8.95pb

THE ART OF IRISH COOKING
by Monica Sheridan
0335 ISBN 0-7818-0454-X $12.95pb

THE ART OF ISRAELI COOKING
by Chef Aldo Nahoum
O252 ISBN 0-7818-0096-X $9.95pb

THE ART OF PERSIAN COOKING
by Forough Hekmat
0125 ISBN 0-7818-0241-5 $9.95pb

THE BEST OF POLISH COOKING
Revised
by Karen West
1071 ISBN 0-87052-123-3 $8.95pb

POLISH HERITAGE COOKERY
by Robert and Maria Strybel
0241 ISBN 0-7818-0069-2 $35.00hc

OLD WARSAW COOKBOOK
by Rysia
0536 ISBN 0-87052-932-3 $12.95pb

THE BEST OF RUSSIAN COOKING
by Alexandra Kropotkin
0251 ISBN 0-7818-0131-1 $9.95pb

THE BEST OF SMORGASBORD COOKING
by Gerda Simonson
0207 ISBN 0-7818-0407-8 $14.95pb

A SPANISH FAMILY COOKBOOK
by Juan and Susan Serrano
0249 ISBN 0-7818-0129-X $19.95hc
0245 ISBN 0-7818-0193-1 $9.95pb

THE BEST OF UKRAINIAN CUISINE
by Bohdan Zahny
0124 ISBN 0-7818-0240-7 $19.95pb

Coming Soon . . .
THE CUISINE OF ARMENIA
THE BEST OF CZECH COOKING

Prices subject to change. **TO PURCHASE HIPPOCRENE BOOKS** contact your local bookstore, or write to: HIPPOCRENE BOOKS, 171 Madison Avenue, New York, NY 10016. Please enclose a check or money order, adding $5.00 shipping (UPS) for first book and .50 for each additional book.

The Art of Turkish Cooking

Neşet Eren

HIPPOCRENE BOOKS
New York

For information, address:
HIPPOCRENE BOOKS, INC.
171 Madison Avenue
New York, NY 10016

ISBN 0-7818-0201-6

Printed in the United States of America.

Author's Note

This book includes the best recipes of the Turkish cuisine. Renowned as the delight of the Ottoman Sultans, historically it rivals that of the Roman epicures. Contemporarily, it embraces the favorite dishes of many Eastern European and Eastern Mediterranean nations, whose gastronomic taste, for more than half a millennium, was inspired by the Imperial Kitchen at the Topkapi Palace in Istanbul.

Foreword

I owe this book to friends in England and in America. Year after year, as they kept returning to our table, their repeated insistence convinced me that I had to undertake the task. I also owe it to all those visitors who went to Turkey and, after tasting our dishes, publicly expressed a desire to try them in their own homes. Finally, I owe it to my husband, whose chronic worry about his diet could never overcome his yen for the varied delights of Turkish cuisine.

The preparation of the manuscript took more time and care than the cooking of each recipe. I am grateful to affable and ever helpful Selma Ekrem, the dean of Turkish writers in America, for her suggestions concerning the traditions of Turkish cooking.

I am also greatly indebted to Lucy Goldthwaite, a tried and trusted friend, for reading the manuscript and making the necessary changes required for American usage.

Neşet Eren

New York, 1969

Contents

Items marked with an asterisk may be located by consulting the Index.

Introduction

My first recollections of childhood often focus on one kitchen of our historic home where we loved to sneak. It was a huge rectangular room with a wall to wall fireplace, dotted with all sizes of cooking pots from a huge cauldron to a teapot. At one end there was a row of high narrow windows. In the absence of the cooks we loved to pull the table over to the windows in order to stand on it and stretch our heads outside. The walls were filled with rows and rows and rows of shelves stacked with jars of jams, herbs, and spices.

But we loved most the corner where the water pump stood, dripping into a large cauldron in which cucumbers, tomatoes, and watermelons floated to cool. We kept away from the end where a whole lamb or mutton with its head cut off hung from a chain on the high black ceiling. On cold winter days when we could not play outside and the cook would not have us in the kitchen we sat on the service window from which food was passed to the dining room and watched the cook chopping the meat, cutting the vegetables, mixing the herbs.

Our home was the headquarters of the Bektaşi Order of Dervişes of which my family were the heads. We lived in a large mansion on a steep hill overlooking the Bosporus. From my window in Europe I could see across to the houses in Asia. We kept open house day and night to all the members of the sect who came our way. We never knew how many would sit around the table or sleep under the roof. As I think about it now it must have been a veritable challenge to any cook to cater for a constantly unknown number of guests. And we were supposed to serve a good meal.

For merrymaking the Aşüre* festival topped all. Three days before the festival the tripods in the fireplace were removed to make space for the huge cauldron that was moved from the pantry to the kitchen. How we loved to watch the cook weigh the twenty different ingredients that went into the cauldron for the Noah's Pudding. We jostled each other, eagerly waiting for the opportunity to light the fire. There would be a big scramble among us for pushing the torch under the cauldron and we would all rush out of the kitchen crying, "I did it," "I did it." The fire would burn for a whole day and a whole night, somebody keeping watch constantly stirring the pudding with a wooden spoon with a long handle. We would all take our turns and many a time drop the heavy spoon in the cauldron to be chased away by the cook but to return soon enough.

And then the morning of the festival, Grandfather would descend from upstairs to make his yearly entry into the kitchen. Everybody would stand apart with his hands folded before him and his head bowed, which we children would imitate. Grandfather would speak a prayer, take the spoon, and serve the pudding into a bowl extended by the cook. Thereafter the poor of the village would come and each would get his bowl filled. Messengers with precious porcelain pitchers filled with the pudding would be dispatched to friends.

I also remember most fondly my grandmother, who every spring would take us for a violet hunt on the hills. We would spend a whole morning gathering wild violets which my grandmother would cook into a sweet purple delicacy. This would be kept in jars for the duration of summer and fall and served on special occasions during long wintry evenings. Cold water added to an inch of violet syrup in a glass would make a delectable drink. Those who were served would know that they were the privileged friends of the family.

We loved hiking with the cooks gathering herbs. During the spring the hills of Istanbul are green and yellow and red and purple with a million flowers, herbs, and grasses. Before we were five we all knew how to pick thyme, oregano, and dandelions. I owe my sense of the use of different herbs in cooking to these jaunts.

Then for many years I forgot about kitchens and food, until I married and went to live in Ankara. My husband was a government official and for the first time I had to do my own cooking. I had never thought I would have to face so many problems. I read cookbooks, I followed instructions from friends—I learned a great deal. My husband helped with his suggestions but his were from hearsay, and often helped to make a good dish inedible. I took a course in cooking. But I knew that I lacked the touch, the proficiency of a good cook. Every now and then I would end with a perfect dish which elated my husband's appetite and my own spirit. But consistency, the ability to repeat the same quality, I could never manage.

After a couple of months of diligent application the knowledge that I had arrived burst upon me one Sunday morning. As we woke up late, after an exacting but successful dinner the previous evening for an uncle and aunt known for their meticulousness, my husband said, "Let us not go out today. Let us eat at home." Since our marriage, supposedly to give me a respite but really to indulge his palate for good food, every Sunday, my husband had insisted we have dinner in a restaurant. This was the first Sunday we dined at home. He has not wanted to dine out since then, stubbornly resisting my requests for a weekend holiday from the kitchen. But I have not minded it.

When the Empress Eugénie, the wife of Napoleon III, was in Istanbul as the guest of Sultan Abdulaziz, the Ottoman emperor, she fell in love with eggplant purée, at that time a specialty of the Topkapi Palace. She asked her host if he would allow his chef to teach her cook how to prepare it. The sultan obliged. The next day the French chef requested an audience with the empress and begged to be excused from this impossible task. "I took my book and my scales to the Turkish chef," he said, "and he threw them out. 'An imperial chef,' he told me, 'cooks with his feelings, his eyes, his nose.'" The empress returned to France without the recipe for her favorite dish but the traditional eggplant purée of the Imperial Topkapi cuisine was named Her Majesty's Favorite and to this day in Turkey it is known as the Hünkar Beğendi*.

Thus the delights of Turkish cooking were known only to those who visited Turkey and to those who were entertained in Turkish homes. But now that the recipe book and the measuring cup have captured the magic of the professional instinct the delights of Turkish cooking can be easily duplicated across the oceans, over the mountains, many leagues away from Turkey. And this is what this book aims to do.

The Turkish peninsula boasts six millennia of ancient and modern cultures. It is the cradle of many civilizations. Peoples from many directions and diverse climes have flocked to its green valleys and blue seas. They have bred many empires and then settled to enjoy the pleasures of its climate, the delights of its many products. The Turkish cuisine is the result of this rich historical experience, fertilized by centuries of continuous crossbreedings from East and West and sustained by an infinite variety of fish, meats, vegetables, and fruits.

Many of the well-known national cuisines rely on one basic element. For instance, French cuisine is based on the sauce. Pasta forms the essence of the Italian cuisine. There is, however, no single dominant feature in the Turkish kitchen. Meats, fish, vegetables, pastries, and fruit are cooked in an infinite variety of ways. Eggplant alone can be prepared in at least forty different ways. Variety might catch the imagination but taste is of the essence. Millennia have worked to refine the Turkish palate. In Istanbul the people choose their drinking water as others would choose their wine. A sip suffices to identify the spring from which the water comes. And the proverb says, choose your friend by the taste of his food.

In Turkey you never order peaches. You must specify whether you want Bursa peaches or Izmir peaches. When you want fish you must specify its age. "Çinakok" is a generation younger than "lüfer." "Torik" is a year older than "Palamut." This sensitivity to nuance reflects the Turkish aesthetic approach to food.

Fresh herbs play an important part in Turkish cuisine. They should always be used when called for in a recipe unless dried herbs are designated as a substitute.

The environment where food is consumed acquires utmost importance. Inevitably the table must overlook the sea, or the hills of an inner court. Food must be consumed leisurely as one's eyes feast on the beauties of nature. The "open-air" restaurant or café so characteristic of Continental Europe has its origin in Ottoman Turkey. The outdoor restaurant was brought to Vienna in the seventeenth century by an Austrian ambassador to the Ottoman court, who had enjoyed open-air cafés on the shores of the Bosporus. French "café" was a child of Turkish coffee, which the Ottomans picked up from the southern extremities of their empire, in Arabia, and learned to enjoy after dinner and offer as a token of friendly welcome to their guests.

In view of the literal injunction of the Koran against wines, the Turks, a Muslim people, have developed raki*—distilled from grapes—as their national drink. Raki is colloquially termed lion's milk because of its potent effect. A formal Turkish dinner, even today, begins with raki and a variety of hors d'oeuvres, called meze, spread on the table. It is the hostess with the mostest of mezes who receives the gold medallion.

In secular republican Turkey, wines also grace many a table. Turkey will be recalled as the cradle of the Sultana raisins. The Aegean still abounds with the amphorae from Roman galleys which, loaded with the famed wines of Asia Minor, were caught between Scylla and Charybdis and never made the return trip. A great proportion of the famed Sultanas are today made into delectable wines, a percentage of which is exported to France for blending with French wines.

Turkish cuisine is the most extensively internationalized. For six hundred years the Ottoman Empire spread from the Danube to the tip of the Arabian Peninsula. It bred fourteen independent modern states. The basics of Turkish cuisine today prevail from the Balkans to the shores of North Africa; Greeks and Turks, for instance, will be found to relish in many instances the same dishes. The further south one travels, the more spicy becomes the taste. The Arabs have a hot palate. Southwest in Greece and Albania olive oil dominates with greater pungency. The Turks like to think that as the founders of the Turkish cuisine theirs is the more refined taste.

Indeed, as one travels in the Eastern Mediterranean one finds that real Turkish cooking is devoid of any extremes of taste and is more agreeable to the international palate. Almost all Turkish dishes can be served without forcing a new taste. They can be combined with international dishes. Many of the vegetable stews provide imaginative and tasteful side dishes. Chicken Walnut or Spinach Boerek always serves as a tasty appetizer.

Preparation also is not inhibitive. For the host and hostess who seek to combine novelty and imagination with exoticism and tastefulness Turkish cuisine offers limitless opportunities.

The Art of
Turkish Cooking

1. Hors d'Oeuvres

Hors d'oeuvres are an intriguing aspect of the Turkish cuisine. They are served with the national drink, raki, which is taken with a ceremony of its own. The preparation of a "raki table" as it is called, provides the measure of the imagination and skill of the hostess, as well as the measure of the hospitality offered to the guests. A raki party can be defined as a prolonged and sedentary cocktail party, confined to a limited group. The hors d'oeuvres, as varied as the generosity of the host allows, are laid on the table and the guests are invited to sit around. A raki party is more than a gustatory affair. In fact, it is a get-together for good talk and for good music, depending on occasion and taste. Often, it can last to the small hours of the morning.

The cold hors d'oeuvres are laid out on the table in advance. Bite-size slices of white cheese, as it is known in Turkey, or feta, as the Greeks call it, Snow Almonds, sliced tomatoes and cucumbers, green and black olives, sardines, and marinated bonito figure among the staples. Caviar—and Turkish caviar is very delectable—is considered especially useful as a blotter at a prolonged raki party. Mussels, Liver Petites, and small boereks are served periodically as they are brought hot from the kitchen.

For regular cocktail parties Cheese Boereks, Liver Petites, and mussels are favored. White Cheese Dip, Snow Almonds, and *Tarama*[1] dip also are served with effect.

[1] *Tarama* is the name for specially prepared fish eggs which are imported from Turkey and sold in 10 ounce jars. *Tarama* may be obtained from groceries and delicatessen shops specializing in Mediterranean foods. For a list of such shops see the Appendix.

Fried Mussels placed on lettuce leaves with Tarator Sauce can be served as an appetizer. Boiled eggs sliced and heavily dipped in *Tarama* and placed on tomato slices also can be served as an appetizer. Rice dolmas decorated with lemon wedges make a good starter.

Tarama, Mashed Chick-peas, White Cheese Walnut on toasted rye or toasted whole wheat bread make good sandwiches for a summer outing or brunch. Cheese Boereks can also be served with tea in the afternoon.

Hors d'Oeuvres

SNOW ALMONDS
Buzlu Badem

6 ounce package plain almonds

Put almonds in plastic container with a lid. Fill container with cold water, cover, and leave in refrigerator 3 to 4 days. The day before serving rub skins off. Wash almonds, put them back into the container and again fill it with fresh cold water. Cover and leave in refrigerator until serving time. This can be kept in the refrigerator up to a week.

The day before serving, fill a 6 inch high glass serving bowl with water to within 2 inches of the top. Place in freezer and freeze solid.

To serve place bowl on a round serving dish. Drain almonds and place on top of ice.

SERVES 10 TO 12 PERSONS.

CHEESE BOEREKS
Peynirli Börek

FILLING:

6 ounces cream cheese	*2 or 3 tablespoons milk*
6 ounces feta or white cheese	*1 cup chopped parsley*
1 cup cottage cheese	*2 tablespoons chopped dill*
2 tablespoons grated	
Parmesan cheese	*½ pound Phyllo pastry*
2 eggs	*sheets*[2]
Pinch salt	*¼ pound butter, melted*

[2] Phyllo pastry sheets, used in many of these recipes, may be obtained from groceries and delicatessen shops specializing in Mediterranean foods. For a list of such shops see the Appendix.

Preheat oven to 350 degrees F. after the boereks have been prepared. *Filling:* Put all the cheese, eggs, salt, and milk in a mixing bowl. With a wooden spoon stir into a smooth paste. Fold in parsley and dill.

The pastry sheets will be piled on top of each other in a block like sheets of paper of equal size. Put them on a flat surface and cut through the block crosswise, making two equal parts as in Figure 1. Cut through again lengthwise making four equal parts, Figure 1. Place all parts on top of each other in an orderly pile and cover with a kitchen towel to prevent drying. Now the cut pastry sheets are ready to use as in Figure 2.

Take one sheet from the pile. Place it in front of you. Using a brush, butter surface. Place a teaspoon of cheese mixture on

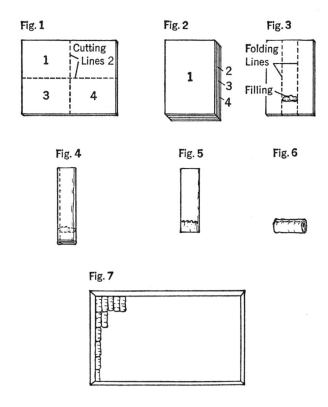

pastry as in Figure 3. Fold both sides over filling as in Figure 4. Fold end of pastry near filling over filling as in Figure 5. Butter surface of folded end. Roll like a cigarette and butter end of pastry so that ends stick together as in Figure 6. Place each rolled boerek on a buttered baking pan, Figure 7. When all pastry sheets have been rolled and placed on the pan, butter the tops. Bake for 25 to 30 minutes until boereks are golden brown. Do not overcook. Transfer to a serving tray and serve warm.

MAKES ABOUT 50 BOEREKS.
SERVES 20 TO 25 PERSONS.

MEAT BOEREKS
Kıymalı Börek

FILLING:

½ pound ground beef	2 tablespoons chopped dill
2 tablespoons butter	Salt and pepper to taste
1 medium onion, grated	
1 small tomato, diced	½ pound Phyllo pastry
1 egg	sheets*
1 cup chopped parsley	¼ pound melted butter

Preheat oven to 350 degrees F. after the boereks have been prepared.

Filling: Put meat, butter, onions and tomatoes in frying pan and cook over medium heat for 15 minutes, stirring occasionally. Remove from heat. Add the egg, parsley, dill, salt and pepper. Mix well.

Prepare pastry as for Cheese Boereks*. Make meat boereks cigarette-shaped like the cheese ones if you are serving only one kind, but if you are serving both meat and cheese boereks, make the meat boereks triangular-shaped so that you can tell them apart.

Take a sheet of pastry from the pile. Butter surface with a brush. Place 1 teaspoon of meat mixture in the middle of pastry as in Figure 1. Fold both sides over filling, Figure 2. Butter surface of folded sides then fold end of pastry over filling, forming a triangle as in Figure 3. Continue folding in triangles until end is reached, Figures 4 to 5. Butter end to hold together. Place each triangle on buttered baking pan, Figure 6. When all pastry sheets are folded and placed in the pan, butter tops and bake 25 to 30 minutes or until the boereks are golden brown. Do not overcook. Transfer into a serving tray and serve warm.

MAKES ABOUT 50 BOEREKS.
SERVES 20 TO 25 PERSONS.

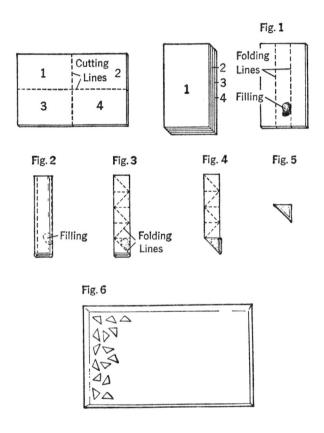

BOEREK STICKS
Kokteyl Böreği

½ *pound Phyllo pastry sheets*
¼ *pound margarine, melted*
4 *tablespoons grated Parmesan cheese*

Preheat oven to 350 degrees F. after the sticks have been prepared. Put pastry sheets on a flat surface. Cut into two equal parts crosswise. Wrap up one half tightly in its own plastic bag and store in refrigerator for future use. It can be kept for several days. Cut the remaining half into four equal parts about 4 by 6 inches. Pile all sheets neatly on top of one another and cover with a kitchen towel to prevent drying.

Take one sheet from the pile. Brush surface with margarine and sprinkle with a half teaspoon of cheese. Roll up from the shorter end very tight, just as if rolling an old-fashioned cigarette. Paste end down with a little extra margarine if necessary. Roll all pastry sheets the same way, placing them in rows in a lightly buttered baking pan. When all sheets are used, brush tops lightly with margarine and bake about 15 minutes, or until light gold. Serve warm or cold with cocktails.

MAKES ABOUT 88 STICKS.
SERVES 30 TO 40 PERSONS.

WHITE CHEESE DIP
Beyaz Peynir Ezmesi

¼ *pound feta or white cheese*	*2 tablespoons milk*
2 tablespoons salad or olive oil	*1 cup chopped parsley*
	Salt and pepper to taste

Soak cheese in cold water and refrigerate for 1 to 2 days to get rid of the excess salt. Drain and break into chunks.

Put 1 tablespoon oil and 1 tablespoon milk into blender container, add cheese and half the parsley. Cover and blend on low for 3 or 4 seconds. Repeat several times adding the rest of the ingredients. Blend until ingredients form a smooth paste. To facilitate blending, turn off blender occasionally and push ingredients down with a rubber spatula. Empty paste into a container with a lid. Cover and refrigerate.

At serving time empty paste into a small bowl. Serve as a dip with fresh vegetables, such as carrots, cauliflower, cucumbers, celery, etc., cut into bite-size pieces. It also may be served with potato chips, or as open canapés on crackers or on small slices of bread.

MAKES 1 CUP PASTE.

WHITE CHEESE WALNUT

Cevizli Beyaz Peynir

½ pound feta or white cheese   *Dash cayenne*
2 tablespoons olive oil   *Salt to taste*
8 tablespoons milk   *1 teaspoon paprika*
1 cup shelled walnut meats

Soak cheese in cold water and refrigerate for 1 to 2 days to get rid of the excess salt. Drain and break into chunks. Put 1 tablespoon oil and 3 tablespoons milk into blender container. Add one-third of cheese and one-third of walnuts, cover, and turn blender on low for a few seconds. Repeat several times. Add rest of oil, 3 tablespoons milk, half of the remaining cheese, and one-half of the remaining walnuts and again turn blender low for a few seconds. Add the remaining milk, cheese, and walnuts, the cayenne, and salt and blend to a smooth paste. To facilitate blending turn off blender occasionally and push ingredients down with a rubber spatula. Empty paste into a container with a lid. Cover and refrigerate.

At serving time empty paste into a small bowl, sprinkle with paprika. Serve as a dip with crackers, as canapés on toasted bread, or as small size sandwiches for tea parties.

MAKES 1½ CUPS PASTE.

MASHED CHICK-PEAS

Nohut Ezmesi

1 cup canned cooked   *Salt to taste*
* chick-peas, skinned*   *1 teaspoon paprika*
¾ cup Tahin[3] oil   *1 tablespoon chopped parsley*
¾ cup lemon juice
3 cloves garlic, crushed

Blender method: Put all ingredients, except paprika and parsley, alternately into a blender, blending a few seconds at a time until

[3] Tahin oil, ground sesame seed oil, may be obtained from groceries and delicatessen shops specializing in Mediterranean foods. For a list of such shops see the Appendix.

all ingredients are used up. The result will be a thick, smooth paste. *Hand method:* Put chick-peas through a sieve or food mill. Add Tahin oil and lemon juice alternately and beat into a smooth paste. Add garlic and salt and beat again until a thick smooth paste is obtained. This may be served several ways:

Pour paste into a bowl, garnish with paprika and parsley. Serve as a dip with crackers.

Make canapés with toasted bread cut into desired shapes, garnishing top with paprika and parsley.

Cut celery stalks into inch long pieces and fill with paste. Sprinkle with paprika and parsley.

Fill romaine lettuce leaves the same way as the celery.

Make sandwiches on toasted or untoasted white bread.

BOTH METHODS MAKE 2 CUPS.

DAINTY FINGERS
Hanım Parmağı

½ pound ground beef	*4 tablespoons bread crumbs*
2 medium onions, grated	*½ cup chopped parsley*
2 eggs	*Salt to taste*
1 tablespoon curry	*2 cups salad oil*

Put beef, onions, eggs, curry, bread crumbs, parsley, and salt in a bowl. Knead mixture well for 5 minutes until it makes a smooth paste. Take a small piece of the paste into your palm and roll to the shape of your little finger. Place each piece on wax paper until all the paste is used.

Heat oil in a frying pan over medium heat. Place fingers in the pan and fry until golden brown. Insert a toothpick in each finger and serve with French mustard. It is a popular hot cocktail dish.

MAKES ABOUT 50 DAINTY FINGERS.
SERVES 20 TO 25 PERSONS.

FISH ROE MIX
Tarama

3 tablespoons lemon juice
3 tablespoons olive oil or
  salad oil
3 tablespoons sour cream

1 tablespoon tarama*
3 tablespoons bread crumbs
1 sprig parsley

Put one-third of each of the ingredients into the blender, except parsley, taking care to put the liquids in first. Turn the blender on high speed for 3 or 4 seconds. Add another third of the ingredients and again turn on the blender for a few seconds. Stop and add the remaining ingredients and blend a few seconds more. You will have a paste the consistency of thick mayonnaise.

Place the paste in a bowl, garnish it with parsley, and serve it with pumpernickel bread or unsalted round crackers.

If it is a big party, the amount of the ingredients may be doubled and the paste placed in a scooped-out cabbage. This makes a very attractive combination.

SERVES 10 TO 12 PERSONS.

STUFFED GRAPEVINE LEAVES
Yalancı Dolma

6 cups water
16 ounce jar grapevine leaves
2 large onions, coarsely grated
1 cup rice
3 tablespoons black currants
2 tablespoons pignolia nuts
¼ cup chopped fresh mint
  leaves
¼ cup chopped parsley (save
  stems)

¼ cup chopped dill (save
  stems)
2 tablespoons lemon juice
⅔ cup olive oil
1 teaspoon sugar
1 tablespoon allspice
Salt to taste
2 cups unseasoned chicken
  broth or water
2 lemons, cut into wedges

Place 6 cups water in a saucepan and bring to a boil. Unroll leaves and place in boiling water. Boil for 2 minutes. Carefully take leaves out with a perforated kitchen spoon and place in a colander to drain. Separate leaves one by one without breaking, remove stem and place around the rim of the colander.

Put onions into a mixing bowl. Add rice, currants, nuts, mint, parsley, dill, lemon juice, oil, sugar, allspice, and salt. Mix well.

Put parsley and dill stems at the bottom of a heavy saucepan.

Take a vine leaf into your left-hand palm, rough side up and the stem end toward you. Place 1 teaspoon of rice mixture, a little more if the leaf is large, on the stem end. Fold stem end over and then fold both sides securely. Roll to end of leaf.

Arrange rolled dolmas in saucepan over dill and parsley stems in close rows. After the first layer start a new layer until all dolmas are rolled.

Pour over broth or water. Cover dolmas with wax paper and place a plate over the wax paper to give weight during cooking. Cover and cook over medium heat until rice is tender and all the water is absorbed, about 1 hour. If necessary more broth or water may be added.

Remove from heat and cool, covered.

Arrange dolmas on a serving platter. Decorate with lemon wedges. Serve cold as hors d'oeuvres. Also very good as a first course.

MAKES 40 DOLMAS.
ALLOW 4 PER PERSON AS A FIRST COURSE.
ALLOW 2 PER PERSON AS HORS D'OEUVRES.

LIVER PETITES
Ciğer Nezesi

½ cup flour	*Salt to taste*
1 pound calf's liver cut up	*2 scallions, chopped*
into ½ inch cubes	*¼ cup chopped parsley*
1½ cups olive or salad oil	*Toothpicks*

Spread flour on wax paper. Dredge liver cubes well.

Heat oil to boiling point in frying pan. Place half the liver cubes in oil and fry 3 to 4 minutes, turning them constantly with a perforated kitchen spoon. Arrange them on a serving platter. Sprinkle over salt, half of the scallions, and half of the parsley. Place a toothpick in each cube and serve hot.

Repeat same process using the same oil for a second serving with the rest of the liver cubes.

MAKES ABOUT 40 CUBES.
SERVES 12 TO 14 PERSONS.

THE RECIPE

Nasrettin Hoca had become very fond of the liver petites his friend the city councilman offered him on several occasions for lunch. Finally, he asked him for the recipe. The councilman brought it to him the next day, carefully described and written up by his wife. Hoca placed it in his pocket and walked to the butcher shop. He bought a pound of calf's liver and had it diced as described. As he came out the dogs that lingered around the shop grabbed the package and ran away.

Unperturbed, Hoca shouted after them, "I wouldn't bother if I were you. It will be of no use. I have the recipe here in my pocket."

FRIED MUSSELS I
Midye Tavası

20 mussels
½ cup flour
1 cup tomato juice
1 can beer
2 eggs, lightly beaten with
  a fork

1½ cups salad oil
Salt and pepper to taste
1 cup Tarator Sauce*
Toothpicks

Open mussel shells by inserting a knife along the flat side and running it along to the other side. Cut off beard. Remove meat. Discard shells. Wash and dry mussels. Flour each one separately. Dip first into the tomato juice, then into beer, and last into the beaten eggs. Fry in hot oil until golden brown on all sides. Sprinkle with salt and pepper. Insert a toothpick into each mussel and serve

immediately with a bowl of tarator sauce. Place a little sauce on
each mussel before eating.

MAKES 20 PIECES.
SERVES 10 PERSONS.

FRIED MUSSELS II
Midye Tavası

20 mussels	1½ cups salad oil
½ cup flour	Salt and pepper to taste
2 eggs, lightly beaten with	Tarator Sauce*
a fork	

Prepare mussels as in Fried Mussels I*. Flour each mussel, dip
into beaten eggs, and fry in hot oil until golden brown on all
sides. Sprinkle with salt and pepper and serve with tarator sauce.

MAKES 20 PIECES.
SERVES 10 PERSONS.

PUMPKIN CHIPS
Bal Kabağı Kızartması

8 tablespoons flour	1 pound pumpkin
1 cup water	1 cup salad oil
Salt and pepper to taste	Yogurt Sauce I*, optional

Beat together the flour, water, salt, and pepper until smooth.
Peel pumpkin and slice into paper-thin chips. Dip into batter
and fry in hot oil. Place each chip into a serving dish making a nice
pile. Sprinkle salt on top of each layer. These may be served hot
or cold, plain or with yogurt sauce.
Place yogurt sauce in a small bowl. Serve with chips as a dip.

SERVES 10 TO 15 PERSONS.

Who drinks on credit gets doubly drunk.

2. Salads

Salads, fresh or cooked, are an important aspect of Turkish cuisine. During the hot, dry summer months they provide a cool, light lunch and at night they serve as refreshing side dishes to the main course.

The most prized and best green is undoubtedly the Turkish *marul* or romaine lettuce, which, unfortunately, has a short season. The romaine grows to very large proportions in Turkey, yet it is tender, sweet with a delicate taste. The heart can be eaten as is with a little salt added. In the old days in Istanbul there were numerous truck gardens which only grew romaine and people from all over the city went there to buy their supply fresh from the source.

Turkey abounds in a variety of greens, watercress, dandelion and mustard greens, many of which are available in the Italian markets in America. The Turkish salad is generally a mixture of these greens and can be varied to suit individual taste.

The dressing is almost always olive oil, lemon or vinegar or both with a dash of wine added if so desired. The Turks are particular when it comes to salad dressing. There is a saying in Turkish that a stingy person pours the oil, a generous one the vinegar, and a crazy one beats the dressing vigorously until well blended. It is then poured over the greens before serving. Often thin slices of green pepper are left to soak in the oil for 24 hours for a delicate flavoring. For those who like garlic chopped garlic can be marinated in the oil for a few hours. Neither the pepper slices nor the garlic is removed before the dressing is used.

The fresh salads are served in small separate dishes along with the main course. The cooked salads provide the hostess with an opportunity to exercise her imagination. *Piyaz, Fava,* and cauliflower can be garnished according to individual taste; green and black olives, hard-boiled eggs, radishes, scallions, tomatoes, cucumbers, parsley, green or red peppers are the ingredients of the artist cook. At a picnic lunch they often decorate the table as effectively as flowers.

The Turkish people prefer to serve green salads with fried fish, poultry, or meat. Spinach, fava, and eggplant are also served as side dishes. With roasts and baked poultry a combination of tomato and cucumber salad is preferred. Jerusalem artichokes and zucchini are acceptable as side dishes.

When green or fresh salads are served for lunch, they are supplemented with white cheese. A light, cooled white wine helps to reinforce their taste.

Salads

MASHED BEAN SALAD
Fasulye Ezmesi

1 can (1 pound, 4 ounces)
   cooked white kidney
   beans, drained
3 tablespoons olive or salad
   oil
3 tablespoons yogurt
2 tablespoons lemon juice

1 tablespoon vinegar
Salt to taste
3 hard-boiled eggs, quartered
2 scallions, chopped with
   green tops
1 tablespoon chopped parsley

Put beans into a bowl and mash with a potato masher. Add olive oil, yogurt, lemon juice, vinegar, and salt one at a time, and continue to mash to a smooth purée. Place in a salad bowl and refrigerate until serving time.

Before serving, decorate with eggs, scallions, and parsley.

Serve as a salad for luncheons with cold cuts or for buffet dinners.

SERVES 6 PERSONS.

BEAN SALAD
Piyaz

4 tablespoons olive or salad
   oil
4 tablespoons lemon juice
1 tablespoon wine vinegar
Salt and black pepper to taste
1 can (1 pound, 4 ounces)
   cooked white kidney
   beans, drained
¼ cup chopped parsley

¼ cup chopped dill
¼ cup chopped fresh mint
   leaves
1 large onion, cut in half
   lengthwise, then finely sliced
1 tomato, sliced
1 green pepper, sliced
8 black olives
2 hard-boiled eggs, quartered

In a large salad bowl place oil, lemon juice, vinegar, salt, and pepper and blend thoroughly. Add the drained beans and mix well. Sprinkle parsley, dill, mint, and onion slices over beans. Garnish with tomato, green pepper, black olives, and quartered eggs.

This is a light luncheon dish for summer. It can be served as a side dish during the summer for a garden brunch. It also can be prepared in advance and taken for picnics.

SERVES 4 TO 6 PERSONS.

BEET SALAD

Pancar Salatası

2 bunches beets, about 10 roots	1 tablespoon vinegar
	2 tablespoons lemon juice
3 teaspoons sugar	¼ teaspoon garlic powder,
¼ teaspoon salt	optional
8 cups water	2 scallions, finely chopped,
2 tablespoons olive oil	whites only

Remove stems and roots from the beets. Scrape the cut ends lightly but leave skin on. Wash in cold water.

Put beets, sugar, salt in 8 cups of water in a saucepan. Bring to a boil. Cook over medium heat until beets are tender and the water is reduced to ⅓ cup. If necessary more water may be added, but it must be reduced to ⅓ cup again.

Cool beets and peel off skins. Slice very thin into a salad bowl.

Put beet juice in a small bowl. Add olive oil, vinegar, lemon juice, and garlic. Mix well, pour over sliced beets, cover and refrigerate.

Serve in individual serving salad bowls and garnish with scallions.

SERVES 6 PERSONS.

CABBAGE SALAD
Lahana Salatası

1 *small white cabbage,*	*Lemon Sauce**
about 1 pound	*¼ cup roasted red peppers*
2 *tablespoons salt*	*(can be bought)*
½ cup chopped parsley	*6 black olives*

Cut cabbage in two and wash. Place on cutting board and shred very fine. Put in a bowl and add salt. Mix and knead by hand for 3 or 4 minutes. Wash several times with cold water. Drain well.

Place drained cabbage in a salad bowl. Add parsley, pour over the sauce, and mix. Decorate with peppers and olives.

SERVES 6 PERSONS.

CAULIFLOWER SALAD
Karnıbahar Salatası

5 *cups water*	2 *black olives*
2 *tablespoons lemon juice*	4 *radishes, finely sliced*
Salt to taste	2 *scallions, chopped*
1 *medium cauliflower*	2 *tablespoons chopped parsley*
2 *hard-boiled eggs, quartered*	*Green Pepper Sauce**

In a saucepan bring to a boil 5 cups of water, add the lemon juice and the salt. Then add the whole cleaned and washed cauliflower. Boil until tender, 20 to 30 minutes. Allow to cool.

Remove cauliflower to salad bowl. Arrange egg slices around it. Decorate with olives, radishes, scallions, and parsley. Pour sauce on top and serve cold as a salad.

Also may be served as a luncheon dish and for cold buffet.

SERVES 6 PERSONS.

CAULIFLOWER TARATOR

Taratorlu Karnıbahar

5 cups water   1 medium cauliflower
2 tablespoons lemon juice   Tarator Sauce*
Salt to taste

Put 5 cups of water into a saucepan with the lemon juice and salt. Bring to a boil and add the whole cauliflower, which has been washed. Boil until tender, 20 to 30 minutes.
Remove cauliflower to a serving bowl, preferably glass. Let cool, then pour tarator sauce on top and serve.

SERVES 6 PERSONS.

DANDELION GREENS

Hindiba Salatası

1 pound dandelion greens   1 tablespoon vinegar
6 cups water   6 black olives
1 teaspoon salt   2 hard-boiled eggs, optional
Lemon Sauce*

Wash greens several times in cold water, discarding damaged outer leaves. Cut off brown part from roots. Cut in half crosswise.
Place 6 cups of water in a saucepan. Add 1 teaspoon salt. When water boils, add the greens and boil 5 to 8 minutes. Drain.
Place dandelion greens in salad bowl. Add lemon sauce and vinegar, mix gently. Garnish with black olives and quartered eggs.

SERVES 4 TO 5 PERSONS.

EGGPLANT SALAD

Patlıcan Salatası

4 large eggplants	1 small onion, cut in half
5 tablespoons lemon juice	lengthwise, then sliced
⅓ cup olive or salad oil	1 small green pepper, sliced
Salt to taste	and seeded
1 tablespoon vinegar	1 small tomato, sliced
6 black olives	1 tablespoon chopped parsley

Insert knife into eggplants about an inch deep at several places. Place them directly over a high gas flame and turn often so they will cook evenly. The skin will burn and turn black. If an electric stove is used, place the eggplant directly on the heating unit. Put lemon juice in a bowl.

When eggplants are soft, skin them with a knife while still hot. Scrape out the seeds and drop eggplants into the lemon juice. Add oil, salt and vinegar and mash with a potato masher into a smooth paste.

Place paste on a platter. Decorate with olives, onions, green pepper, and tomato slices. Sprinkle parsley on top.

SERVES 6 PERSONS.

DRIED FAVA BEAN SALAD

Fava

1½ cups shelled dry fava	2 tablespoons salad oil
beans	1 tablespoon sour cream
1 large onion, quartered	1 bunch scallions chopped
2 quarts water	2 tablespoons chopped dill
1 teaspoon sugar	2 tablespoons chopped parsley
Salt to taste	6 black olives
2 tablespoons lemon juice	6 radishes

Soak beans overnight in cold water. Next day wash them and place in a saucepan with the onion and 2 quarts of cold water.

Cook until beans can be mashed easily, stirring occasionally to prevent scorching. Add more water if necessary. When beans are well cooked and all the water is absorbed, remove from heat, add sugar, salt, lemon juice, salad oil, and sour cream. Mash with a potato masher or put through food mill until they reach the consistency of mashed potatoes. Place in a flat serving platter, smooth the top, and allow to cool.

Garnish with scallions, dill, and parsley, and the olives and radishes. When chilled, the beans may be cut like a cake.

If desired, additional lemon and oil may be served with the salad.

SERVES 6 TO 8 PERSONS.

JERUSALEM ARTICHOKE SALAD
Yerelması Salatası

1 pound Jerusalem artichokes	*2 scallions, chopped*
2 tablespoons lemon juice	*¼ cup chopped fresh mint*
4 cups water	*leaves*
4 large lettuce leaves	*Lemon Sauce**

Pare artichokes and cut into two or three pieces, depending on the size of the artichoke. Place in cold water.

Add lemon juice to 4 cups of water in a saucepan. Bring to a boil. Add drained artichokes, cover and cook over medium heat until tender, 15 to 20 minutes. Drain them and cool.

Place whole lettuce leaves at the bottom of a salad bowl. Fill with artichokes. Decorate top with scallions and mint leaves. Pour sauce over and serve.

SERVES 4 PERSONS.

MASHED POTATO SALAD
Patates Ezmesi

8 medium potatoes	3 tablespoons lemon juice
3 cups water	Salt to taste
¼ cup olive oil	1 cup finely chopped dill
1 egg yolk	8 black olives
1 very small onion, grated	

Peel, quarter, and wash potatoes and place in a saucepan. Add 3 cups of cold water. Cook over high heat until potatoes are very tender and almost all the water is absorbed. Mash with a potato masher. While still hot, add oil and blend well with the masher. Continue to mash and add, one at a time, egg yolk, onion, lemon juice, salt, and dill until a smooth but not too thick purée is obtained. Place in a serving bowl with a flat bottom. Cool, then set in refrigerator for a few hours. Decorate with olives before serving.

Serve as a salad for luncheons with cold cuts or for buffet dinners.

SERVES 6 PERSONS.

POTATO A LA TURCA
Patates Salatası

6 medium potatoes	1 tablespoon chopped dill
4 tablespoons vinegar	Salt and pepper to taste
1 teaspoon ground mustard	Dash cayenne
4 tablespoons salad or olive oil	2 medium onions, cut in half lengthwise, then sliced
2 tablespoons lemon juice	10 black olives
2 tablespoons chopped parsley	

Wash potatoes and cook in boiling water until tender. Drain and skin. Cut into halves and then slice halves very thin into a salad bowl. Add vinegar, cover and set aside.

Put mustard, oil, lemon juice, parsley, dill, salt, pepper, and cayenne in a separate bowl. Mix well and add to the potatoes.

Put onions in a bowl with 1 tablespoon salt and knead well with hands to remove juice. Wash away salt under cold water several times. Squeeze out water and add to the potatoes. Blend without mashing the potatoes. Garnish top of bowl with olives and serve.

SERVES 8 PERSONS.

ROMAINE LETTUCE SALAD
Marul Salatası

1 romaine lettuce
2 scallions, chopped
¼ cup chopped fresh mint
    leaves

Lemon Sauce*

Discard the damaged and coarse outer leaves of the lettuce. Separate the rest one by one. Wash well.

Shred the large green leaves and place in a salad bowl. Arrange the small heart leaves over the top in an attractive pattern. Decorate with scallions and mint leaves. Pour sauce over the greens.

Serve with fish, boiled chicken, or meat dishes.

SERVES 4 TO 6 PERSONS.

SHEPHERDS' SALAD
Çoban Salatası

½ head Boston lettuce, thinly
    sliced
3 leaves romaine lettuce,
    thinly sliced
1 green pepper, seeded and
    thinly sliced
½ cucumber, peeled and
    thinly sliced
1 tomato, thinly sliced
2 scallions with green tops,
    thinly sliced

2 radishes, thinly sliced
6 slices roasted red peppers
    (can be bought)
6 green olives
2 tablespoons chopped parsley
2 tablespoons chopped dill
2 tablespoons chopped fresh
    mint leaves
Lemon Sauce* with
    1 tablespoon vinegar added

Place all ingredients except lemon sauce into a salad bowl. Add sauce and toss well.

Very good with fish dishes, especially with broiled fish.

SERVES 5 TO 6 PERSONS.

SPINACH ROOT SALAD
Ispanakkökü Salatası

2 pounds fresh spinach	Juice 1 lemon
5 cups water	Pepper to taste
Salt to taste	2 hard-boiled eggs, chopped
¼ cup olive or salad oil	8 black olives

Prepare spinach as in Fried Spinach*. Use only roots. (Save leaves for frying. See Vegetables as Side Dishes*.)

Drop roots into 5 cups boiling salted water. Boil for 5 minutes or until roots are almost tender but not too soft. Drain.

Place oil and lemon juice in a bowl, add salt and pepper. Beat well.

Place spinach roots in a salad bowl. Pour sauce over roots and mix. Sprinkle chopped eggs on top and garnish with olives.

SERVES 4 TO 6 PERSONS.

TOMATO AND CUCUMBER SALAD
Domates Ve Hiyar Salatası

1 large tomato, peeled and sliced	1 tablespoon chopped fresh dill
1 medium cucumber, peeled and sliced	Lemon Sauce* with 1 tablespoon vinegar added
1 tablespoon chopped fresh mint	

Arrange tomatoes and cucumber slices on a flat serving platter. Decorate with mint and dill. Pour sauce over and serve.

Very good with fish dishes, also with *Şiş Kebab*, *Şiş Köfte*, and *Kuru Köfte*.

SERVES 4 TO 5 PERSONS.

TOMATO AND ONION SALAD
Sovanlı Domates Salatası

1 large onion
1 tablespoon salt
2 large tomatoes
1 small can (2 ounce)
    rolled fillets of anchovies

2 tablespoons chopped mint
    or parsley
Lemon Sauce*

Peel and wash the onion. Cut lengthwise into two pieces, then place each piece flat side down on cutting board and cut into very fine slices. Place in a bowl with salt and knead well with hands. Wash with cold water several times to get rid of all the salt. Then squeeze onions in palm of hand until dry. Spread on a flat serving platter.

Wash, peel, and seed tomatoes. Cut crosswise slices ⅓ inch thick. Arrange over onions in platter. Decorate with fillets of anchovies and mint or parsley.

Pour sauce over and serve with beef, chicken, mushrooms, or *Talash Boereks**, or with fish and meat dishes.

SERVES 6 PERSONS.

ZUCCHINI SALAD
Kabak Salatası

6 medium tender zucchini
1 teaspoon salt
2 medium tomatoes, peeled
    and sliced
3 hard-boiled eggs, quartered
1 green pepper, seeded and
    chopped

2 scallions, chopped
2 tablespoons chopped dill
6 black olives
Lemon Sauce*

Scrape and wash zucchini. Cook in boiling salted water until tender, about 15 to 20 minutes. Cool, drain well, and cut in slices ⅓ inch thick. Arrange in the middle of a large platter. Place tomato slices around zucchini, then the egg slices over the tomatoes. Mix green pepper, scallions, and dill together and spread over zucchini. Decorate with olives. Pour sauce over and serve.

This is a summer luncheon salad good with cold cuts.

SERVES 6 PERSONS.

ZUCCHINI YOGURT SALAD
Yoğurtlu Kabak Salatası

4 medium zucchini, unpeeled
1 tablespoon margarine
¼ cup water
½ cup yogurt
2 cloves garlic, crushed
¼ teaspoon dried mint leaves
  or 1 teaspoon finely
  chopped dill

Salt to taste
1 teaspoon vinegar
1 tablespoon olive or salad oil
Paprika to taste, optional

Grate zucchini coarsely. Place in a saucepan with margarine and ¼ cup water. Cook over medium heat, stirring occasionally until all the water is absorbed, and the zucchini is well cooked. Remove from heat, let cool.

Add yogurt, garlic, mint or dill leaves, salt, vinegar, and oil. Mix well, then refrigerate for about an hour or until serving time. Sprinkle paprika on top if desired.

SERVES 4 PERSONS.

A hungry stomach has no ears.

3. Sauces

Unlike the Americans, who usually boil or steam their vegetables, the Turks like to cook most of theirs with tomatoes, onions, seasoning, and a little water or broth thus producing their own sauce.

The principal Turkish sauce is *Terbiye* (lemon and egg sauce), which is easy to make and gives a special flavor to many main dishes and soups. Tarator Sauce adds an exotic flavor to fish and vegetables. Walnut Sauce is inevitable with boiled chicken.

Yogurt flavored with garlic is served on fried eggplant, zucchini, and carrots. It not only lightens their taste but helps in their digestion. Yogurt with powdered sugar is served with many kinds of berries. Without sugar it can top sweets such as baba-rhum. Lighter than cream it provides a special flavor. Finally Rose Sauce and Rose Water are recommended for an unusual touch for desserts.

Sauces

LEMON SAUCE
Limon Salçası

¼ cup salad or olive oil
5 tablespoons lemon juice

Salt and pepper to taste
½ cup chopped parsley

Place oil in a bowl, add lemon juice, salt, and pepper. Beat with rotary beater. Add parsley and mix well.

For all salads, baked, broiled, or boiled fish, boiled or fresh vegetables.

MAKES ABOUT ½ CUP SAUCE.

LEMON AND EGG SAUCE I
Terbiye

2 egg yolks
2 tablespoons lemon juice
2 tablespoons cold water

Place egg yolks in a bowl and beat well with a rotary beater. Add lemon juice and water and continue beating until well mixed.

This is a light lemon and egg sauce. It may be used with soups, some meat stews, and other meat dishes. It is poured over before serving.

MAKES ½ CUP SAUCE.

LEMON AND EGG SAUCE II
Terbiye

2 eggs
3 tablespoons lemon juice
1 cup clear chicken or meat stock (water may be substituted)

In a small saucepan, beat eggs until frothy. Add lemon juice and stir. Place over very low heat. Add stock slowly, stirring constantly. Continue to stir and cook until sauce is thickened, 10 to 15 minutes.

This sauce may be used over boiled fish and over meat stew, meatballs, meat dolmas. It is poured over before serving.

MAKES 1 CUP SAUCE.

ONION SAUCE
Piyaz

4 small onions
2 tablespoons salt
½ cup chopped parsley

Peel and wash the onions. Cut lengthwise into two pieces, then place each piece flat side down on cutting board and cut into very fine slices.

Place in a bowl with salt and knead well with hands. Wash with cold water several times to get rid of all the salt. Then squeeze onions in palm of hand until dry.

Place onions in a small serving bowl. Add parsley and mix.

For broiled and fried fish, bean salad, or fried calf's liver. Use 1 or 2 tablespoons per serving.

MAKES 1 CUP SAUCE.

GREEN PEPPER SAUCE
Yeşil Büberli Salça

1 green pepper	¼ tablespoon mustard
⅓ cup olive or salad oil	Salt to taste
5 tablespoons lemon juice	

Wash and cut pepper into two. Remove seeds. Slice on cutting board horizontally into very thin slices. Place in a bowl. Add oil, lemon juice, mustard, and salt. Mix well.

May be prepared several hours ahead of serving time or overnight.

This sauce may be served with all kinds of green salads such as lettuce, etc., or with boiled potatoes and boiled zucchini.

MAKES A LITTLE OVER ½ CUP SAUCE.

TOMATO SAUCE
Tomates Salçası

5 medium ripe tomatoes or	1 bay leaf
1 can (16 ounce) whole	Salt and pepper to taste
tomatoes and juice	2 cups water
3 tablespoons olive oil	2 tablespoons vinegar
1 tablespoon sugar	
1 clove garlic, crushed,	
optional	

Place tomatoes in saucepan with oil, sugar, garlic, bay leaf, salt, and pepper. Add 1 cup water and cook over medium heat, uncovered, stirring and mashing tomatoes occasionally. Cook until tomatoes are soft, about 1 hour.

Add another cup of water and continue to cook, stirring occasionally, 30 to 40 minutes. Add vinegar. Stir and remove from heat.

Use cold on fried eggplant, boiled green beans, boiled pinto beans, and white kidney beans.

MAKES 1 CUP SAUCE.

TARATOR SAUCE
Tarator

1 cup pignolia nuts	*2 cloves garlic, optional*
1 cup olive oil	*1 teaspoon salt*
4 slices white bread with crusts removed and soaked in water and squeezed dry	*½ cup white vinegar*

Soak pignolia nuts in cold water for 10 minutes; drain and dry on paper towel.

Place one-third of the nuts into blender. Add one-third of the oil, 2 slices of bread, cover and turn blender for several seconds. Switch the blender on and off several times. Add half of the remaining nuts and half the remaining oil, the rest of the bread, garlic, and salt. Cover and turn blender on low for a few seconds. Turn it on and off a few times.

Last, add the remaining ingredients and vinegar. Turn blender on low until the sauce is smooth but not too thick.

Empty sauce into a container with a lid. Cover and refrigerate until ready to use.

This sauce is used frequently with boiled vegetables, such as cauliflower, boiled pinto beans, and boiled green beans. It may also be served over other vegetables and with Fried Mussels*.

MAKES 2 CUPS SAUCE.

WALNUT SAUCE
Ceviz Salçası

1¼ cups clear unseasoned chicken stock	*1 clove garlic or ¼ small onion, optional*
2 cups walnut meats	*Salt and pepper to taste*
3 thin slices white bread with crusts removed and soaked in ¼ cup of the chicken stock	*1 teaspoon paprika for decoration, optional*

Put one-quarter of the stock into blender, add one-half of the walnuts, 1 slice of bread (do not squeeze out liquid), cover and turn blender on low for a few seconds. Turn off.

Add half of the remaining stock, half of the remaining walnuts, another slice of bread; cover and turn blender on low. Turn it on and off a few times.

Last, add the remaining ingredients, garlic or onion, salt and pepper, and turn blender on and off a few times until sauce becomes a smooth paste the consistency of mayonnaise. If a lighter consistency is desired more stock may be added.

Serve on cold boiled chicken, on boiled vegetables, or on open toast for lunch. Decorate top with paprika.

MAKES 2 CUPS SAUCE.

YOGURT SAUCE I
Yoğurt Salçası

½ *pint plain yogurt*
½ *teaspoon salt*
1 clove garlic, crushed, optional

Empty yogurt into a bowl, add salt, garlic. Beat well.

Use on fried vegetables, on some meat kebabs, and some meat dolmas.

MAKES 1 CUP SAUCE.

YOGURT SAUCE II
Yoğurt Salçası

½ *pint plain yogurt*
3 or 4 tablespoons confectioners' sugar

Empty yogurt into a bowl, add sugar and beat well.

Use on berries and other fresh fruit.

MAKES 1 CUP SAUCE.

ORANGE SAUCE

Portakal Salçası

6 *medium oranges*	2 *cups sugar*
12 *cups water*	2 *tablespoons lemon juice*

Peel oranges, then cut peel into thin strips, $\frac{1}{10}$ inch wide and 1½ inches long. Bring 10 cups of water to a boil in a saucepan, add orange peel and cook for 30 minutes. Reserve 1 cup cooking water for later use, if desired. Drain.

Place sugar in a saucepan, add 2 cups of water, and dissolve over medium heat, stirring occasionally. If a stronger orange flavor is desired, use 1 cup of plain water and 1 cup of the water in which peel was first cooked. Add orange peel and cook over low heat for about 1 hour or until a light syrupy sauce is achieved. Add lemon juice and cook for another 5 minutes. Remove from heat and cool.

May be served with plain milk puddings, custards, vanilla ice cream, or orange sherbet.

MAKES 3 CUPS SAUCE.

Honey loosens one's tongue.

4. Soups

Soups are an important part of the Turkish cuisine. In the cold months, the farmers begin their day with *tarhana,* which is a mixture of yogurt, mashed tomatoes, and wheat flour. This is dried in the sun during the summer and stored for the winter.

The Turks divide their soups into two categories: the substantial, such as Lentil Soup, Tripe, and the Wedding Soup, which are served for lunch when the meal is a light one as they are good fortifiers on a cold day.

As the Americans reach for Alka Seltzer after imbibing too much, the Turks rely on Tripe Soup, which is supposed to settle a queasy stomach and sober up a man.

The second category, which comprises the light soups, is reserved for more formal occasions. Chicken Vermicelli, Cultured Chicken, Yogurt Beef Soup, constitute the first course of a dinner.

Turquoise, the famous cold Turkish soup, deserves a special mention. During the hot summer months it can be served for lunch or as an appetizer. In the old Turkish tradition, turquoise is also served as a salad to accompany barbecued meats.

Soups

CHICKEN VERMICELLI SOUP
Şehriyeli Tavuk Suyu

2 tablespoons butter
2 cups broken vermicelli pieces
4 cups chicken broth

Salt and pepper to taste
¼ cup chopped parsley
½ lemon

Melt butter in a saucepan. Fry vermicelli over medium heat until golden brown, stirring with a wooden spoon. Add broth and cook for 15 minutes or until vermicelli is tender. Add salt and pepper.

Sprinkle parsley on top and serve with a slice of lemon on the side.

This is a light soup. It can be served for dinner even in summer. It is good for people who are ill and should eat lightly.

SERVES 6 PERSONS.

CULTURED CHICKEN SOUP
Terbiyeli Tavuk Suyu

4 cups clear seasoned chicken
    broth (canned or instant
    chicken broth may be used)
2 eggs

3 tablespoons lemon juice
1 tablespoon finely chopped
    parsley

Heat broth to boiling point. Lower heat.

Beat eggs in a bowl with a rotary beater until frothy. Add lemon juice and beat again. Add a few spoonfuls of hot broth to eggs and continue to beat. Do this 4 or 5 times, beating each time. Remove broth from heat. Add egg mixture to broth slowly, stirring all the time.

Serve in teacups topped with parsley, and Cigarette Boereks*.

SERVES 6 PERSONS.

FALL SOUP
Domatesli Pirinç Çorbası

¼ cup rice	4 cups beef broth
1 onion, grated	1 tablespoon butter
2 green peppers, chopped	1 cup milk
4 large tomatoes or	Salt and pepper to taste
3 tablespoons tomato paste	½ cup chopped parsley

Wash rice and place in a saucepan. Add onion, green peppers, cut-up tomatoes, beef broth, butter and simmer over medium heat for 45 minutes. Add milk, salt and pepper to taste and continue simmering for 20 minutes, or until rice is well cooked. Add parsley, stir, and cook for 5 minutes more. If the soup is too thick a little broth or water may be added. Serve with Toasted Bread Cubes.

SERVES 6 PERSONS.

TOASTED BREAD CUBES: Cut white bread into half inch cubes, place on an oven tray, and toast in hot preheated 400 degree F. oven until golden brown.

FARINA SOUP
İrmik Çorbası

5 fresh or canned whole	8 cups chicken stock
tomatoes, diced	Salt to taste
¼ cup water	3 eggs
4 tablespoons butter	½ cup milk
½ cup farina	

Place tomatoes in a small saucepan, add ¼ cup water and cook over medium heat about 30 minutes, stirring occasionally until tomatoes are very soft. Set aside.

Place butter in a saucepan, add farina, sauté over medium heat, stirring all the time for 4 minutes. Add stock and stir. Simmer over medium heat for 20 minutes. Add salt and the cooked tomatoes. Stir and simmer for another 5 minutes.

Beat eggs well. Add milk and beat again. Beat a little of the hot soup into egg mixture. Repeat this several times. Then fold egg mixture slowly into soup, stirring constantly. Serve immediately with warmed sesame crackers.

SERVES 8 TO 10 PERSONS.

HITTITE SOUP

Domatesli Mercimek Çorbası

1 cup red lentils	*2 tablespoons flour*
3 cups beef broth	*3 cups tomato juice*
1 medium onion, grated	*Dash cayenne*
3 tablespoons butter	*Salt and pepper to taste*

Place lentils and beef broth in a saucepan. Cook until lentils are tender, about 30 minutes.

Sauté onions in butter for 3 minutes. Add flour and continue sautéing over medium heat for 5 minutes more, stirring all the time with a wooden spoon.

Add tomato juice gradually, stirring all the time until it starts bubbling. Still stirring, add the cooked lentils, cayenne, salt, and pepper. Let soup simmer for 30 minutes over low heat.

If the soup is too thick, a little broth or water may be added. Serve in individual bowls with Toasted Bread Cubes*.

SERVES 6 TO 8 PERSONS.

LENTIL SOUP I
Mercimek Çorbası

2 cups dried lentils	¼ pound beef, cut into ¼
4 cups water	inch cubes
1 tablespoon butter	3 large tomatoes, chopped
1 onion, grated	1 tablespoon tomato paste
1 tablespoon rice	5 cups beef broth
1 small carrot, grated	Salt and pepper to taste

Wash lentils and boil in a saucepan with 4 cups of water for 15 minutes. Drain and set aside.

Place butter in a saucepan, add onions and sauté about 3 minutes. Add rice, carrot, beef, lentils, tomatoes, tomato paste, and broth. Cook over medium heat, stirring occasionally until all ingredients are cooked, about 20 to 30 minutes. Add salt and pepper and continue cooking for 3 minutes more.

SERVES 8 TO 10 PERSONS.

LENTIL SOUP II
Mercimek Çorbası

3 cups dried lentils	2 tablespoons butter
13 cups water	3 tablespoons flour
1 carrot, diced	2 eggs
2 large onions, grated	3 tablespoons vinegar
3 cups beef broth	1 teaspoon paprika
Salt and pepper to taste	

Soak lentils in 6 cups of cold water for 2 hours. Drain.

Place lentils in a saucepan with the carrot, 1 grated onion, and 7 cups of cold water. Boil until all ingredients are done, about 30 minutes, then put through a food mill. Add hot broth, salt, and pepper, and simmer over very low heat.

Place 1 tablespoon butter in a saucepan, add the remaining grated onion, and sauté for 2 minutes over low heat, stirring constantly with a wooden spoon. Add the flour and continue cooking for 5 minutes more, stirring constantly. Add the flour mixture to the soup a little at a time, stirring constantly. Simmer 10 to 15 minutes on low heat.

Beat 2 eggs with a rotary beater. Add vinegar and beat well. Slowly add egg mixture to the soup, stirring all the time. Remove from heat and empty into a hot soup tureen.

If soup is too thick, a little broth or water may be added.

Heat 1 tablespoon butter, add paprika, stir and pour over the soup and serve.

SERVES 10 TO 12 PERSONS.

A heavy cauldron takes long to boil.

RED LENTIL SOUP
Kırmızı Mercimek Çorbası

2 medium onions, chopped	*4 cups chicken or beef broth*
4 tablespoons butter	*2 tablespoons flour*
½ pound red lentils	*2 egg yolks*
4 cups water	*1 cup milk*
Salt and red pepper to taste	

Place onions in saucepan, add 2 tablespoons butter, and sauté over medium heat for 5 minutes. Add red lentils and 4 cups of water. Cook over medium heat, stirring occasionally, until lentils are tender, about 30 minutes. Add salt, red pepper, and the 4 cups of hot broth and boil for another 2 minutes. Remove from heat, strain through food mill. Return to saucepan and keep warm.

Put 2 tablespoons of butter in a saucepan, add flour and cook over medium heat, stirring constantly with a wooden spoon for 5 minutes. Remove from heat. Beat egg yolks and add to flour mixture, a little at a time, stirring constantly. Add milk the same way, a little at a time.

Now add this mixture to the lentils, again a little at a time, stirring constantly. Heat and serve with Toasted Bread Cubes*.

This is a good winter soup. With salad it is a good luncheon dish.

SERVES 8 PERSONS.

COLD TOMATO SOUP
Soğuk Domates Çorbası

½ pint yogurt	2 tablespoons vinegar
3 cups pure tomato juice	½ tablespoon curry
1 tablespoon olive or salad oil	Salt to taste
2 tablespoons lemon juice	2 tablespoons chopped parsley

Whip yogurt until smooth, then add tomato juice, oil, lemon juice, vinegar, curry, and salt. Blend well. Cover bowl and refrigerate for 4 or 5 hours.

Serve in small bowls and sprinkle with chopped parsley.

This makes a good summer soup followed by grilled meat, hamburgers, or frankfurters.

SERVES 6 PERSONS.

TRIPE SOUP
Işkembe Çorbası

4 pounds tripe, frozen preferred	2 eggs
5 cups water	Juice 2 lemons
Salt and pepper to taste	1 teaspoon paprika
4 tablespoons butter	Dash cayenne
2 tablespoons flour	4 slices white bread for Toasted Bread Cubes*

FOR VINEGAR SAUCE:
  6 tablespoons vinegar
  4 cloves garlic, crushed

Wash tripe thoroughly and place in saucepan. Add 5 cups of water, cover, and cook over medium heat for 3 hours, adding more water as it boils away. Remove tripe and save stock; put tripe through meat grinder or chop into small pieces. Return it to stock. Season with salt and pepper. Cook over medium heat for 2 hours more.

Melt 2 tablespoons butter in a small saucepan, add flour and cook for 3 minutes, stirring all the time with a wooden spoon.

Gradually add a little soup to the butter and flour mixture and stir well to prevent lumps. Blend this into the soup slowly. Cook 10 minutes longer, stirring all the time. If less thick soup is desired, flour and butter mixture may be omitted. Keep soup warm.

Beat eggs well with a rotary beater, add lemon juice and beat again.

Remove soup from heat, add the lemon and egg mixture slowly so as not to curdle the eggs, stirring all the time.

Melt remaining 2 tablespoons butter until very hot. Add paprika and a dash of cayenne. Stir well.

Pour soup into a serving bowl, decorate top with the hot butter and paprika. When serving, sprinkle a few toasted bread cubes and a little vinegar sauce on each soup plate.

This is a cold weather soup, good after cocktails or late in the evening after the theater.

SERVES 10 TO 12 PERSONS.

VINEGAR SAUCE: Place vinegar in a sauceboat, add crushed garlic, and stir well.

TURQUOISE
Cacık

1 large cucumber	*2 tablespoons chopped fresh*
Salt to taste	*mint or 1 tablespoon*
1 clove garlic	*dried mint*
1 tablespoon vinegar	*3 tablespoons salad or olive*
1 pint yogurt	*oil (preferably olive)*
2 tablespoons chopped dill	

Peel cucumber, grate finely into a bowl, and sprinkle with salt. Rub a soup bowl with garlic, discard, and swish the vinegar in it to collect flavor.

Add yogurt, grated cucumber, dill, mint, and oil to the garlic-vinegar bowl and stir until mixture is consistency of thick soup. If too thick add 3 tablespoons of plain water. Cover and place bowl in refrigerator.

Serve very cold in small individual bowls.

SERVES 4 TO 6 PERSONS.

WEDDING SOUP
Düğün Çorbası

2 pounds lamb or beef bones with a little meat on them	8 tablespoons butter
	½ cup flour
1 onion	2 egg yolks
1 medium carrot	Juice ½ lemon
5 cups water	½ tablespoon paprika
Salt to taste	Dash cayenne

Place meat and bones in a saucepan, adding the peeled onion and scraped carrot. Add 5 cups of cold water and the salt, cover and cook over medium heat until meat is tender, about 1 hour. Remove from heat, strain stock, shred the meat and add to the stock.

In a saucepan melt 6 tablespoons of the butter, add flour and stir constantly over low heat until mixture is thoroughly blended, about 6 minutes. Add the meat stock to this mixture gradually, stirring constantly. Simmer for about 10 minutes. Remove from heat, but keep warm.

Beat egg yolks with a rotary beater, add lemon juice and gradually stir 2 tablespoons of hot soup into this mixture. Then pour it into the soup gradually, stirring all the time. Melt the remaining 2 tablespoons of butter in a small saucepan, add paprika and cayenne. Garnish soup with this mixture. Serve with Toasted Bread Cubes*.

This is a rich soup. Traditionally it is served at wedding meals. It makes a good first course for a more formal dinner. It also can be served as a light lunch with crackers.

If soup is too thick a little broth or water may be added.

SERVES 6 TO 8 PERSONS.

THE WEDDING SOUP

On his way to preach at a mountain village Nasrettin Hoca, the Turkish sage, was lost in an unexpected snowstorm. The next morning the villagers found him half frozen under an oak tree, a mile beyond the village inn. When he came to himself he thanked the people at the inn for saving his life. *"I warmed myself by watching the glow of the inn's light,"* he said.

Thereupon, the villagers rejoiced for saving Hoca's life and asked him for a show of true appreciation. Hoca accepted the challenge and offered to prepare a feast for them.

Next evening the elders of the village gathered at the inn. They sang and danced, praising Hoca's hospitality. Hours passed, and the guests began to cluster around the empty table. Hoca kept dashing in and out of the kitchen but returned always empty-handed. Finally, their patience exhausted, they pressed Hoca to serve them. "A festive occasion like this calls for a wedding soup. Come and see how it is being prepared," he said, smiling, and led them to the kitchen.

They saw a huge cauldron hanging from the ceiling with a tiny candle underneath.

"You don't expect this candle to cook the soup," they shouted.

"Why not, if the glow of the inn's light warmed me. Why not?" remonstrated Hoca. *"If the glow of the inn's light can keep a poor soul in the forest warmed up, surely, a candle can cook a cauldron of wedding soup."*

YOGURT BEEF SOUP
Yayla Çorbası

1 pint yogurt	6 tablespoons butter
¼ teaspoon garlic salt, optional	¾ cup flour
Salt and pepper to taste	2 tablespoons dried mint leaves
4 cups beef broth	

Put yogurt, garlic salt, salt, and pepper in a mixing bowl. Add cold broth slowly, stirring to smooth consistency. Melt butter in saucepan, add flour slowly, stirring constantly over low heat for 5 minutes. Add yogurt and broth mixture gradually, stirring constantly, until it boils. Boil for 5 minutes, remove from heat, and pour into soup bowls. Garnish top with dried mint leaves.

This is a creamy soup with an unusual sourish flavor. It is a good appetizer for a formal dinner.

SERVES 6 PERSONS.

5. *Eggs*

Eggs are an invaluable part of Turkish cuisine and they are the ingredient of many dishes. Fish and several vegetables are first dipped in egg batter and fried.

In the past, they were served as a first course. During Ramadan, a sacred month in the Mohammedan calendar, when people fasted from sunup to sundown, eggs fried with chopped meat and onions were offered to break the fast. Hardly ever eaten at breakfast, eggs constitute the main course for lunch. When served for lunch they are accompanied by a green salad, romaine lettuce in season, with tomatoes and scallions. At formal dinners egg dishes are served as appetizers but only in winter.

The Turkish hostess prides herself on owning a variety of colorful enameled skillets. Eggs are brought to the table in the skillet they are cooked in, which also prevents the breaking of the eggs.

Eggs

BAKED EGGS
Fırında Yumurta

4 *large ripe tomatoes*   4 *teaspoons chopped parsley*
4 *teaspoons butter*   *Salt and pepper to taste*
4 *eggs*
4 *tablespoons grated*
 Parmesan cheese

Preheat oven to 400 degrees F.

Slice through top of tomatoes, but do not sever it, for it will serve as a cover. Scoop out inside and discard. Place 1 teaspoon butter into each tomato, cover with top, place tomatoes in baking dish and bake for 15 minutes.

Remove tomatoes from oven, lift cover, break 1 egg into each tomato. Top eggs with 1 tablespoon cheese and 1 teaspoon parsley, salt, and pepper. Replace cover, put back into oven and bake for 10 minutes more or until eggs are cooked. Serve immediately.

SERVES 4 PERSONS AS AN APPETIZER.

GROUND MEAT EGGS
Kıymalı Yumurta

1 *large onion cut in half,*   1 *tablespoon chopped parsley*
 then sliced   *Salt and pepper to taste*
2 *tablespoons butter*   6 *eggs*
1 *pound ground lamb or beef*   1 *teaspoon paprika*
2 *tomatoes, diced*

Place onions in a frying pan, add butter and sauté for 2 minutes, stirring constantly with a wooden spoon. Add meat and continue to sauté until meat turns brown and is crumbly, about 10 minutes.

Add tomatoes, parsley, salt, and pepper, mix well, cover and simmer for 10 minutes.

Uncover, make six spaces for the eggs by separating the meat mixture. Break 1 egg into each space. Sprinkle eggs with paprika. Cover and cook over low heat for 4 minutes and serve.

SERVES 6 PERSONS AS AN APPETIZER,
OR 3 PERSONS AS A LUNCHEON DISH.

ONION EGGS
Sovanlı Yumurta

4 medium onions cut in half,   ½ teaspoon sugar
   then sliced   4 eggs
2 tablespoons butter   Salt, pepper, and allspice to
½ cup water   taste

Place onions in a frying pan, add butter and sauté lightly over medium heat. Add the water and sugar, cover and cook until all the water is absorbed and the onions are tender.

Make four spaces for the eggs by separating onions. Break eggs into these spaces. Sprinkle salt, pepper, and allspice on top of eggs. Cover and cook until eggs are set. Serve immediately.

SERVES 4 PERSONS AS AN
APPETIZER, OR 2 PERSONS
AS A LUNCHEON DISH.

PASTIRMA EGGS
Pastırmalı Yumurta

2 onions cut in half, then   ½ pound pastirma[1], sliced
   sliced   thin
3 tablespoons butter   4 eggs
3 tablespoons tomato juice   Salt and pepper to taste

[1] Pastirma, a dried meat covered with garlic paste, may be obtained from groceries and delicatessens specializing in Mediterranean foods. For a list of such shops see the Appendix.

Put onions in a frying pan. Add butter and sauté lightly over medium heat for about 5 minutes. Add tomato juice and cook for 3 minutes. Add pastirma slices, stir and cook for 2 minutes more.

Make four spaces by separating the pastirma and onion mixture. Break 1 egg into each space. Sprinkle eggs with salt and pepper. Cover and cook over medium heat for 5 minutes and serve.

SERVES 4 PERSONS AS AN
APPETIZER, OR 2 PERSONS
AS A LUNCHEON DISH.

SPINACH EGGS

Ispanaklı Yumurta

1 package (10 ounce) frozen chopped spinach	*Salt to taste*
4 tablespoons butter or margarine	*4 tablespoons grated Parmesan cheese*
1 medium onion, grated	*4 eggs*
1 teaspoon sugar	*Pepper to taste*

Place frozen spinach in a frying pan. Add butter and onion and sauté over medium heat, stirring frequently for about 30 minutes. The spinach will defrost as it cooks. Add sugar, salt, and cheese, and blend all ingredients thoroughly.

Make four spaces for the eggs by separating the mixture. Break eggs into these spaces. Sprinkle them with pepper, cover, and cook until eggs are set. Serve immediately.

SERVES 4 PERSONS AS AN
APPETIZER, OR 2 PERSONS AS
A LUNCHEON DISH.

SUMMER EGGS
Yaz Yumurtası

2 medium onions cut in half,   ½ cup chopped parsley
   then sliced   ½ cup water
3 tablespoons butter   Salt and pepper to taste
3 green peppers, sliced thin   6 eggs
3 medium tomatoes, sliced   1 teaspoon paprika
   thin

Place onions in a frying pan. Add butter and sauté lightly over medium heat for about 5 minutes. Add green peppers, tomatoes, parsley, ½ cup water, salt, and pepper. Stir. Cook covered until peppers and tomatoes are soft and no water is left in the pan, about 30 minutes.

Remove lid, make six spaces for the eggs by separating the vegetable mixture. Break 1 egg into each space. Sprinkle eggs with paprika. Cover and cook over medium heat for 5 minutes and serve.

SERVES 6 PERSONS AS AN APPETIZER,
OR 3 PERSONS AS A LUNCHEON DISH.

EGGS WITH YOGURT
Çilbır

1 clove garlic   ½ tablespoon vinegar
2 cups yogurt   2 tablespoons butter
Salt to taste   1 teaspoon paprika
4 eggs   Dash red pepper

Rub a bowl with garlic and discard; add yogurt and salt. (If stronger garlic flavor is desired crush garlic and mix with yogurt.) Place bowl on a hot plate and stir occasionally until yogurt is warm, not hot.

Poach eggs in water to which vinegar has been added. Pour

L'Ibriktar-Agassi.

Officier qui donne à laver du Grand Seigneur.

yogurt on a hot platter, drain eggs with a perforated large kitchen spoon, and place on top of yogurt.

Heat butter in a small pan, add paprika and a dash of red pepper. Pour on top of the eggs and yogurt. Serve immediately.

SERVES 4 PERSONS AS AN
APPETIZER, OR 2 PERSONS AS A LUNCHEON
DISH.

6. Fish

Fish is a top culinary delight in Turkey. Every region prides itself
on its own particular type. The Black Sea with its cold and dark
waters yields the sturgeon. Underneath the towers of Trebizond
fresh Turkish caviar with the Turkish brand of vodka competes with
the best Russian variety. The same waters produce the "Kalkan," a
kind of turbot which fried or steamed is a delight to taste. But
the Black Sea people are mostly associated with the Hamsi, the
brisling, and the Turks say, "allowed the opportunity the Black
Sea-ers will use the brisling even in their jam." The people of the
Aegean pride themselves on the Chipura, a pompano-like flat fish
which is broiled and served with a lemon and oil sauce. Taken
with raki a Chipura dinner ends inevitably with the men taking the
floor to dance the "Zeybek." The red mullet of the Aegean is the
aristocrat but is offered at more official occasions. The Iskenderun
coastline, the Riviera of Turkey, yields a good crop of shrimp. The
shipful or two that reaches the New York market once or twice a
year commands the highest prices.

Above all, Istanbul is the fish city par excellence. In the Bosporus,
the cold waters of the Black Sea mix with the warm currents of
the Mediterranean and provide the best varieties of both. In fact,
it is the fish that determine the change of seasons in Istanbul. "The
Uskumru is back," they say, and they mean that the summer has
ended. When they see myriad lights sparkling the dark waters of
the Bosporus at night, they know that the fishermen have gone to
meet the "lüfer," a kind of cross between bluefish and trout, and
take out their topcoats for the first bite of the winter. The "Palamut,"
a kind of bonito, announces the coming of the first snows, and

when its elder brother the "Torik" makes its appearance there are piles of snow on the ground and at times ice in the Bosporus. The "Kalkan" is the harbinger of spring. When the "Tekir," the freckled redhead with its shining colors, takes its place in the fish stalls, summer with all its Ottoman glory has burst upon the Istanbulites.

Truly, the fishmongers are among the most interesting characters and their shops rank as the most colorful in the city. The fish are displayed in large wooden trays, three to four feet in diameter, placed in semi-inclining positions in front of the store. They are organized in rows of two or three trays. Depending on the size of the shop they can be three or four trays deep. The shops have no windows, no doors, winter and summer they are completely exposed. In the interior, white marble slabs serve for the cutting and cleaning of the fish. With their copious moustaches fishermen affect virility and each has his individual expression in declaiming loudly to the passing public the delights of his fish.

Fish in the Turkish cuisine is served broiled, steamed, fried, baked. It is served as a main course. The Uskumru, the Palamut, and the sturgeon are available smoked in season. The Palamut transforms itself into Lakerda under a special treatment of semi-salting. With an oil-lemon sauce it serves as a delightful accompaniment to raki. "Chiroz," a dried mackerel, beaten soft and soaked in vinegar, garnished with dill, is cherished as an Istanbul specialty.

Only mussels have demanded special treatment. The Turks have really applied their culinary imagination to them. And almost all of the mussel courses appeal to the American taste.

I have often served Fried Mussels with Tarator Sauce as a first course, provoking real gourmet appreciation. I have also discovered that Mussel Pilav elicits considerable approval as a buffet dish.

In many cases I have substituted for some of the Turkish varieties fish more commonly found in America. The Turkish manner of cooking them, indeed, gives them a new flavor worth tasting. Salmon or flounder in casserole are two good examples. Swordfish on Spits served as a first course adds distinction to your meals. Striped Bass Plaki, or Mussel Plaki are equally serviceable as first courses or at buffet dinners. Turkish Fish Balls, altogether different from American fish balls, served hot or cold, provide variety as appetizers at formal cocktail parties.

Baked, fried, or broiled varieties included in my recipes make good main courses, especially for luncheons. Baked dishes should be cooked preferably in dishes that can be brought to the table. Although white wine is the universal prescription for fish many of the Turkish fish recipes go well with rosés and the fried variety goes well with beer.

Fish

BAKED BASS
Levrek Fırında

2 medium onions cut in half
  lengthwise, then finely sliced
4 tablespoons salad or olive
  oil
1 clove garlic, crushed,
  optional

Paprika to taste
4 bass steaks, 1 inch thick
Salt to taste
4 tablespoons lemon juice
4 tablespoons tomato juice
¼ cup chopped parsley

Preheat oven to 400 degrees F.

Place onions in a frying pan with oil and sauté until golden brown. Add garlic and paprika.

Place fish steaks in greased baking dish and sprinkle with salt. Spread onion mixture over them. Then pour lemon and tomato juices over the top. Bake for 20 to 25 minutes or until fish is cooked.

Decorate with chopped parsley and serve.

SERVES 4 PERSONS.

STRIPED BASS PLAKI
Levrek Plaki

3 medium onions cut in half
  lengthwise, then finely sliced
1 large carrot, sliced thin
  crosswise
1 stalk celery, chopped
2 parsley roots, chopped
¼ cup salad or olive oil
3 cloves garlic, chopped
2 medium potatoes, peeled
  and diced

½ cup water
1 medium striped bass
½ lemon, sliced
2 tablespoons tomato paste
  diluted with ¾ cup water
  or 2 medium tomatoes,
  sliced
Salt and pepper to taste
¾ cup white wine
2 tablespoons chopped parsley

Place onions, carrots, celery, and parsley roots in a frying pan. Add oil and sauté over medium heat for about 8 minutes, stirring constantly. Add garlic and potatoes and sauté 5 minutes more. Add ½ cup water, cover, and cook for 10 minutes. Remove from heat.

Slice fish crosswise into pieces 1½ to 2 inches thick. Wash and drain.

Place slices in a shallow casserole that can be brought to the table. Put onion mixture around the fish and place a slice of lemon on each piece. Pour diluted tomato paste or place fresh tomato slices over the fish. Add salt and pepper. Cover and cook over medium heat for 25 minutes or until fish and vegetables are tender.

Add wine 3 minutes before removing from heat.

Uncover and let cool 10 to 15 minutes. Sprinkle with parsley before serving.

May also be served cold.

SERVES 4 TO 6 PERSONS.

BROILED COD FILLETS
Morina Isgarası

1 tablespoon oil	*About 40 bay leaves*
6 slices cod fillets, ½ inch	*12 small onions, peeled,*
thick	*cleaned and cut into halves*
Salt and pepper to taste	*Lemon Sauce**

Preheat broiler.

Grease an oven pan with the oil, place each fillet on the greased pan, and sprinkle with salt and pepper. Cover fillets completely with bay leaves.

Place onion halves between fillets. Broil under the broiler until bay leaves turn black, 10 to 15 minutes. Then put pan in the oven for 5 to 10 minutes right over the broiler flame, so that the under side of the fillets are cooked. If using an electric stove, broil top side first, then turn off broiler. Set oven at 400 degrees F. and bake for 5 to 10 minutes.

Discard bay leaves. Remove fillets to a serving platter. Decorate with onions. Serve with lemon sauce.

SERVES 6 PERSONS.

BAKED COD FILLETS
Morina Fırında

2 tablespoons olive or salad
    oil
4 slices cod fillets, 1 inch
    thick
Salt and pepper to taste
5 scallions, including green
    tops, coarsely chopped

2 tablespoons tomato paste
    diluted in ½ cup water
    or 2 fresh tomatoes, sliced
½ lemon, sliced thin
½ cup chopped parsley
½ cup white wine

Preheat oven to 350 degrees F.

Oil a baking dish that can be brought to the table. Place fillets in the baking dish next to each other. Sprinkle with salt and pepper and spread the scallions over them. Pour on tomato paste or place tomato slices on top of fillets.

Decorate with lemon slices. Sprinkle with parsley. Bake 30 minutes or until fish is tender. Add wine and bake 3 minutes more.

Serve hot or cold with Mashed Potato Salad*.

SERVES 4 PERSONS.

FRIED COD FILLETS
Morina Tavası

Salt to taste
4 slices fish fillets, ½ inch
    thick
½ cup flour

1½ cups salad or olive oil
½ cup Onion Sauce*[1]
1 lemon, quartered

Salt fillets.

Spread flour on a piece of wax paper and coat fillets on both sides. Fry in very hot oil until golden brown, about 4 minutes on each side.

Serve hot with a tablespoon of onion sauce on top of each fillet

[1] The amounts called for in recipe for onion sauce can be halved to yield the smaller amount needed here for less waste.

and a piece of lemon on the side. Serve boiled or fried potatoes
and Romaine Lettuce Salad* with the fillets.

SERVES 4 PERSONS.

FISH BALLS
Balık Köftesi

FOR BOILING FISH:

1½ cups water	1 bay leaf
1 small onion, quartered	Salt and 5 peppercorns
2 sprigs parsley	Approximately ¾ pound
1 small carrot	mackerel or halibut or
2 lemon slices	sea bass

FOR FISH BALLS:

1 cup boiled fish meat	2 tablespoons chopped parsley
1 slice white bread, soaked	2 tablespoons black currants
in water and squeezed dry	2 tablespoons pignolia nuts
2 eggs	½ teaspoon allspice
2 scallions, including green	Salt and pepper to taste
tops, chopped	½ cup flour
2 tablespoons chopped dill	1 cup salad oil or shortening

Bring to a boil 1½ cups water, with the onion, sprigs of parsley,
carrot, lemon slices, bay leaf, salt, and peppercorns. Add cleaned
and washed fish, cover and cook 10 to 15 minutes or until fish is
tender. Remove fish from pan and cool. Then remove all bones
and skin from the fish.

Place fish in a bowl. Add bread, eggs, scallions, dill, parsley,
currants, nuts, allspice, salt, and pepper. Mash with a fork, working
into a smooth paste. With the paste form croquettes about 2½
inches long and roll in flour.

Fry in hot fat until golden brown on all sides. Shake pan often
to prevent scorching.

Serve hot or cold with Romaine Lettuce Salad*.

MAKES 10 BALLS.
SERVES 5 PERSONS AS AN APPETIZER.
MAKES 30 SMALL ROUND BALLS FOR COCKTAILS.

FIVE FINGERS
Hamsi Kızartması

1½ pounds fresh brislings or   1½ cups olive or salad oil
   whitebait   Few lettuce leaves
Salt to taste   1 lemon, sliced
½ cup flour

Wash and clean fish. Keep heads and tails on. Salt.

Dredge fish in flour spread on wax paper. Hold 5 brislings together by the tails in a fan shape. Add a little more flour to tails
and wet so that tails stick together. Prepare rest the same way.

Heat oil in frying pan to boiling point. Fry each fan-shaped fish
group a light golden brown 1 minute on each side.

Serve on lettuce leaves and decorate with lemon slices.

Serve hot as an appetizer.

SERVES 6 PERSONS.

FLOUNDER CASSEROLE
Dil Domatesli

2 tablespoons salad or olive   Paprika to taste
   oil   1 can (8 ounce) tomato
Salt to taste   sauce
2 pounds flounder fillets   2 tablespoons butter
6 to 8 bay leaves   ½ cup chopped parsley
1 tablespoon flour

Preheat oven to 350 degrees F.

Grease a shallow casserole with oil. Salt fillets. Place 1 bay leaf
in the center of each fillet and fold once or twice depending on the
size of the fillet. Place each finished fillet in casserole.

Sprinkle folded fillets with flour and paprika, pour tomato sauce
on top, and dot with butter.

Bake for 25 minutes. Decorate with parsley and serve.

SERVES 4 PERSONS.

BAKED HALIBUT WITH GREEN PEPPER
Halibut Fırında

2 medium onions, cut in half lengthwise, then finely sliced	*Salt to taste*
4 tablespoons salad or olive oil	*4 halibut steaks 1 inch thick*
	Black pepper to taste
2 large green peppers, seeded and sliced thin	*1 large tomato, cut into 4 slices*
½ cup water	*4 lemon slices*
	1 cup chopped parsley

Preheat oven to 350 degrees F.

Place onions in a saucepan with the oil. Sauté over medium heat for 5 minutes, stirring with a wooden spoon. Add green peppers and continue to sauté for 5 minutes more, stirring occasionally. Add ½ cup water, cover, and cook for 10 minutes.

Salt fish and place in greased baking dish. Sprinkle with black pepper. Spread the onion and green pepper mixture over the steaks. Place 1 tomato and 1 lemon slice on each steak. Cover steaks with parsley.

Bake for 25 minutes or until cooked.

SERVES 4 PERSONS.

BROILED MACKEREL
Uskumru Isgarası

Salt to taste	*6 to 12 bay leaves*
12 very small or 6 medium mackerel	*Onion Sauce**
	Lemon Sauce*
1 tablespoon oil	

Preheat broiler.

Salt mackerel, leaving them whole.

Place fish on an oiled oven pan. Put bay leaves on the fish. Broil under the broiler until top side is done, 10 to 15 minutes. Then place pan in the oven right over the broiler flame for 5 to

10 minutes so that the underside of the fish is cooked. If using an electric stove, broil top side first, then turn off broiler. Set oven at 400 degrees F. and bake for 5 to 10 minutes.

Remove fish to a serving platter. Decorate with onion sauce and serve lemon sauce separately.

SERVES 6 PERSONS.

MACKEREL PAPILLOTE

Uskumru Kağıtta

12 very small or 6 medium mackerel
Salt to taste
10 scallions with green tops, chopped
3 tablespoons chopped parsley
3 tablespoons chopped dill
2 tablespoons salad or olive oil

6 pieces 12 inch square wax paper
Pepper to taste
2 tablespoons tomato paste diluted in 4 tablespoons water or 2 tomatoes, thinly sliced
6 thin lemon slices, cut crosswise

Preheat oven to 350 degrees F.

Cut off the heads and the tails of each mackerel. Then cut each fish into 2 fillets lengthwise. Wash, salt, and drain.

Mix scallions, parsley, and dill together in a bowl and set aside.

Oil each square of wax paper with a brush. Place 4 small fillets or 2 medium-sized ones in a row on each square of paper. Sprinkle with pepper. Place 1 tablespoon of diluted tomato paste or 2 tomato slices on the fillets. Spread the scallion mixture generously over the fillets. Place 1 lemon slice on the scallions.

Make a package by folding the ends of paper over the fish. Then roll up. Wet top of package with water.

Place packages on an oven tray and bake for 25 minutes.

Serve 1 package per person.

Very good with baked or boiled potatoes.

SERVES 6 PERSONS.

MUSSEL PILAV
Midye Pilavı

1 cup rice	*1 tablespoon sugar*
1½ tablespoons salt	*2 tablespoons black currants*
40 medium mussels	*1 tablespoon allspice*
4 medium onions, coarsely	*¼ teaspoon pepper*
grated	*1½ cups beef stock or water*
½ cup olive or salad oil	*½ cup chopped dill*
2 tablespoons pignolia nuts	*2 sprigs dill*
2 medium tomatoes, fresh	
or canned, diced	

Place rice in a bowl, add 1 tablespoon salt and cover with hot water. Stir and allow to cool. Drain and set aside.

Select the 12 largest mussels. Scrub surface well with a knife or metal brush. Rinse and soak in cold water. Set aside.

Open the rest of the mussel shells by inserting a knife along the flat side and running it along to the other side. Cut off beard. Remove the meat and discard shells.

Put onions in a frying pan with oil and ½ tablespoon salt. Sauté over medium heat, stirring constantly for 10 to 15 minutes.

Add nuts and rice and sauté, stirring constantly, for 10 minutes more.

Add tomatoes and continue to sauté, stirring constantly for 5 minutes. Add sugar, black currants, allspice, and pepper. Stir and remove from heat.

Place stock in a heavy saucepan and bring to a boil. Add the rice mixture and the opened mussels. Stir once carefully. Add the unopened mussels, placing each one into rice here and there. Cover and cook for 5 minutes on high heat, then on low for 15 minutes, or until all stock is absorbed. Add chopped dill and stir once.

Remove from heat. Take off cover, place a napkin or a dish towel over saucepan, and replace cover. Let stand for 40 minutes in a warm place.

Pile rice in a serving bowl, taking care not to break the rice. Arrange mussels in shells, which now will be open and filled with rice, around rice pile. Decorate with sprigs of dill.

Serve cold as an appetizer.

SERVES 8 PERSONS.

MUSSEL PLAKI
Midye Plakisi

40 medium mussels
3 cups water
2 medium onions, coarsely
   grated
½ cup olive or salad oil
2 medium carrots, diced
1 medium potato, diced

2 cloves garlic, diced, optional
1 teaspoon sugar
Salt to taste
1 medium tomato, diced
1 cup chopped parsley
1 tablespoon lemon juice

Open mussel shells by inserting knife along the flat side and running it along to the other side. Cut off beard. Remove meat and wash. Discard shells.

Bring 3 cups of water to a boil in a saucepan. Add mussels and boil vigorously for 3 minutes. Drain and set mussels aside, reserving 1 cup of the drained water.

In a saucepan, sauté onions in oil over medium heat, stirring constantly for 10 minutes. Add carrots and sauté 2 minutes more. Add potatoes, garlic, sugar, salt, reserved mussel water, and tomato. Cover and cook over medium heat until vegetables are tender and almost all the water is absorbed. If vegetables do not become tender, more water may be added.

Add parsley, mussels, and lemon juice and mix well. Remove from heat and cool.

Serve cold (room temperature) as an appetizer.

SERVES 6 PERSONS.

STUFFED MUSSELS
Midye Dolması

½ cup rice
3 teaspoons salt
40 to 45 very large mussels
6 medium onions, coarsely
  grated
⅔ cup olive or salad oil
2 tablespoons pignolia nuts
2 small tomatoes, fresh or
  canned, diced

2 tablespoons black currants
1 teaspoon allspice
2 teaspoons sugar
Pepper to taste
1 cup beef stock or water
1 cup mussel liquid or water
2 lemons, cut into wedges
Few parsley sprigs

Place rice in a bowl, add 2 teaspoons salt, and cover with hot water. Stir, and allow to cool. Drain and set aside.

Scrub mussel shells well with a knife or metal brush. Rinse and soak in cold water. Set aside until ready to use.

Place onions into a frying pan. Add 1 teaspoon salt, oil, sauté over medium heat, stirring constantly for 15 to 20 minutes.

Add nuts and rice, sauté, stirring constantly for 10 minutes. Add tomatoes and sauté 3 minutes.

Add currants, allspice, sugar, pepper, 1 cup boiling stock. Stir, cover, and cook over medium heat until all stock is absorbed, about 15 minutes. Remove from heat. Stir once.

Open the mussels by inserting a knife along the flat side and running it along to the other side. Save mussel liquid. Cut off beard. Open shells until they are loosened but not separated, otherwise mussels will not close.

Fill shells lightly with rice mixture, using a small spoon. Close shells and place in a shallow saucepan in layers, arranging them close to each other. When bottom layer is full start next layer over first. When all mussels are filled, add 1 cup mussel liquid or water. Cover with wax paper. Place a plate over wax paper to give weight during cooking.

Cover saucepan and place over medium heat and cook for 30 minutes. Turn heat to low and cook 40 minutes more.

Remove from heat and cool, covered.

Wipe each mussel shell with paper towel and arrange in a

serving platter. Surface of shells may be oiled to give them luster. Decorate platter with lemon wedges and parsley sprigs.

Serve cold as an appetizer, or at buffet dinners.

ALLOW 3 OR 4 PER PERSON.

SALMON GREEN PEPPER CASSEROLE
Som Fırında

2 *medium onions, chopped*	½ *cup water*
1 *clove garlic, crushed*	*Salt and pepper to taste*
4 *tablespoons olive or salad*	4 *salmon steaks, 1 inch thick*
oil	4 *lemon slices*
2 *large green peppers,*	½ *cup chopped parsley*
seeded and sliced thin	

Preheat oven to 350 degrees F.

Place onions and garlic in a saucepan and add oil. Sauté over medium heat for 5 minutes, stirring with a wooden spoon. Add green peppers and continue to sauté for another 5 minutes, stirring occasionally.

Add ½ cup water, cover, and cook for 10 minutes. Sprinkle salt and pepper over fish. Place in a greased casserole. Spread the onion and green pepper mixture on top. Decorate with lemon slices and parsley.

Bake for 25 minutes or until steaks are cooked. Serve hot.

SERVES 4 PERSONS.

SARDINES IN GRAPEVINE LEAVES
Asma Yaprağında Balık Isgarası

8 *fresh sardines or small*	8 *large fresh grapevine leaves*
mackerel	6 *tablespoons olive oil*
Salt to taste	2 *lemons, cut into wedges*

Preheat broiler or have charcoal fire ready.

Clean and wash fish. Sprinkle with salt and set aside for ½ hour. Take 1 grape leaf, shiny side up, and oil surface. Place 1 fish horizontally near the stem and oil surface of fish. Roll like a cigarette to the end of the leaf. Tuck end of leaf under so that it will not open up. Repeat until all leaves have been rolled up. Place rolled fish on broiler tray or over charcoal rack, taking care to place fish 3 inches from the coals, which should be red hot but not flaming. Broil about 5 minutes on both sides.

Decorate with lemon wedges and serve as an appetizer.

To eat, open up grape leaves and squeeze lemon over fish. Do not eat leaves. Grape leaves give fish a nice flavor.

ALLOW 2 PER PERSON.

SOLE ORIENTAL
Dil Domatesli

1 bunch scallions with green tops, chopped	*½ cup water*
2 green peppers, seeded and sliced thin	*2 pounds fillets of sole*
	Salt and pepper to taste
3 tablespoons salad or olive oil	*2 fresh tomatoes, sliced thin*
	1 lemon, sliced thin
	½ cup chopped parsley

Preheat oven to 350 degrees F.

Place scallions and green peppers in a saucepan. Add oil and ½ cup water, cover and cook for 10 minutes over medium heat.

Wash and dry fillets. Fold them over and place in a greased casserole. Sprinkle with salt and pepper. Spread the cooked scallion and pepper mixture over the fillets. Place tomato and lemon slices over the pepper mixture.

Bake for 25 minutes or until fillets are cooked. Decorate with parsley and serve.

SERVES 4 PERSONS.

BAKED SWORDFISH
Kılıç Fırında

4 swordfish steaks, 1 inch
   thick
Salt and pepper to taste
4 tablespoons salad or olive
   oil
2 bunches scallions, with green
   tops, chopped

¼ cup chopped parsley
¼ cup chopped dill
4 tablespoons tomato juice
4 tablespoons lemon juice
6 green pitted olives, optional

Preheat oven to 350 degrees F.

Wash and place fish steaks in a greased baking dish. Sprinkle with salt and pepper and pour on oil.

Mix scallions, parsley, and dill and spread on fish. Pour tomato and lemon juice on top. Decorate with green olives.

Bake for 25 minutes or until fish is cooked. Serve hot.

SERVES 4 PERSONS.

The fish that gets away is always big.

SWORDFISH ON SPITS
Kılıç Şişte

2 pounds swordfish
¼ tablespoon paprika
4 tablespoons lemon juice
2 tablespoons olive or salad
   oil
Salt and pepper to taste

10 bay leaves
3 tomatoes
2 green peppers
2 medium onions
Lemon Sauce*

Preheat broiler or have charcoal fire ready after the fish is marinated.

Skin fish, cut into 1 inch cubes, and place in a shallow container with a cover. Mix paprika, lemon juice, oil, salt, pepper, and half the bay leaves and marinate fish with this mixture. Place in refrigerator and leave for 3 hours.

Slice tomatoes, peppers, and onions into 2 or 3 pieces, depending on their size. Place fish on spit with peppers, onions, bay leaves, and tomatoes interspersed. Make a spit for each person to be served. Broil on both sides over flameless charcoal or under broiler at a distance of 3 inches. This takes about 10 minutes.

Serve immediately with lemon sauce.

SERVES 4 PERSONS.

7. Poultry

If in Rome one awakes with the chime of bells, in Istanbul one rises with the chant of the cocks. Istanbul is one of the few cities in the world where some people continue to raise their own chickens. Although a rapid industrialization of poultry farming is under way, chicken continues to be scarce and still holds its supreme position as a treat in the Turkish menu. Whenever a Turkish hostess seeks to favor a guest she concentrates on a chicken dish. As in the past, in the small towns in the countryside in the evening one can still catch glimpses of small boys carrying on a copper tray a chicken freshly roasted in the village bakery. In the larger cities people have their own ovens and roast turkey stuffed with rice serves as the pièce de résistance at a formal dinner party. During the summer many prefer the *Tavuklu Güveç*, or *Tavuklu Beğendi* to the roast. In America the *Tavuklu Güveç, Tavuk Yahni,* or Chicken with Chick-peas can provide a delectable and original main dish for a buffet supper.

Among all the Turkish chicken recipes Chicken Walnut enjoys universal recognition. It appeals to every taste and it serves many purposes. Served on romaine lettuce it makes a good first course. But it is also excellent for buffet dinners and it is often used as an appetizing sandwich-filling spread for picnics and motor rides with cold beer as an appropriate chaser.

Turkey is a bird hunter's paradise. Thousands of tourists come to shoot duck, geese, quail, partridge, pheasant. In the fall as darkness descends on the Black Sea coast the hills are illuminated by men waving flaming torches into the sky. They are there to guide the quail into their nets as they cross from the Crimea to the south and fall exhausted on Turkish soil from their long trip over the Black Sea. They come well fed, and charcoal broiled they are a delicacy rarely forgotten once tasted.

I have not included any recipes for game birds because duck and geese and the rest are cooked the same way as everywhere. But turkey has its own rituals. Stuffed with chestnuts and roasted, it is served on New Year's Eve when Turkish families gather around the hearth to eat, drink, and dance and try their luck at the card table; they watch the break of the dawn on a New Year, in new hopes and wishes.

Incidentally, turkey is not a Turkish bird. It is native to America. The conquistadores took it to Spain from whence it traveled across Europe, when people still thought of the Western Hemisphere as the Indies. The Turks called it *Hindi,* just as the French named it dindon attributing it to India. But to the British the East was the Ottoman Empire and the new bird was named turkey.

Poultry

CHICKEN WITH EGGPLANT PUREE
Tavuklu Beğendi

6 medium chicken breasts
2 tablespoons olive or salad
   oil
1 tablespoon salt
1 teaspoon black pepper

1 teaspoon paprika
1 tablespoon thyme leaves
1 teaspoon rosemary leaves
Eggplant Purée*

Preheat oven to 400 degrees F.

Brush breasts on both sides with oil. Combine salt, pepper, paprika, thyme, and rosemary leaves and sprinkle on breasts. Arrange breasts in a baking pan.

Bake ½ hour. Lower oven heat to 350 degrees F. and continue to bake ½ hour more. Turn breasts when one side is browned. Baste occasionally with drippings.

Arrange breasts on one side of a serving platter and pour over drippings. Place warm eggplant purée on the opposite side of the platter.

Serve immediately.

SERVES 6 PERSONS.

CHICKEN WITH CHICK-PEAS
Nohutlu Tavuk

1 frying or broiling chicken,
   about 3 pounds
12 pearl onions
6 tablespoons butter
4 medium fresh tomatoes or
   4 whole canned tomatoes,
   sliced

1 cup tomato juice
1 cup water
2 cans (1 pound 4 ounces
   each) ready-cooked
   chick-peas
Salt, pepper, and paprika to
   taste

Cut chicken into serving pieces. Wash and dry with paper towel. Set aside.

Skin onions whole. Melt 3 tablespoons butter in a large frying pan. Add onions and sauté, stirring constantly for 6 minutes. Remove onions to a plate, leaving butter in pan.

Sauté chicken pieces in the same pan until light brown on both sides, about 15 minutes. Remove pan with chicken from heat and set aside.

Put tomatoes, tomato juice, 1 cup water, and 3 tablespoons butter in a saucepan; cover and cook over medium heat until tomatoes are soft, about 30 minutes.

Drain and wash chick-peas under running hot water. Add to tomatoes. Add the onions; cover and simmer over low heat for 10 minutes.

Pour the whole tomato and chick-pea mixture over chicken in frying pan. Add salt, pepper, and paprika. If necessary add ½ cup more water. This dish should not be too dry. It must have its own juice as sauce.

Cover pan and cook over medium heat for 20 minutes.

Serve hot as main course with Tomato Pilav* and mixed pickles.

SERVES 6 PERSONS.

CHICKEN WITH OKRA
Bamyalı Tavuk

1 medium frying or broiling chicken	1 pound okra or 2 frozen packages (10 ounce) whole, defrosted
3 tablespoons butter	
4 large tomatoes, diced	½ cup water
Salt and pepper to taste	2 tablespoons lemon juice

Clean and cut chicken into serving pieces. Place in a shallow saucepan with the butter. Place tomatoes on top of chicken. Add salt and pepper, cover, and cook over medium heat for about 15 or 20 minutes.

If using fresh okra, peel the cone-shaped end without piercing the vegetable. Wash and arrange okra on top of the chicken. Add ½ cup of water, cover, and cook over medium heat for 20 minutes or until chicken and okra are tender. Add lemon juice and cook 5 minutes more. Remove from heat, transfer to a serving dish, and serve with Tomato Pilav*.

This dish should not be too dry. If necessary a little more water can be added.

SERVES 4 TO 5 PERSONS.

SPRING CHICKEN PAPILLOTE
Piliç Kağıtta

1 young spring chicken	*½ lemon*
Salt to taste	*3 tablespoons butter*

Preheat oven to 350 degrees F.

Wash chicken and rub with salt and lemon juice.

Brush the center of a double layer of large wax paper with 1 tablespoon butter. Brush the rest of the butter on the chicken. Press the legs of the chicken close to the body and wrap it tightly in wax paper, tying it with a piece of string. Wet the outside of the package with water. Bake for 2 hours.

Remove from oven, open package, cut the chicken into portions, and serve with egg noodles.

SERVES 4 PERSONS.

STUFFED ROAST CHICKEN
Piliç Dolması

1 cup rice	*2 tablespoons black currants*
Salt	*Pepper to taste*
1 roasting chicken about 4 pounds, with liver, heart, and gizzard	*1½ cups chicken stock or water*
8 tablespoons butter	*1 bunch scallions, whites only, finely chopped*
2 tablespoons pignolia nuts	*½ bunch watercress*

Preheat oven to 400 degrees F. after the rice stuffing is ready.

Place rice in a bowl, add 1 tablespoon salt, and cover with hot water. Stir and allow to cool. Drain and set aside.

Prepare chicken for roasting; melt 2 tablespoons butter and brush chicken. Place in baking pan and set aside.

Dice liver, heart, and gizzard. Melt 2 tablespoons butter in a small saucepan, add diced giblets, and sauté over medium heat, stirring constantly, for 5 minutes. Set aside.

Melt 4 tablespoons butter in a heavy saucepan, add nuts and rice. Sauté over medium heat, stirring constantly for 10 minutes. Add currants, salt, pepper, and 1 cup boiling stock. Stir. Cover and cook over medium heat until all stock is absorbed, about 15 minutes. Remove from heat. Add sautéed liver mixture with its butter; add scallions and stir.

Stuff the body cavity of the chicken with as much of the rice mixture as it will hold. Sew up the opening. Leave any leftover rice in the saucepan.

Place chicken in oven and reduce heat to 325 degrees F. Baste with drippings every 15 minutes. Roast about 1½ hours or until chicken is golden brown.

Add ½ cup boiling stock to leftover rice in saucepan. Cover and cook over medium heat until stock is absorbed, about 10 minutes. Remove from heat. Take off cover, place a napkin over the saucepan, and replace cover. Leave covered for 40 minutes, or until serving time, in a warm place.

Remove chicken to a serving platter and decorate with watercress.

Spoon out rice filling as you serve. The leftover cooked rice may be served for second portions in a separate dish.

Serve warm with boiled green vegetables.

SERVES 4 TO 5 PERSONS.

CHICKEN CASSEROLE WITH VEGETABLES
Tavuklu Güveç

4 *large chicken breasts, halved*	1 *package (10 ounce) frozen*
6 *tablespoons butter*	*French-cut beans, defrosted*
1 *medium eggplant*	1 *package (10 ounce) frozen*
2 *medium zucchini*	*okra, defrosted*
3 *green peppers*	3 *medium tomatoes, fresh or*
⅓ *cup olive or salad oil*	*canned, peeled and sliced*
2 *medium onions, coarsely*	*Salt and pepper to taste*
sliced	

Preheat oven to 350 degrees F.

Sauté chicken breasts in 4 tablespoons butter very lightly on both sides for about 10 minutes. Arrange in the bottom of an earthenware casserole with a lid.

Prepare vegetables as follows: Wash and cut the stem off eggplant. Then peel off a half inch wide strip of the black skin lengthwise, leaving the next half inch with the skin on. Repeat until you have a striped effect. Then cut the eggplant lengthwise into 4 equal pieces and each piece crosswise into 2 inch pieces.

Scrape and wash zucchini. Cut each lengthwise into 2 equal pieces and each piece crosswise into 2 inch pieces.

Wash peppers. Cut each into 4 equal parts. Remove seeds.

Dry all vegetables with paper towels.

Place oil in the same frying pan that you used for chicken pieces. Heat until very hot. Add eggplant and sauté a few minutes on both sides. Remove with a perforated kitchen spoon, and arrange over chicken in the casserole.

Sauté peppers. If necessary more oil may be used. Place a few pieces over eggplant with a few pieces of onions.

Sauté zucchini and arrange over eggplant. Again add a few peppers and onion slices.

Arrange beans over zucchini and cover with the rest of peppers and onion slices.

Last, arrange okra and place tomatoes over okra. Add salt and pepper. Dot with 2 tablespoons butter. Cover and bake until tender, about 1 hour and 15 minutes.

Serve hot with Mashed Potato Salad*.

SERVES 8 PERSONS.

CHICKEN WALNUT
Cevizli Tavuk

1 boiling chicken, about 3½ pounds	*Salt and white pepper to taste*
2 quarts water	*2 cups shelled walnuts*
1 large onion, quartered	*3 thin slices white bread, crusts removed*
1 carrot, scraped and cut into four	*1 clove garlic, crushed, optional*
1 stalk celery, cut into four	*1 teaspoon paprika*
3 sprigs parsley	*1 tablespoon salad oil*

Wash and place chicken in a saucepan with 2 quarts of water, onion, carrot, celery, parsley, salt, and pepper. Bring to a boil and skim foam off top. Cover and cook on medium heat until chicken is tender. Remove chicken from saucepan and cool. Remove skin and bones. Cut meat into thin pieces about 2 to 3 inches long. Set aside. Strain stock and save.

Put walnuts through meat grinder twice. Soak bread slices in a little chicken stock, squeeze dry. Place in a mixing bowl, add walnuts, salt, and pepper and put mixture through meat grinder again. Then add 1 cup of chicken stock a little at a time and work into a paste the consistency of mayonnaise. More stock may be added if the paste is too thick. If desired, garlic may be added. Mix chicken parts with one-fourth of the sauce. Place on a serving platter. Then spread the rest of the paste over the chicken smoothly (like a chocolate frosting spread on a cake).

In a small saucepan over a low flame, heat paprika and oil until the oil turns red. Pour this over the paste carefully, leaving the paprika powder in saucepan.

This is an interesting surprise as an appetizer served with romaine lettuce hearts or with White Pilav*.

When served with rice, place chicken in the middle of a large round platter and make a ring with rice around it.

Always serve at room temperature. Never refrigerate because the chicken stock in the walnut paste congeals and loses its creaminess when chilled.

A blender may be used instead of a meat grinder for making the walnut paste. Then the walnuts need not be ground separately. All ingredients, walnuts, bread, stock, and garlic, are placed into the blender at the same time. But care must be taken to follow blender rules. Ingredients, stock first, must be placed in the blender in small proportions and the rest gradually added as the first lump is ground to paste.

SERVES 6 PERSONS.

WALNUTS OR WATERMELONS

One summer afternoon, Nasrettin Hoca, working on his vegetable garden, stopped to rest his tired bones. The shade of his walnut trees beckoned him to a siesta. With his legs outstretched and his back resting on the trunk, he relaxed. As he did so, he caught sight of a huge watermelon outgrowing its slender stem.

"Strange are the ways of the Almighty," he mumbled to himself. "Look at this magnificent tree with only a small measly little nut and the measly watermelon plant with a magnificent . . ." and he dozed away.

All of a sudden there was a thump on his bald head and he found himself on his feet. Fondling the growing lump, he viewed the delinquent walnut and thanked God for his infinite wisdom.

"Oh, Lord," he said, "if the tree had produced the watermelon as I thought it should I would have joined you sooner than you expected"; and he proceeded to gather the fallen walnuts, his mouth watering in anticipation of the chicken walnut dinner promised by his good wife.

CHICKEN STEW
Tavuk Yahni

1 medium frying or broiling chicken	1 tablespoon flour
12 small white onions	1 can (8 ounce) whole tomatoes and juice
2 tablespoons butter	½ cup water
Salt, pepper, and paprika to taste	4 tablespoons red wine

Clean and cut the chicken into serving pieces. Place in a shallow casserole. Leave the onions whole but remove the outer skins. Wash and place them between the pieces of chicken in the casserole.

Dot with butter. Add salt, pepper, and paprika and sprinkle flour on top of the chicken pieces.

Put tomatoes and ½ cup water over the chicken. Cover and cook over medium heat until the chicken is tender, about 30 minutes.

Add wine and cook for another 2 minutes.

Serve hot with Vermicelli Pilav* and watercress salad.

SERVES 4 TO 5 PERSONS.

CHICKEN ZUCCHINI
Tavuklu Kabak

6 large fat zucchini, about 6 inches long	1 can (3 ounce) sliced mushrooms, drained
5 cups water	⅓ cup flour
Salt	2 cups milk
4 tablespoons butter	1 cup coarsely grated Gruyère cheese
2 medium chicken breasts	Pepper to taste
6 peppercorns	
1 small carrot, diced	

Preheat oven to 400 degrees F. after the chicken filling has been prepared.

Scrape and wash zucchini and trim both ends. Cut through lengthwise and scrape out seeds and pulp making a ½ inch thick, canoe-shaped shell.

Place rack in a large saucepan and on it arrange shells side by side in a row. Add 3 cups water and ½ teaspoon salt. Cover and cook over medium heat until shells are tender but not soft, about 15 minutes.

Grease an oven-proof dish with 1 tablespoon butter. Take shells out carefully and arrange them side by side in the oven-proof dish with hollow sides up. Set aside.

Place chicken breasts in a saucepan. Add 2 cups of water, a pinch of salt, peppercorns, and carrot. Cover and cook over medium heat until chicken is tender, about 25 minutes. Remove chicken from saucepan. Discard bones and skin. Cut meat into thin, 1 inch long strips. Add the diced carrots and mushroom slices. Mix and set aside.

Melt the rest of the butter in a saucepan over low heat. Add flour and sauté for 2 minutes, stirring constantly. Add milk and continue to cook, stirring constantly until milk thickens, about 6 minutes. Add ⅔ cup cheese, salt, pepper, and continue to stir until cheese melts. Remove from heat.

Thoroughly mix half of the sauce with the chicken. Heap zucchini shells with this mixure. Spoon the other half of the sauce over the filled shells. Smooth tops and sprinkle the remaining cheese over the sauce, dividing it equally over each shell.

Bake zucchini until cheese turns brown, about 25 minutes.

Serve as a luncheon dish.

SERVES 6 PERSONS.

STUFFED TURKEY

Hindi Dolması

1 cup rice	*5 cups water*
Salt	*9 medium green apples*
Young turkey about 7 pounds, with neck, liver, heart, and gizzard	*10 tablespoons butter*
	2 tablespoons pignolia nuts
	Pepper to taste
1 carrot, quartered	*2 tablespoons black currants*
1 onion, quartered	*1 bunch scallions, whites*
1 stalk celery, quartered	*only, finely chopped*
Few peppercorns	

Preheat oven to 400 degrees F.

Place rice in a bowl, add 1 tablespoon salt, and cover with hot water. Stir and allow to cool. Drain and set aside.

Place neck of turkey in a saucepan. Add carrot, onion, celery, peppercorns, dash of salt, and 5 cups of water. Cook over medium heat until stock is reduced to 3 cups. Strain and set aside.

Place turkey, prepared for roasting, in a large baking pan, breast upward. Later, apples will be added to pan. Stick 1 apple into the neck cavity. Brush turkey with 4 tablespoons melted butter. Cover with aluminum foil.

Place turkey in oven and reduce heat to 325 degrees F. Add 1 cup of stock to the pan and roast for 1 hour.

Dice liver, heart, black meat of gizzard, and sauté with 2 tablespoons of butter in a small saucepan over medium heat, stirring constantly for 5 minutes. Set aside.

Melt 4 tablespoons butter in a heavy saucepan, add nuts and rice, sauté over medium heat, stirring constantly for 10 minutes. Add salt, pepper, currants, and 1 cup of boiling stock. Stir, cover, and cook over medium heat until all stock is absorbed, about 15 minutes. Remove from heat, add scallions and sautéed liver with its butter and mix together.

After turkey has been roasted for 1 hour, remove from oven. Remove foil and stuff body cavity with as much rice mixture as you can, leaving the rest in the saucepan. Sew up opening. Place apples in pan around turkey. Continue to roast, basting every 15 minutes, for 1½ hours or until turkey is tender and golden brown. Add more stock as it evaporates.

Add ½ cup boiling stock to leftover rice in saucepan. Cover and cook until stock is absorbed, about 10 minutes. Remove from heat. Take off cover, place a napkin over the saucepan, and replace cover. Leave covered in a warm place for 40 minutes, or until serving time.

To serve, place apples around turkey, or serve them in a separate vegetable dish. The leftover cooked rice may be served in a separate dish for second helpings.

Strain juices remaining in pan and serve.

SERVES 8 PERSONS.

TURKEY WITH CHESTNUTS
Kestaneli Hindi

7 *pound turkey, with neck,*	7 *tablespoons butter*
liver, heart, and gizzard	1½ *pounds large chestnuts*
1 *carrot, quartered*	1 *teaspoon sugar*
3 *medium onions, quartered*	½ *bunch watercress*
1 *stalk celery, quartered*	1 *tablespoon flour*
Few peppercorns	*Pepper to taste*
Salt	1 *teaspoon mixed herbs*
7 *cups water*	

Preheat oven to 400 degrees F.

Make a stock with neck of turkey, carrot, 1 onion, celery, pepper-corns, dash of salt, and 5 cups of water. Cover saucepan and cook over medium heat until stock reduces to 4 cups. Strain and set aside.

Prepare turkey for roasting and place in a roasting pan breast side up. Fill body cavity with 2 quartered onions and the diced liver, heart, and gizzard. Brush turkey with 4 tablespoons melted butter and cover with aluminum foil.

Place turkey in oven and reduce heat to 325 degrees F. Add 1 cup of stock to pan. Roast for 1 hour, remove foil and continue to roast, basting with drippings every 15 minutes, until turkey is tender and golden brown, about 1½ hours. Add more stock as it evaporates.

Slash chestnut shells without cutting the meat. Place in pan and roast in oven until they open up (a few minutes). Remove outer shells and peel off inner skins with a knife, leaving chestnuts whole.

Place chestnuts in a saucepan with 1 cup of stock, 2 cups water, 1 tablespoon butter, 1 teaspoon salt, and 1 teaspoon sugar. Cover and cook over medium heat until chestnuts are soft, but not crumbling, about 30 minutes. Remove chestnuts with a perforated kitchen spoon. Keep in a warm place until serving time.

Remove turkey when done to a serving platter. Place chestnuts around platter. Decorate with watercress.

Place 2 tablespoons butter in the pan in which turkey was roasted. Add 1 tablespoon flour and 1 or 2 cups of stock or water.

Cook over medium heat, stirring constantly until sauce boils and thickens. Add salt, pepper, and herbs. Serve separately in a sauce-boat.

SERVES 8 PERSONS.

Eat and drink with your friends but do not trade with them.

THE TURKEY

Among the household pets, birds are especially loved by the Turks. Many families take pride in their canaries.

Singing contests among the canaries are the joy of bird-fanciers. On the Aegean coast lovebirds carry on their amorous dialogue in their colorful cages swinging from almost every balcony. There are also pigeon fanciers who specialize in different types of the species. More practical-minded types raise their own chickens and ducks. In the open markets hens and cocks are sold alive.

The story is told of Nasrettin Hoca, the sage, who particularly liked turkeys. One day he was in the market for his weekly shopping. He found his way blocked by a crowd. They were watching an argument between two men about the price of a parrot.

"Twenty gold coins," insisted the owner.

"Eighteen," said the customer.

"For a small bird like that?" said Hoca.

"Yes," answered the owner. "You know what it can do? It can talk."

Next week Hoca was in the marketplace with one of his turkeys.

"Fifty gold coins," he shouted, gathering a crowd around him.

"Are you mad?" they said. "Fifty gold coins for a turkey!"

"Why not? Compared with twenty gold pieces for a parrot— this is cheap."

"But the parrot can talk. What does the turkey do?"

"Aha!" said Hoca. "The turkey thinks."

8. *Meats*

Kebab is a word that has figured prominently in the Turkish cuisine for more than ten centuries. Naturally, as the different recipes will prove, it has developed to include broiled, baked, and stewed versions of different kinds of cubed meat. Indeed, a distinguishing feature of Turkish cooking is the cubing of meat into small, bite-size morsels. Sliced thus, meats are broiled as in Shish Kebab, or stewed as in Steam Kebab.

Another feature of the Turkish preparation of meat is its mixture with vegetables in such a way as to allow for an interchange of flavors. For instance, the meat in Turkish Shish Kebab is always placed between a morsel of tomato and a morsel of green pepper or onion.

Lamb is the meat par excellence in Turkey. During the spring, baby lambs no older than a couple weeks are a special delight. In the countryside they are placed in a pit with smoldering charcoal at the bottom. Then the top is covered with earth and the lamb left to roast gradually in the enclosed chamber. At home and in the restaurants spring lamb chops charcoal-broiled should not be overcooked. Many of the meat dishes in this collection which require lamb in Turkey can be cooked with veal and beef in this country. However, delicate and choice pieces of these meats should be used for tenderness and juiciness.

Chopped meats constitute an important ingredient of the Turkish cuisine. For the many types of dolmas, they are indispensable. Meat for these should not be too lean. A certain amount of meat fat is necessary for succulence. Lemon and Egg Sauce, which the Turks call terbiye, enhances the flavor of these dishes. Dolmas are exotic and at the same time constitute an excellent main course for lunch. They also add to the variety of a buffet dinner. Chilled white wine or beer can be served with the dolmas very pleasantly.

Some meat dishes are cooked with a plate on top in order to keep them in shape. Any ordinary plate can be used.

Shopping for the daily entrails in Turkey a stranger will notice a special shop where variety meats are sold. Indeed, they occupy a niche in the Turkish kitchen. There are also restaurants that specialize in variety meats. Many of the late merrymakers will be found in an *Iskembeci* shop in the early hours of the morning drinking a huge bowl of Tripe Soup. The same establishments also specialize in liver and brains. Liver Petites are recommended for hors d'oeuvres. The various brain dishes are excellent lunch servings. Preferably they can be served with chilled white wine or beer.

Meats

MEAT DISHES

BEEF WITH ONIONS
Sovanlı Yahni

2 pounds beef, cut into 1 inch
cubes
3 tablespoons butter
2 tomatoes, diced
1 pound pearl onions, only
first coat removed and
trimmed whole

2 cloves garlic, optional
½ teaspoon allspice
2 tablespoons vinegar
Salt and pepper to taste
1 cup tomato juice

Cook meat and butter in a covered saucepan over low heat for 1
hour. Shake saucepan occasionally to prevent scorching. Add tomatoes, onions, garlic, allspice, vinegar, salt, pepper, and tomato
juice. Cover and continue to cook over low heat for 1 hour more or
until meat is tender. This dish should not be dry but must have its
own sauce. If necessary a little warm water may be added. Serve
warm with boiled Brussels sprouts or noodles.

SERVES 4 TO 5 PERSONS.

SHORT RIBS IN POT
Kavurma

2 pounds short ribs of beef
Salt to taste

Cut short ribs into pieces 1 inch wide and 2 inches long. Place in
2 quart saucepan. The size of the pan is of prime importance for
the ribs should fill three-fourths of the saucepan, otherwise they
will not cook properly. Cover and cook over medium heat until
meat is juicy. Reduce heat to very low and cook covered until all
the juice is absorbed and the meat is tender, about 1½ hours. This

dish requires very slow cooking. When the meat is tender and all the juice absorbed, uncover, add salt, and cook another 15 minutes, stirring occasionally.

This is an easy dish to prepare and very palatable. It can be served on every occasion with numerous side dishes, but is best served with Cracked Wheat Pilav* and Shepherds' Salad*.

SERVES 4 PERSONS.

EGGPLANT KEBAB

Patlıcanlı Kebab

1½ pounds boneless, fat-free cubed lamb, veal, or beef
2 medium onions, chopped
4 tablespoons butter
3 medium tomatoes, 2 diced, 1 sliced
Salt and pepper to taste
4 medium eggplants
2 green peppers, seeded and cut into rings

In a saucepan sauté the meat and onions in 1 tablespoon butter, stirring occasionally until meat is browned, about 10 minutes. Add the diced tomatoes, salt, and pepper, cover, and cook over low heat until meat is tender.

Cut the stem off the eggplant. Then peel off a half inch wide strip of the black skin lengthwise leaving the next half inch with the skin on. Repeat until you make a striped effect. Then cut vegetable crosswise into 1 inch thick round slices. Place slices in a deep tray and salt them generously. Fill tray with cold water. Leave about 30 minutes. Squeeze out the bitter juice, wash with cold water and dry.

Place 3 tablespoons butter in a frying pan. Heat and sauté eggplant slices on both sides. Place in a shallow flat cooking pot in one layer. Spread the cooked meat on top. Garnish with green pepper rings and tomato slices.

Cover and cook over a medium heat for about 20 to 25 minutes. Serve hot with Tomato Pilav*.

SERVES 8 TO 10 PERSONS.

GARDENER'S KEBAB
Bahcıvan Kebabı

2 pounds lamb or beef,   1 pound pearl onions, whole
   cut into 1 inch cubes   1 cup shelled green peas
6 tablespoons butter   Salt and red pepper to taste
2 large carrots, sliced   1 tablespoon fresh chopped
4 medium tomatoes, diced   dill

Brown meat in butter. Add carrots, cover tightly, and cook over low heat until meat is dry, about 1 hour, shaking saucepan occasionally to prevent scorching. Add tomatoes, onions, peas, salt, and red pepper to taste. Cover and cook for ½ hour. Add a little water, not more than a cup, if necessary, to prevent scorching.
When meat is tender, add dill, stir, and serve.
May be served with egg noodles or Tomato Pilav*.

SERVES 5 TO 6 PERSONS.

KEBAB PAPILLOTE
Kağıt Kebabı

1½ pounds boneless beef,   2 medium tomatoes, fresh
   veal, or lamb, cut into 1   or canned, diced
   inch cubes   2 tablespoons rosé wine
3 tablespoons butter   1 cup hot water
1 large onion, grated   3 tablespoons margarine
2 medium carrots, cut into   2 medium potatoes, peeled
   ½ inch pieces   and cut into ½ inch cubes
2 cups chopped dill or parsley ½ cup cooked peas
Salt and pepper to taste   ½ teaspoon thyme leaves

Preheat oven to 375 degrees F. after the meat has been prepared.
Place meat in saucepan with 3 tablespoons butter. Sauté until light brown, about 10 minutes. Add onion, carrots, 1 cup dill, salt, and pepper. Continue to sauté 10 minutes more, stirring occasionally. Add tomatoes, wine, and sauté 5 minutes more. Add 1 cup hot

water, a little at a time, cover, and cook over medium heat until meat is tender and about 8 tablespoons of juice remain in the saucepan. If necessary, a little more hot water may be added.

Remove meat and carrots with a perforated spoon into a plate, leaving juice in saucepan.

Melt margarine in a small saucepan. Add potatoes and sauté over high heat until browned and done. Add to carrots with the margarine remaining in saucepan. Add peas and the remaining dill, and then the thyme. Mix well.

Put on a table 4 pieces of 14 inch square double-fold wax paper. Divide meat into 4 portions. Place each portion in the center of a piece of wax paper. Divide vegetables into 4 portions and add to meat. Pour one-quarter of the sauce from the saucepan over each pile of meat and vegetables. Bring ends of wax paper together crosswise over the meat, making a square package. With a few tablespoons of water wet a baking pan large enough for the 4 packages. Place packages in pan, loose ends securely tucked under. Wet package tops with a little water. Bake packages for 20 minutes.

Remove packages to a serving platter and serve hot with your favorite salad. Or place each package on dinner plate, loose end up, open paper and crush it into a ring around the meat.

SERVE 1 PACKAGE PER PERSON.

SHISH KEBAB
Şiş Kebab

2 pounds boned leg of lamb or beef, cut into 1 inch cubes	½ tablespoon thyme leaves
	6 long skewers
	3 medium tomatoes, halved
2 tablespoons olive oil	2 green peppers, seeded and quartered
3 tablespoons lemon juice	
1 large onion, grated	8 medium mushrooms, peeled
Salt and pepper to taste	6 pearl onions, peeled

Preheat broiler or have charcoal fire ready after the meat has been marinated.

Place meat in a bowl, add olive oil, lemon juice, grated onion, salt, pepper, and thyme leaves. Mix well, cover, and refrigerate for

4 to 5 hours for lamb, overnight for beef. Remove from refrigerator 2 hours before cooking.

Arrange meat on skewers alternately with tomatoes, peppers, mushrooms, and pearl onions. Broil, preferably over charcoal, taking care to place skewers 3 inches above the coals, which should be red hot but not flaming. Broil about 5 minutes on each side, turning the skewers so that meat browns evenly.

Place skewers on a serving platter and serve with Tomato Pilav*, Cracked Wheat Pilav*, and Shepherds' Salad*.

SERVES 6 PERSONS.

STEAM KEBAB

Islim Kebabı

1½ pounds lamb or beef, cut into 1 inch cubes	2 cups hot water
2 tablespoons butter	Salt and pepper to taste
1 onion, coarsely grated	2 large eggplants
2 tomatoes, 1 diced, 1 sliced into 4 pieces	2 green peppers
	2 cups olive or salad oil

Preheat oven to 400 degrees F. after the meat has been cooked.

Sautè meat in butter and onion over medium heat in a saucepan, stirring occasionally until meat turns brown, 30 minutes. Add diced tomato and continue to sauté and stir occasionally for 10 minutes more. Add 2 cups hot water, salt, pepper. Cover and cook over low heat until meat is tender and just a few tablespoons juice are left, about 1½ hours. If necessary more water may be added. Set aside.

Cut stems off the eggplants. Peel and cut lengthwise into ½ inch slices.

Cut peppers into 4 equal pieces and remove seeds.

Place 1½ cups of the oil into frying pan and heat to boiling point. Fry eggplant slices on both sides until golden brown. Take care that slices are well cooked and soft. Drain on absorbent paper to get rid of excess oil. After the first panful of eggplant slices is cooked add the rest of the oil.

Fry peppers in the same way in the oil used for the eggplant. Lay half the fried eggplant slices next to one another on the bottom of an 8×8 inch oven-proof dish. Place some meat cubes over each slice and spoon a little sauce over meat cubes, leaving butter in saucepan. Cover meat cubes with the remaining eggplant slices, placing each slice on top of the bottom one with meat in between. Place peppers on top and decorate each slice with a piece of tomato. Spoon remaining butter over the whole dish. Wrap dish tightly with aluminum foil.

Bake for 20 minutes. Unwrap foil and serve right away.
Serve with Tomato and Cucumber Salad*.

SERVES 4 PERSONS.

YOGURT KEBAB
Yoğurtlu Kebab

1½ pounds boneless lamb or	*2 pints yogurt*
beef, cut into 1 inch cubes	*2 cloves garlic, crushed,*
1 medium onion, grated	*optional*
3 tablespoons olive oil	*4 medium very ripe tomatoes*
2 tablespoons lemon juice	*4 English muffins*
1 teaspoon thyme leaves	*5 tablespoons butter*
Salt and pepper to taste	*1 teaspoon paprika*
4 long skewers	

Put meat in a bowl with onion, 2 tablespoons oil, lemon juice, thyme, salt, and pepper. Mix well. Cover and refrigerate for 4 to 5 hours for lamb, overnight for beef. Remove from refrigerator 2 hours before cooking.

Preheat broiler or have charcoal fire ready.

When ready to cook, divide and arrange meat on 4 oiled skewers. (Use remaining tablespoon of oil for this.) Place skewers on tray and put aside.

Pour yogurt into a bowl. Add salt and garlic and leave in a warm place.

Warm 4 individual earthenware or oven-proof shallow dishes, such as pie dishes. Keep them warm.

Peel, seed, and dice 2 tomatoes. Place in a small saucepan and cook over medium heat, stirring and mashing occasionally until they are cooked well. Keep warm.

Broil meat preferably over charcoal, taking care to place skewers 3 inches above the coals, which should be red hot but not flaming. Broil about 5 minutes on each side, turning skewers so meat browns evenly. If cooked under the broiler, it will take a few minutes longer. While meat is cooking, quarter the remaining 2 tomatoes and broil.

Place muffins under the broiler or on charcoal fire and toast both sides a few minutes.

While the meat is broiling take serving dishes out of oven. Place 1 toasted muffin, cut into 4 pieces, on each dish.

Melt butter in saucepan but do not brown. Pour 1 tablespoon on each muffin. Spoon the cooked tomatoes over buttered muffins. Then pour yogurt sauce generously, filling the dish.

Stir 1 teaspoon paprika into the remaining melted butter. Heat but do not burn. Keep warm.

Take meat from skewers. Place a skewer of meat over each dish of yogurt and muffins. Decorate with broiled tomato pieces and paprika butter.

Serve at once.

This is a delicious summer dish for an informal family dinner. It is quite filling, so a light dessert, such as Melon Dolma*, should follow, or fresh fruit in season is perfect.

SERVES 4 PERSONS.

POTTED LAMB WITH RICE
Tas Kebab

2 cups rice	1 small green pepper,
Salt to taste	seeded and chopped
1 pound lamb or beef, cubed	¼ teaspoon allspice
6 tablespoons butter	Black pepper to taste
2 medium tomatoes, cubed	3 cups water
1 medium onion, chopped	2 sprigs parsley

Place rice in a bowl, add 1 tablespoon salt, and cover with hot water. Stir and allow to cool. Drain and set aside.

Place meat in a saucepan, add 1 tablespoon butter, tomatoes, onion, green pepper, allspice, salt, and black pepper to taste. Add 3 cups of water. Cover and cook over a medium heat until meat is tender, about 1 hour.

Strain meat and save broth. Place meat in middle of a large saucepan with plenty of space around it. Cover meat with a metal bowl, placing a heavy object on top of the bowl to prevent displacement. Bring to boil 2 cups of broth, adding water if necessary to make 2 cups, with 4 tablespoons of butter. Pour into the saucepan with the meat.

Pour rice into the boiling broth. Stir, cover saucepan, and cook on medium heat for 5 minutes. Then turn heat on low and cook until rice absorbs all the broth, about 15 minutes. Remove from heat. Take off cover, place a napkin over the saucepan and replace cover. Leave covered for 40 minutes in a warm place. When ready to transfer to a serving dish, remove the metal bowl carefully. Stir rice with a wooden spoon gently, taking care not to break it, keeping meat in the middle. Place a round serving dish on the saucepan and invert. The meat should be in the middle of the dish and the rice around it. Decorate with parsley and serve.

SERVES 6 PERSONS.

CULTURED MEATBALLS
Terbiyeli Köfte

1 pound ground beef	*3 cups water*
1 onion, grated	*2 eggs*
3 tablespoons rice	*Juice ½ lemon*
Salt and pepper to taste	*1 tablespoon dry crushed*
2 tablespoons flour	*mint leaves*

Place meat in a bowl, add onion, rice, salt, and pepper. Knead mixture well. Form round, half-dollar size meatballs and place on wax paper.

In a saucepan mix flour with 3 cups of water. Cook over slow heat, stirring constantly. When flour mixture starts bubbling, add meatballs one by one and continue cooking over medium heat for 45 minutes uncovered, or until the meatballs are done. Remove from heat.

Break eggs into a bowl, beat well with an eggbeater; add lemon juice and beat 1 minute more. Gradually add a few tablespoons of the hot meatball sauce to the egg mixture and continue to beat. Then pour egg mixture over the meatballs. Transfer to a deep serving dish, sprinkle mint leaves on top and serve.

This is an informal lunch dish. Serve with asparagus. It can also be served on toast.

SERVES 4 PERSONS.

LADY MEATBALLS
Kadin Budu

½ cup rice	¼ cup chopped dill
2 cups water	Salt and pepper to taste
1 pound lean beef, ground	½ cup flour
1 large onion, grated	3 eggs, beaten
½ cup grated Parmesan cheese	½ cup shortening
¼ cup chopped parsley	2 cups Lemon and Egg Sauce II*

Boil rice with 2 cups of water over medium heat until tender. Remove from heat, drain well. Place meat in a bowl, add rice, onions, cheese, parsley, dill, salt, and pepper. Knead mixture for 5 minutes. Form into egg-shaped ovals and roll in flour.

Dip the balls into the eggs, which have been beaten until frothy. Fry on both sides in hot shortening.

Makes about 12 large meatballs.

This is a dish which agrees with almost every palate. Pour sauce over and serve with asparagus or broccoli.

SERVES 6 PERSONS.

FRIED MEATBALLS
Kuru Köfte

1 pound lean beef, ground twice	2 eggs
1 large onion, grated	2 tablespoons chopped parsley
2 slices stale white bread, soaked in water and squeezed dry	Salt and black pepper to taste
	1 tablespoon flour
	2 tablespoons butter

Combine meat, onion, bread, eggs, parsley, salt, and pepper in a bowl. Knead well for 10 minutes. Wet palms with warm water and shape meat into round rolls about 3 inches long, like thick fingers. Roll in flour. Heat butter in frying pan over medium heat and brown meatballs evenly on both sides.

Serve hot with french fried potatoes and Shepherds' Salad*.

SERVES 6 TO 8 PERSONS.

MEATBALLS IN TOMATO SAUCE
Izmir Köftesi

1 pound lean beef, ground twice	1 tablespoon flour
1 large onion, grated	2 tablespoons butter
2 slices stale white bread, soaked in water and squeezed dry	3 medium tomatoes, cubed, or ¼ cup tomato paste
2 eggs	2 green peppers, seeded and diced
Salt and pepper to taste	½ tablespoon sugar
2 tablespoons chopped parsley	½ tablespoon oil
	1 cup water

Prepare and sauté meatballs as for Fried Meatballs*, but the meatballs should be larger and either round or egg-shaped.

Strain butter in which the meatballs were sautéed into a saucepan, add tomatoes, green peppers, sugar, oil, salt, black pepper, and 1 cup of water. Cook over medium heat for 20 minutes.

Place meatballs in a shallow saucepan. Pour over the tomato sauce, cook over medium heat for 15 minutes.

Serve hot with fried potatoes and mixed pickles.

MAKES ABOUT 8 TO 10 MEATBALLS.
SERVES 4 TO 5 PERSONS.

SHISH MEATBALLS
Şiş Köfte

1 large onion, grated	*8 small skewers*
2 tablespoons salt	
2 pounds lamb or beef,	OPTIONAL:
ground twice	*4 slices white bread*
2 eggs	*2 cups Yogurt Sauce I**
Pepper to taste	*2 tablespoons butter*
1 tablespoon salad or olive oil	*1 tablespoon paprika*

Preheat broiler or have charcoal fire ready.

Place onion and 2 tablespoons salt in a bowl. Let stand 15 minutes.

Place meat in a bowl and squeeze onion juice through cheesecloth into the bowl. Add eggs and pepper and knead well. Shape into 8 sausages, 1 inch in diameter and 4 inches long. Oil surface of each. Oil skewers and put them through the meatballs. Broil, preferably over charcoal, taking care to place skewers 3 inches above coals, which should be red hot but not flaming. Broil about 5 minutes on each side until meatballs are evenly browned.

May be served on skewers with chilled tomato juice and corn on the cob.

Another way of serving: Toast 4 slices of white bread and put 1 slice on each serving plate. Remove meatballs from skewers and place 2 on each piece of toast. Pour yogurt sauce on top. Put butter and paprika in a small pan and heat until very hot but do not allow to burn. Pour over yogurt and serve immediately.

SERVES 4 PERSONS.

TURKISH MEAT LOAF
Sucuklu Köfte

1½ pounds ground meat,
half beef and half veal
1 egg
2 thin slices white bread,
soaked in water and
squeezed dry
1 onion, grated
1 tablespoon salad or olive oil

2 cloves garlic, crushed
1 teaspoon allspice
1 tablespoon ground caraway
seed
2 tablespoons chopped dill
Salt and pepper to taste
½ cup water

Preheat oven to 350 degrees F.

Place meat and other ingredients except water in a bowl and knead well. Form into a meat loaf. Place in a baking pan and add ½ cup of water; bake for 45 or 50 minutes.

Slice and serve with ketchup and any desired vegetable.

May also be served cold.

SERVES 6 TO 8 PERSONS.

LAMB CHOPS THYME
Kuzu Pirzolası

1 medium onion
1 teaspoon salt
2 tablespoons olive oil

8 lamb chops
1 tablespoon thyme leaves
Few sprigs parsley

Preheat broiler or have charcoal fire ready.

Grate onion into a bowl and sprinkle salt over. Leave 10 minutes. Then extract onion juice by squeezing onions between palms. Add juice to olive oil.

Lay chops on wax paper. Rub olive oil and onion juice mixture on both sides of chops. Sprinkle thyme leaves generously on both sides. Cover with another piece of wax paper and leave for 2 hours.

Broil, preferably, over charcoal, taking care to place chops 3

inches from the coals, which should be red hot but not flaming.
Broil 5 minutes on each side.

Arrange on serving platter, garnish with sprigs of parsley, and
serve.

ALLOW 2 CHOPS PER PERSON.

ROAST LEG OF LAMB
Kuzu Budu Rostosu

1 leg of lamb, about	*1 teaspoon black pepper*
6½ pounds	*3 cloves garlic, optional*
1 lemon	*2 tablespoons olive oil*
½ tablespoon salt	*2 tablespoons thyme leaves*
1 tablespoon paprika	*1 bunch watercress*

Preheat oven to 350 degrees F. when lamb is ready.

Trim all the fat from the lamb. Squeeze juice of lemon over meat
and rub in. Combine salt, paprika, and pepper and rub in. Insert
cloves in several spots. Spread oil and sprinkle thyme leaves on both
sides.

Place leg in baking pan and cover pan with aluminum foil.
Leave at room temperature for 2 hours.

Place leg of lamb in oven and bake for 1 hour. Then remove
foil and cook until surface is well browned, about 1 hour, basting
occasionally with drippings in the pan. Remove from oven and
slice, keeping in the shape of the leg.

Decorate with watercress. Serve with a vegetable and Chicken
Liver Pilav*.

SERVES 12 PERSONS.

SPRING LAMB WITH LETTUCE LEAVES
Kapama

2 bunches scallions, using
  green tops, cut into 2
  inch lengths
1 medium onion, cut into 8
  pieces
1 medium carrot, scraped
  and cut into 2 inch pieces
2 large Boston lettuce
2 large romaine lettuce

6 pound leg of young spring
  lamb
½ lemon
2 tablespoons butter
½ tablespoon sugar
Salt to taste
1 cup water
1 bunch dill, chopped

Spread scallions, onion, and carrot pieces on the bottom of a large
heavy saucepan.

Separate leaves of Boston and romaine lettuces one by one. Wash
well. Place evenly over the carrots and scallions. Do not be alarmed
by the bulk; lettuce diminishes as it cooks.

Have your butcher cut the leg of lamb into 3 inch chunks, with
the bones. Trim all the fat from the chunks and rub with lemon.
Place over lettuce leaves. Add butter, sugar, salt, and 1 cup water.
Cover and cook over very low heat, until meat is tender, about 2½
to 3 hours, and about 2 cups of the juices remain at the bottom of
the saucepan. Add dill and cook 5 minutes more.

Serve immediately, placing 1 piece of meat and some lettuce leaves
on each plate. Pour 1 or 2 spoonfuls of juice over it. Serve with
warmed French or Italian bread.

SERVES 8 PERSONS.

*If skill could be acquired by watching, dogs would become
butchers.*

SULTAN'S DELIGHT
Hünhâr Beğendi

1½ pounds lamb, beef, or	*2 small tomatoes, diced*
veal, cut into 1 inch cubes	*Salt and pepper to taste*
2 small onions, chopped	*Eggplant Purée**
2 tablespoons butter	*1 tablespoon chopped parsley*

Place meat, onions, and butter in a saucepan. Sauté over medium heat until meat turns brown, about 10 minutes, stirring occasionally.

Add tomatoes and sauté 5 minutes more. Add salt and pepper, cover, and cook over low heat until meat is tender. Add a little warm water if necessary.

Place meat in the middle of a round serving platter. Arrange eggplant purée around the meat. Decorate meat with parsley and serve hot.

SERVES 6 PERSONS.

ARTICHOKE MEAT DOLMA
Etli Enginar Dolması

1 pound lamb or beef, ground	*2 egg whites*
1 large onion, grated	*Salt and pepper to taste*
¼ cup rice	*2 tablespoons flour*
½ cup diced canned whole	*Juice 1 lemon*
tomatoes	*10 medium artichokes*
2 tablespoons chopped parsley,	*4 tablespoons butter*
save stems	*1 cup Lemon and Egg*
2 tablespoons chopped dill,	*Sauce II**
save stems	

Place meat, onion, rice, tomatoes, parsley, dill, egg whites, salt, and pepper in a bowl. Mix well. Set aside.

Fill a large bowl with cold water; sprinkle with flour and lemon juice and mix well. Set aside.

Prepare artichokes by removing the outer leaves until only tender ones remain. Trim off tough upper portions of the remaining leaves, leaving about 2 inches attached to the heart of the artichoke. The heart is concealed by the choke, a fuzz which must be spooned out. Also remove the thorny pinkish inner leaves. Trim off bottom. Drop artichokes into the bowl of water with lemon juice and flour to prevent discoloration. When all artichokes are ready, shake off excess water and stuff hearts with the meat mixture. (Save 5 cups of this water.) Repeat until all artichokes are filled. Dot with 3 tablespoons butter.

Place rack at the bottom of a heavy saucepan. Place 1 tablespoon butter and dill and parsley stems on rack.

Cut out 10 pieces of 12×12 inch wax paper.

Place 1 artichoke in the middle of a sheet of paper. Gather ends together and twist. Place each wrapped artichoke, bottom down, into the saucepan over dill stems. Add 2 cups of the saved flour water. Put a plate on top to give weight during cooking. Cover and cook over medium heat until water is absorbed. Add 2 more cups of the flour water. Continue to cook. Add the last cup of flour water and cook until artichokes are tender, about 1½ hours.

Unwrap artichokes while still hot and arrange on a serving platter. Pour lemon and egg sauce over.

Serve as a second course after fish or chicken, or as a main luncheon dish.

Note: If any water remains in the saucepan it can be used for making the lemon and egg sauce.

ALLOW 2 PER PERSON
AS MAIN COURSE
AND 1 AS SECOND
COURSE.

CABBAGE MEAT DOLMA
Etli Lahana Dolması

1 pound ground lamb or beef	*Salt and cayenne to taste*
1 large onion, coarsely grated	*11½ cups water*
¼ cup rice	*3 to 3½ pounds white*
1½ cups canned, whole	*cabbage*
tomatoes with juice, diced	*3 tablespoons butter*
2 tablespoons fresh chopped	*1 cup Lemon and Egg*
mint leaves	*Sauce II**
½ cup chopped parsley	

Place meat, onion, rice, tomatoes, mint, parsley, salt, and cayenne in a bowl. Knead well. Set aside.

On high heat bring to a boil 10 cups of water in a large saucepan and 1 teaspoon salt.

Wash cabbage. Cut around core where leaves join it by inserting a sharp knife deep enough to loosen the leaves from the core but not detach them. Place whole cabbage, core upward, into boiling water. Cover, let boil for 3 minutes. Remove cover and take out a few of the outer leaves. Tilt cabbage with the aid of a spoon and take leaves out with tongs, being careful not to break them. Cover saucepan and let boil 3 minutes more. Again take out a few leaves. Continue same process until you come to the heart of the cabbage. Pile leaves in a colander to drain and cool.

Cut leaves into palm-size sections, discarding the hard vein in the middle and the curled parts near the core. Reserve discarded leaves. Pile prepared leaf sections on a dish.

Place several layers of discarded cabbage leaves at the bottom of a heavy saucepan.

Take 1 leaf section from the prepared pile in your palm. Place 1½ to 2 tablespoonfuls of the meat mixture on the thicker end of the leaf 1½ inches away from the edge. Fold thick part over filling. Then fold sides over and roll toward the end of the leaf. Place in saucepan over layers of leaves, loose end facing downward so that ends are securely tucked under. Repeat same process with each leaf, placing dolmas close to each other in rows. When one layer is finished start next layer over the first, and so on until all the meat mixture is used.

Dot with butter. Cover top of dolmas with a layer of discarded leaves. Place a plate over to give weight during cooking. Add 1½ cups water. Cover and place saucepan over medium heat and cook 50 to 60 minutes. All the water does not have to be absorbed. If any remains use it for making the lemon and egg sauce.

Remove dolmas to serving platter. Pour hot sauce over.

Serve warm as an appetizer, or as the main course for lunch.

MAKES 30 DOLMAS.
ALLOW 3 OR 4 PER PERSON AS AN
APPETIZER AND 5 OR 6 AS
MAIN COURSE.

EGGPLANT MEAT DOLMA

Etli Patlıcan Dolması

1 pound ground lamb or beef
1 large onion, coarsely grated
¼ cup rice
⅓ cup tomato juice
1 cup chopped parsley, save stems
Salt and pepper to taste

6 to 7 short narrow eggplants
1 cup oil
3 tablespoons butter
1½ cups water
1 cup Lemon and Egg Sauce II*

Place meat, onion, rice, tomato juice, parsley, salt, and pepper in a bowl. Knead well.

Cut off stem end of eggplants and shape into a cover to be used later. Peel off a half inch wide strip of the black skin lengthwise leaving the next half inch with the skin on. Repeat until you make a striped effect. If the stem end is too narrow, cut off ½ inch from the opposite end and start scooping the inside from there. Leave about ½ inch thick shell. Discard scooped out pulp. Heat oil to boiling in frying pan. Sauté eggplant shells on each side, about 2 minutes per side. Fill shell with meat mixture a little at a time, pushing down with the handle of a spoon. When filled replace stem and cover. Repeat until all eggplants are filled.

Place rack at the bottom of a heavy saucepan and place parsley stems on rack. Arrange eggplants over parsley stems side by side.

If any filling is left, shape into balls 1 inch in diameter and place between or on eggplants.

Dot with butter, add 1½ cups water, place wax paper on top and cover. Cook over medium heat until eggplants are tender, about 1 hour. If necessary more water may be added.

Transfer to a warmed serving platter and keep warm. Put sauce remaining in saucepan into a cup and use this for making lemon and egg sauce. Pour sauce over eggplants.

Serve hot as a luncheon dish, or as a second course after fish or chicken.

SERVE 1 EGGPLANT PER PERSON AS A
LUNCHEON COURSE. SERVES UP
TO 12 PERSONS AS A SECOND
COURSE IF EGGPLANTS ARE
CUT IN HALF.

GRAPEVINE LEAF MEAT DOLMA
Etli Yaprak Dolması

7½ cups water	½ cup tomato juice
16 ounce jar grapevine leaves	1 cup chopped dill, save stems
1 pound ground lamb or beef	Salt and pepper to taste
1 large onion, coarsely grated	3 tablespoons butter
¼ cup rice	2 cups Yogurt Sauce I*

In a saucepan bring to a boil 6 cups of water. Unroll leaves and place in boiling water for 2 minutes. Carefully take leaves out with perforated kitchen spoon. Place in colander to drain. Separate leaves one by one without breaking, remove stem, and leave around the rim of the colander.

Put the meat, onion, rice, tomato juice, dill, salt, and pepper in a bowl and knead well.

Place dill stems at the bottom of a heavy saucepan.

Take a vine leaf, rough side up and the stem end toward you, into the palm of your left hand. Place 1 to 1½ tablespoonfuls of the meat mixture on the stem end of the leaf 1½ inches away from the edge. Fold stem end over filling. Then fold sides over and roll toward the end of the leaf. Put into saucepan on dill stems, loose end downward so that it is securely tucked under. Repeat process with each leaf, placing dolmas close to each other in rows. When one layer is finished start next layer over the first, and so on, until all the meat mixture is used.

Dot with butter. Cover top layer of dolmas with wax paper. Place a plate over to give weight during cooking. Add 1½ cups water. Cover saucepan and cook over medium heat for 50 to 60 minutes.

Pour sauce remaining in pan over the dolmas. Serve hot with yogurt sauce I on the side.

MAKES 40 DOLMAS.
ALLOW 4 TO 5 PER PERSON.

GREEN PEPPER MEAT DOLMA
Etli Büber Dolması

1 pound ground lamb or beef	*Salt and pepper to taste*
1 large onion, coarsely grated	*7 green peppers*
¼ cup rice	*3 tablespoons butter*
½ cup tomato juice	*1½ cups water*
¼ cup chopped dill, save stems	*1 cup Yogurt Sauce I**
¼ cup chopped parsley, save stems	

Place meat in a bowl with the onion, rice, tomato juice, dill, parsley, salt, and pepper and knead well.

Wash and slice almost through tops of peppers but do not sever as they will serve as covers. Remove seeds. Fill peppers with meat mixture and put tops in place.

Place a rack in the bottom of a heavy saucepan. Put dill and parsley stems over rack. Arrange peppers upright over stems.

If any filling is left, shape into balls 1 inch in diameter and place between or on peppers.

Dot with butter. Add 1½ cups water, cover with wax paper, and put lid in place. Cook over medium heat until peppers are tender, about 1 hour.

Transfer peppers into a serving platter and pour over them sauce remaining in pan.

Serve hot with yogurt sauce I on the side as a luncheon dish or as a second course after fish or chicken.

ALLOW 2 PEPPERS PER PERSON FOR A MAIN COURSE,
1 PEPPER FOR A SECOND COURSE.

TOMATO MEAT DOLMA

Etli Domates Dolması

10 large half ripe tomatoes	*1 cup chicken or beef broth*
1 large onion, coarsely grated	*2 tablespoons black currants*
5 tablespoons butter	*½ cup chopped parsley*
5 tablespoons pignolia nuts	*2 tablespoons chopped fresh*
¼ cup rice	*mint leaves*
1 pound ground lamb or beef	*Salt and pepper to taste*

Preheat oven to 350 degrees F.

Slice almost through the stem end of each tomato, but do not sever as it will serve as a cover. Scoop out inside with a teaspoon. Save pulp from 4 tomatoes and dice. Set aside.

Arrange scooped tomatoes lid side up in a baking dish.

Sauté onion in a frying pan with 4 tablespoons of butter over medium heat, stirring constantly, for 5 minutes. Add nuts, sauté 3 minutes more. Add rice and sauté another 3 minutes. Add meat and sauté, always stirring, for 8 minutes. Add diced tomato pulp, stir, and sauté 5 minutes.

Bring to a boil chicken or meat stock. Add to meat mixture, stir, cover, and cook over medium heat until all stock is absorbed, about 20 minutes.

Remove from heat. Add currants, parsley, mint, salt, and pepper. Mix well.

Stuff tomatoes with meat mixture, pressing down with a spoon. Adjust top and dot with the remaining butter. Bake for 50 minutes.

Serve in the baking dish.

ALLOW 1 PER PERSON AS AN APPETIZER,
2 FOR A MAIN COURSE.
MAKES A GOOD LUNCHEON DISH.

ZUCCHINI MEAT DOLMA
Etli Kabak Dolması

1 pound ground lamb or beef
1 large onion, coarsely grated
¼ cup rice
⅓ cup tomato juice
¼ cup chopped dill, save
  stems
¼ cup chopped fresh mint
  leaves

Salt and pepper to taste
8 to 9 fat zucchini (about
  6 inches long)
3 tablespoons butter
1½ cups water

Place meat, onion, rice, tomato juice, dill, mint, salt, and pepper in a bowl. Knead well.

Scrape and wash zucchini, cut off stem end and shape into a cover to be used later. Trim opposite end. Scoop out and discard inside leaving ⅓ inch shell. If stem end is too narrow, cut off ½ inch from opposite end and shape into a cover. Scoop from the cover end. Fill shell with a little of the meat mixture at a time, pushing down with the handle of a spoon. When full, replace stem end as cover. Repeat until all the zucchini are stuffed.

Place a rack at the bottom of a heavy saucepan. Place dill stems on rack. Arrange zucchini over dill stems.

If any filling is left, shape into 1 inch balls and place between or on zucchini.

Dot with butter, add 1½ cups water, cover with wax paper. Place a plate on top to give weight during cooking. Cover and cook over medium heat until zucchini are tender, about 1 hour. If necessary more water may be added.

Transfer to a serving platter and pour over sauce remaining in saucepan.

Serve hot as a luncheon dish with potato salad, or as a second course after fish.

SERVES 6 TO 8 PERSONS.

ARTICHOKES WITH BEEF
Etli Enginar

⅛ *pound butter*	*Salt and pepper to taste*
1 *onion, diced*	2 *tablespoons flour*
1 *pound beef, cut into 1 inch*	*Juice 1 lemon*
cubes	4 *large artichokes*
1 *large tomato, diced*	1 *tablespoon chopped dill*
1 *cup water*	

Put butter, onions, beef, tomatoes, 1 cup water, salt, and pepper in a saucepan and cook over medium heat until meat is almost tender.

Fill a large bowl with cold water, sprinkle with flour, and add lemon juice. Mix and set aside.

Prepare artichokes as in Artichoke Meat Dolma*.

Drain well and add to the meat. Cook over medium heat until the artichokes and the meat are tender, about 25 minutes.

Sprinkle dill over and serve with egg noodles.

SERVES 4 PERSONS.

ARTICHOKE BURGER I
Peynirli Enginar I

½ *pound ground beef*	6 *tablespoons lemon juice*
3 *scallions, chopped*	6 *large artichokes*
2 *small tomatoes, diced*	2⅓ *cups water*
3 *tablespoons butter*	½ *teaspoon sugar*
½ *cup chopped dill*	6 *slices cheese for melting*
Salt and pepper to taste	1 *teaspoon paprika*
2 *tablespoons flour*	

Cook ground meat, scallions, and tomatoes with 1 tablespoon butter, over medium heat, stirring constantly for the first 5 minutes, then occasionally for 10 minutes more. Add dill, salt, and pepper and stir well. Remove from heat and set aside.

Fill a large bowl with cold water. Sprinkle with flour and add 4 tablespoons lemon juice. Cleaned artichokes must be dipped into this to prevent discoloration.

Prepare artichokes by removing all of the leaves one by one. Scoop out the fuzz in the heart with a teaspoon. Cut stem flat so that the artichoke will stand up. Cut a thin layer from the bottom with a knife, smoothing the rough surface, and drop it into the bowl of water. Repeat until all artichokes are ready.

Place artichokes in a shallow saucepan, bottoms down. Add 2 tablespoons butter, 2 cups water, and sugar. Sprinkle with 2 tablespoons of lemon juice. Cover with wax paper, put on the lid, and cook over medium heat until artichokes are tender, about 30 minutes.

Remove artichokes to a baking dish, again with bottoms down. If there is any water left in the saucepan, add it; if not add ⅓ cup water.

Fill the hearts of the artichokes generously with the beef mixture. Place a slice of cheese on top. Sprinkle with paprika. Broil under a hot broiler until cheese melts. Serve hot.

Serve as an appetizer for dinners or as main course for luncheons with Romaine Lettuce Salad*.

SERVES 6 PERSONS.

ARTICHOKE BURGER II

Peynirli Enginar II

1 pound lamb or beef, cut into ½ inch cubes	*6 large artichokes*
	2 tablespoons flour
3 scallions, chopped	*6 tablespoons lemon juice*
2 small tomatoes, diced	*2⅓ cups water*
3 tablespoons butter	*½ teaspoon sugar*
3⅓ cups water	*6 slices cheese for melting*
½ cup chopped dill	*1 teaspoon paprika*
Salt and pepper to taste	

Put meat, scallions, tomatoes, 1 tablespoon butter, and 1 cup of water in a saucepan. Cover and cook over medium heat until meat is tender. Mix in dill, salt, and pepper. The meat should be on the dry side, not watery.

Prepare and cook artichokes as in Artichoke Burger I*. Remove to a baking dish with bottoms down. Fill the hearts with cubed meat. Place a slice of cheese on top. Sprinkle with paprika. Add ⅓ cup water. Broil under a hot broiler until cheese melts. Serve hot.

Serve as an appetizer for dinners or as a main course for luncheons with Shepherds' Salad*.

SERVES 6 PERSONS.

GREEN BEAN STEW I
Kıymalı Çalı Fasulyesi

2 pounds fresh green string beans or 2 packages (10 ounce) frozen French-cut beans, defrosted	½ pound ground beef
	2 tomatoes sliced, or
	2 tablespoons tomato paste
	Salt and pepper to taste
1 onion, grated	1 cup water
2 tablespoons butter	

If fresh beans are used, remove strings from beans and wash. Then cut in two lengthwise.

In a saucepan sauté onion with butter over medium heat for 3 minutes. Add meat and sauté 5 minutes more, stirring all the time. Add beans and place tomatoes on top of beans. If tomato paste is used, dilute with a little water before adding. Add salt and pepper and 1 cup of water. Cover and cook for about 45 minutes or until beans are tender.

Serve with egg noodles.

SERVES 4 TO 5 PERSONS.

GREEN BEAN STEW II
Etli Çalı Fasulyesi

2 pounds fresh green string
  beans or 2 packages (10
  ounce) frozen French-cut
  beans, defrosted
1 onion, grated
2 tablespoons butter

1 pound beef or lamb,
  cubed
2 cups water
2 tomatoes sliced, or 2
  tablespoons tomato paste
Salt and pepper to taste

Prepare beans as in Green Bean Stew I*.

In a saucepan sauté the onion with butter over medium heat for 3 minutes. Add meat and sauté for 10 minutes. Add 1 cup of water, cover, and cook over medium heat for 30 minutes. Add the beans, place tomatoes on top of beans. If tomato paste is used, dilute with a little water. Add salt, pepper, and remaining cup of water. Cover and cook for about 45 minutes or until meat and beans are tender.

Serve with Macaroni with White Cheese or Feta*.

SERVES 4 TO 5 PERSONS.

YANISSARY STEW
Etli Kuru Fasulye

2 cups dried kidney beans
  or 2 cans (1 pound each)
  ready-cooked white kidney
  beans, drained
6½ cups water
Salt to taste
2 medium onions, chopped
5 tablespoons butter

1 pound lamb or beef, cut
  into 1 inch cubes
2 tablespoons tomato paste
  or 1 can (1 pound)
  stewed tomatoes with
  juice
Pepper to taste

If dried beans are used soak them overnight in cold water. Drain. Bring 5 cups of water to a boil in a saucepan. Add 1 teaspoon salt and the beans. Cook over medium heat until beans are almost cooked but not too soft, about 20 minutes.

Sauté onions in butter for 5 minutes in a saucepan. Add meat and continue to sauté for 10 minutes more. Add tomato paste or stewed tomatoes and stir, then add 1½ cups water, salt, and pepper to taste. Cover saucepan and cook over medium heat until meat is almost tender, about 40 minutes. Add beans and more water as necessary, cover and cook over medium heat until meat and beans are tender. If cooked beans are used, add them after the meat is well cooked and cook only 10 minutes more.

Serve hot with Tomato Pilav* and Beet Salad*.

SERVES 6 TO 8 PERSONS.

CABBAGE WITH MEAT
Etli Kapuska

1 pound boneless beef, cut into 1 inch cubes	¼ teaspoon cayenne
	Salt to taste
¼ pound butter	1 medium cabbage, about
2 medium onions, diced	3 pounds
⅓ cup tomato juice	1 tablespoon sugar
2 cups water	

Preheat oven to 350 degrees F. after the meat and cabbage have been cooked.

Put meat, butter, and onions in a saucepan. Cover and cook over medium heat, stirring occasionally, for 30 minutes.

Add tomato juice, 1 cup hot water, cayenne, and salt. Cover and cook over low heat for 40 minutes more.

Wash and cut cabbage into 4 equal pieces and cut into shreds. Add to meat along with sugar and 1 cup hot water. Cover and cook until meat and cabbage are tender and all the water is absorbed, about 1½ hours. More water may be added as necessary.

Transfer to a baking dish and bake for about 8 minutes before serving.

SERVES 6 PERSONS.

CABBAGE IN THE POT

Lahana Kapaması

3 medium onions, chopped
⅛ pound butter
1 pound ground beef
½ cup rice
1 tablespoon pignolia nuts
2 tablespoons black currants
1 teaspoon sugar
Salt and pepper to taste

4 cups water
1 tablespoon lemon juice
1 cup mixed chopped
  parsley, dill, and fresh or
  dried mint leaves
1 medium-size cabbage, as
  loose and straight-leaved
  as possible

Sauté onions lightly in a saucepan with half of the butter, add ground meat and continue to sauté, stirring constantly, until meat is browned. Add rice and pignolia nuts and continue to sauté, stirring constantly, until rice is transparent, about 10 minutes. Add currants, sugar, salt, and pepper and ½ cup of boiling water. Cover and cook over medium heat until rice absorbs all the water. Remove from heat, add lemon juice and herbs, stir, cover and put aside.

Use a pot, preferably one you can bring to the table, such as a deep casserole, just large enough to hold the cabbage. Put 2 cups of water in the pot, add a pinch of salt, and bring to a boil. Wash the cabbage, discarding damaged outer leaves. When water boils, put in the cabbage, bottom down. Cover and cook for 10 minutes. Remove from heat and drain, leaving cabbage in the pot.

Open the leaves of the cabbage one by one, taking care not to tear them from the root and rest them over the edge of the pot. Continue opening until the heart of small leaves is reached. Remove these without disturbing the rest of the leaves. Raise the cabbage and place half of the heart leaves at the bottom of the pot as support for the cabbage. Rest cabbage on the heart leaves.

Fill the heart of the cabbage with the rice and meat mixture, pressing down gently to make room for all the mixture. Spread the other half of the heart leaves on top and fold over the larger leaves that are over the edge of the pot, cover the whole until you have a round cabbage. Spread the rest of the butter on top. Place a plate on top of the stuffed cabbage to keep the leaves in place.

Add 1½ cups of hot water, cover, and cook over medium heat until the cabbage is tender, about 40 minutes.

Serve hot. Take the pot to the table, cut individual portions with a knife and serve with a spoon.

SERVES 6 PERSONS.

CHICK-PEA STEW
Etli Nohut

2 cups dried chick-peas, or	3 tablespoons butter
2 cans (1 pound 4 ounces	1 pound lamb or beef, cut
each) chick-peas, drained	into 1 inch cubes
6½ cups water	2 tablespoons tomato paste
Salt to taste	Red pepper to taste
2 medium onions, chopped	

If using dried chick-peas soak overnight in cold water. Drain. Bring 5 cups of water to a boil in a saucepan. Add salt and chick-peas. Cook over medium heat until chick-peas are almost cooked but not soft, about 20 minutes. Drain.

Place onions in saucepan, add butter and sauté very lightly. Add meat and continue to sauté about 10 minutes. Stir in tomato paste and add 1½ cups water, salt, and pepper. Cover saucepan and cook over medium heat until meat is almost tender, 40 minutes. Add chick-peas and more water if necessary. Cover and cook over medium heat until meat and chick-peas are tender.

Serve hot with Tomato Pilav*.

SERVES 4 TO 5 PERSONS.

CULTURED ROOT CELERY
Terbiyeli Kerevizkökü

1 large onion, grated	*2 cups beef broth or water,*
3 tablespoons butter	*plus 1 additional cup*
½ pound beef or lamb, cut	*broth or water, if needed*
into 1 inch cubes	*2 eggs*
Salt and pepper to taste	*2 tablespoons lemon juice*
4 pounds root celery	

Place onion in a saucepan large enough for both meat and the celery. Add 1 tablespoon butter, meat, salt, and pepper. Cover and cook on medium heat, stirring occasionally for 20 to 25 minutes. Remove from heat. If meat is very tough add a little water and cook 15 minutes more.

Pare the dark outer skin from each celery root until the white part is reached. Divide each root into 4 equal parts lengthwise. Scrape off the soft pulp inside. Place pieces into a bowl of cold water to prevent discoloration.

Place 2 tablespoons butter in a second saucepan. Drain and add the celery pieces. Add ½ cup broth or water. Cover and cook on high heat for 10 minutes. Shake saucepan occasionally to prevent scorching. Remove from heat, uncover, and cool.

Gather meat into the center of the first saucepan. Place cooked celery pieces on top of and around the meat. Measure the remaining broth from the cooked roots and add more broth or water to make 1½ cups and add this to the meat and celery roots.

Add dash of salt, cover, and cook first on high heat for 10 minutes, then on medium heat until celery roots and meat are tender, about 30 minutes. If all broth is absorbed, add 1 cup more broth or water. Remove from heat.

Remove ¾ cup celery stock from the saucepan without disarranging the meat and the celery roots. Then transfer meat and celery roots to a serving platter by placing the platter over the saucepan and quickly inverting it. You may serve this dish in a stove-to-table saucepan, omitting the transferring step.

Beat eggs in a small saucepan, add lemon juice. Place on very low heat, then slowly add ¾ cup stock from the cooked celery roots and meat, stirring constantly. Continue stirring until sauce is thickened, 10 to 15 minutes. Pour sauce over platter and serve immediately.

SERVES 6 PERSONS.

EGGPLANT CASSEROLE
Oturtma

2 eggplants	1 large onion, diced
Salt	1 large tomato, diced
3 tablespoons butter	2 cups water
1 pound beef or lamb, cut into 1 inch cubes	2 tablespoons chopped parsley
	Pepper to taste

Preheat oven to 350 degrees F. after the meat has been cooked.

Prepare and sauté eggplants as in Musakka Eggplant*. Place in baking dish or cooking pot as described.

Put 1 tablespoon butter in a saucepan, add meat, onion, tomatoes, and 1 cup water. Cook until meat is almost tender. Add parsley, salt, and pepper and stir.

Place cooked meat over the eggplants, add remaining 1 cup water, cover and cook over medium heat for 30 minutes, or bake covered for 40 minutes.

Serve hot with Bulgur Pilav*.

SERVES 4 TO 6 PERSONS.

Ast-chi
Cuisinier du Grand Seigneur.

B. 12.

Ant. Grand. du Roi.

MUSAKKA EGGPLANT
Patlıcan Musakka

2 eggplants	1 large tomato, diced
Salt	2 tablespoons chopped parsley
3 tablespoons butter	Pepper to taste
1 large onion, diced	1 cup water
½ pound ground beef	

Preheat oven to 350 degrees F. after the eggplants have been sautéed.

Cut the stems off the eggplants. Then peel a half inch wide strip of the black skin lengthwise, leaving the next half inch with the skin on. Repeat until you make a striped effect.

Then cut eggplants crosswise into 1 inch thick slices. Place slices in a deep tray, salting generously. Fill tray with cold water. Leave 30 minutes. Squeeze out the bitter juice, wash with cold water and dry.

Melt 2 tablespoons butter in a frying pan and sauté the slices on both sides. Place them in a single layer in a baking dish or a small saucepan.

In the same frying pan sauté the onions for 3 minutes in an additional tablespoon of butter. Add meat and sauté another 10 minutes, stirring continually. Add tomatoes and sauté 5 minutes more. Add parsley, salt, and pepper; stir and remove from heat.

Spoon meat mixture over the eggplant slices. Add 1 cup water. Cover and cook on medium heat for 30 minutes, or bake covered for 40 minutes.

Serve hot with Tomato Pilav*.

SERVES 4 TO 6 PERSONS.

SLASHED EGGPLANT
Karnı Yarık

6 medium eggplants, long
  and thin
½ cup salad oil
2 tablespoons butter
2 medium onions, diced
½ pound ground beef
2 medium tomatoes,
  1 chopped, 1 cut into
  6 slices

1 green pepper, seeded and
  chopped, optional
2 tablespoons chopped parsley
Salt and pepper to taste
½ cup water

Preheat oven to 350 degrees F. after the eggplants have been sautéed.

Cut the stems off the eggplants. Then peel off a half inch wide strip of the black skin lengthwise, leaving the next half inch with the skin on. Repeat until you make a striped effect. Then slash them lengthwise on one side only, starting and ending 1 inch from both ends so that the eggplants can be stuffed. Sauté eggplants very lightly on both sides in oil. Place them in a single layer in a baking dish or a shallow saucepan, slashed sides up.

Add butter to the same pan the eggplants were sautéed in and sauté onions lightly. Add meat, cook for 10 minutes, stirring constantly. Add the chopped tomato and green pepper and cook for 5 minutes more. Add parsley, salt, and pepper; stir and remove from heat.

Stuff slashed eggplants with meat mixture. Place a slice of tomato on top of each eggplant. Add ½ cup water, cover, and cook over medium heat for 30 minutes or bake covered for 40 minutes.

Serve with Tomato Pilav* or egg noodles.

SERVES 6 PERSONS.

CULTURED LEEKS
Terbiyeli Pirasa

1 large onion, grated	*Salt and pepper to taste*
3 tablespoons butter	*2 cups broth*
1 pound boneless beef or	*4 pounds leeks*
veal, cut into 1 inch cubes	*2 eggs*
1 tablespoon tomato paste	*2 tablespoons lemon juice*

Place onion, 1 tablespoon butter, meat, tomato paste, salt, and pepper in a saucepan large enough for meat and leeks. Cover and cook over medium heat, stirring occasionally, 20 to 25 minutes. Remove from heat. (If meat is very tough add ½ cup broth and cook 15 minutes more.)

To prepare leeks, first cut off the roots. Then remove 2 or 3 outer skins. Cut leeks crosswise into 2 inch long pieces. Wash and drain.

Put leeks and 2 tablespoons butter in a saucepan. Cover and cook over low heat for 20 minutes, shaking saucepan every 3 or 4 minutes. Remove from heat, uncover, and cool.

Arrange meat pieces in center of saucepan in which it was cooked. Arrange leeks in an orderly fashion over and around meat. Add 1½ cups broth, salt, and pepper. Place wet wax paper over the top. Cover and cook on medium heat for 1 hour, or until leeks and meat are tender. Remove from heat. Take about 1 cup of the hot stock from saucepan without disarranging the meat and the leeks. Transfer meat and leeks to a serving platter by placing the platter over the saucepan and quickly inverting it. An easier way to serve this dish is to cook it in a stove-to-table saucepan, which does away with the transferring step.

Beat eggs in a small saucepan, add lemon juice. Place over very low heat. Add slowly, stirring constantly, 1 cup stock from the cooked leeks and meat. Continue stirring until sauce is thickened, 10 to 15 minutes. Pour over leeks and serve right away.

SERVES 6 PERSONS.

LENTIL STEW
Etli Mercimek

1 cup lentils
4 cups water
1 large onion, chopped
2 tablespoons butter
1 pound lamb or beef, cut
  into 1 inch cubes or
  ½ pound ground beef

1 tablespoon rice
Salt and pepper to taste
1 tablespoon vinegar

Wash lentils and place in a saucepan, adding 3 cups water. Boil for 15 minutes and drain.

Brown onion lightly in butter in a saucepan. Add meat and sauté 10 minutes longer, stirring occasionally. Add 1 cup water, cover, and cook over medium heat until meat is almost tender.

Add lentils, rice, salt, and pepper. If necessary, add a little more water. Cook over medium heat until tender, about 25 minutes.

Add vinegar, stir, and put into a serving dish. Serve hot with Vermicelli Pilav* or egg noodles.

SERVES 4 TO 5 PERSONS.

MEAT WITH OKRA
Etli Bamya

1 pound lamb or beef, cut
  into 1 inch cubes
3 tablespoons butter
1 large onion, grated
4 large tomatoes diced, or
  1 cup canned stewed
  tomatoes

1½ cups water
Salt and pepper to taste
1 pound fresh okra or
  2 packages (10 ounce)
  frozen okra, defrosted
2 tablespoons lemon juice

Sauté meat in butter in a saucepan large enough for meat and okra over medium heat until light brown, about 10 minutes. Add onion and sauté 5 minutes more. Add tomatoes, 1 cup water, salt, and pepper, cover and cook until tender, about 1 hour. If necessary, more water may be added.

Trim okra by peeling the cone-shaped end without piercing the pod. Wash and place on top of the meat in a neat arrangement. Add ½ cup of water, cover, and cook over medium heat for 20 minutes. Add lemon juice and cook 10 minutes more or until okra is tender. This dish should not be too dry. If necessary, a little more water should be added.

Serve with Tomato Pilav*.

SERVES 4 TO 6 PERSONS.

PEAS A LA TURCA
Etli Bezelye

1 pound boneless beef, cut into 1 inch cubes	*1 cup chopped dill*
	2 cups hot water
2 medium onions, coarsely grated	*2 pounds unshelled fresh peas*
	1 teaspoon sugar
4 tablespoons butter	*Salt and pepper to taste*

Place meat in a saucepan. Add onions, 2 tablespoons butter, and half of the dill. Cover and cook over medium heat, stirring occasionally for 20 to 25 minutes. Add 1 cup hot water and cook until meat is almost tender, about 40 to 45 minutes. If necessary, more water may be added.

Shell and wash peas and add to meat. Add sugar, the remaining butter, salt, and pepper, the rest of the dill, and 1 cup hot water. Cover and cook over medium heat until meat and peas are tender, about 40 minutes.

Serve hot in a deep platter with White Pilav* or egg noodles and a green salad.

SERVES 6 PERSONS.

POTATO WITH GROUND MEAT
Kıymalı Patates

8 medium potatoes	2 tomatoes, sliced
2 tablespoons butter	1 cup water
2 medium onions, diced	½ teaspoon thyme leaves
½ pound ground beef	Salt and pepper to taste

Peel and cut potatoes into ½ inch thick round slices. Wash and dry.

In a frying pan sauté potato slices lightly in butter on both sides and arrange them in a saucepan. Set aside.

Place onions in the same frying pan and sauté them with the butter left in the pan for 2 minutes. Add ground meat and sauté together with the onions, stirring constantly, until meat turns brown, 10 minutes.

Spread the meat mixture over the potatoes evenly. Place tomato slices on top and add 1 cup water. Sprinkle with thyme leaves. Add salt and pepper. Cover and cook over medium heat until potatoes are cooked, 45 minutes. If necessary, more water may be added.

Serve with lettuce or watercress salad.

SERVES 6 PERSONS.

MEAT WITH POTATOES
Etli Patates

2 medium onions, coarsely grated	10 medium potatoes
2 tablespoons butter	2 tablespoons margarine
1 pound beef, cut into 1 inch cubes	2 green peppers, seeded and diced
3 medium fresh tomatoes or 1 can (10 ounce), peeled tomatoes, sliced and with juice	Salt and pepper to taste
	1 cup water

Sauté onions with butter in a saucepan over medium heat for 5 minutes, stirring all the time. Add meat and continue to sauté, stirring occasionally, for 15 minutes more. Add tomatoes, cover, and cook until meat is almost tender, about 40 minutes. If necessary, a little water may be added.

Peel, quarter, and wash potatoes. Drain and dry.

In a frying pan, heat margarine to boiling point over high heat. Add potatoes and fry very lightly, stirring with a large spoon.

Add potatoes and leftover margarine in the pan to meat. Add green peppers, salt, pepper, and 1 cup water. Cover and cook over medium heat until potatoes are tender, 30 minutes.

Serve hot with Cabbage Salad*.

SERVES 6 PERSONS.

SPINACH WITH MEAT
Etli Ispanak

4 pounds fresh spinach, or 6 packages (10 ounce) frozen leaf spinach, defrosted	*4 tablespoons butter*
	2 medium onions, grated
	2 tablespoons tomato paste
	2 cups water or beef broth
Salt to taste	*Dash sugar*
1 pound beef, cut into 1 inch cubes	*Pepper to taste*

Cut off spinach roots and cut leaves into 2 or 3 parts crosswise, each part being no longer than 3 inches. Wash spinach several times, then cook in boiling salted water for 5 minutes. Drain and set aside.

Sauté meat with butter in a saucepan large enough for meat and spinach, over high heat, stirring occasionally, for 10 minutes. Add onions and cook over medium heat 5 minutes more. Add tomato paste and continue to sauté, stirring occasionally, for another 5 minutes. Add 1 cup water or beef broth, cover, and cook over medium heat until meat is almost tender, 30 to 40 minutes. If meat requires more cooking, add more water or beef broth. Put spinach on top of meat. Season with sugar, salt, and pepper. Add ½ to 1 cup of water or broth, cover, and cook for 20 to 25 minutes.

Serve hot with a bowl of plain yogurt, placing 1 or 2 tablespoons on the plate with each serving.

SERVES 6 TO 8 PERSONS.

CULTURED SPINACH ROOTS
Terbiyeli Ispanakkökü

1 medium onion, grated	*4 pounds fresh spinach with*
3 tablespoons butter	*large roots*
1 pound lamb or beef, cut	*2 eggs*
into 1 inch cubes	*2 tablespoons lemon juice*
Salt and pepper to taste	

Put onion in a saucepan with 1 tablespoon butter, meat, salt, and pepper. Cover and cook on medium heat, stirring occasionally for 20 to 25 minutes. Remove from heat. If meat is tough, add a little more water and cook 15 minutes more.

Prepare spinach by discarding damaged outer stems and leaves. Cut off roots that come from under the soil. Do not separate stems from the pinkish roots that are going to be used. Then cut the pinkish roots 3 inches long. While doing this soak the cleaned roots in cold water. Save leaves to use in making Fried Spinach*. Wash roots several times in cold water.

In a saucepan sauté roots for 10 to 15 minutes in 2 tablespoons of butter, stirring occasionally. Lift out roots with a perforated kitchen spoon. Leave to cool. Save stock.

Gather meat to the middle of the saucepan in which it was cooked. Place roots in an orderly fashion on top of meat. Add 1 to 1½ cups of the stock left from sautéed roots. If there is not enough stock, water may be used. Cover saucepan and cook until roots and meat are tender, first for 5 minutes over high heat, then on low for 25 to 30 minutes.

When ready take ¾ cup of stock from saucepan without disarranging the meat and the roots. Then transfer roots and meat to a serving platter by placing platter over the saucepan and quickly inverting.

Beat eggs in a small saucepan; add lemon juice. Place on very low heat and add slowly the ¾ cup of stock from the meat and roots, stirring constantly, until sauce is thickened, 10 to 15 minutes. Pour this sauce over the meat and roots and serve at once.

SERVES 5 TO 6 PERSONS.

SHEPHERD'S SPINACH

Kıymalı Ispanak

2 pounds fresh spinach, or	*½ pound ground beef*
3 packages (10 ounce)	*1 tablespoon tomato paste*
frozen leaf spinach,	*2 tablespoons rice*
defrosted	*½ teaspoon sugar*
Salt	*Pepper to taste*
1 medium onion, grated	*1 cup beef broth or water*
3 tablespoons butter	

Prepare the spinach as in Spinach with Meat*. Set aside.

Sauté onion in butter over medium heat, stirring constantly for 5 minutes. Add ground meat and continue to sauté until meat is brown, 10 minutes. Add tomato paste, stir, and sauté 3 minutes more. Add spinach and cook over medium heat 20 minutes. Add rice, sugar, salt, and pepper and 1 cup broth. Cover and continue cooking until rice is tender, 15 minutes.

Pour into deep serving dish. Serve hot with a bowl of plain yogurt, placing 1 or 2 tablespoons on the plate with each serving.

SERVES 4 TO 5 PERSONS.

BEEF CASSEROLE WITH VEGETABLES
Etli Güveç

2 pounds boneless beef, cut
  into 1 inch cubes
4 tablespoons butter
2 medium onions, 1 diced, 1
  cut coarsely into round
  slices
3 medium tomatoes fresh or
  canned, 1 diced, 2 peeled
  and sliced
Salt and pepper to taste

2 cups water
1 medium eggplant
2 medium zucchini
3 green peppers
⅓ cup olive or salad oil
1 package (10 ounce) frozen
  green beans, defrosted
1 package (10 ounce) frozen
  okra, defrosted

Preheat oven to 350 degrees F. after the meat has been cooked.

Place in a saucepan the meat, 2 tablespoons butter, 1 diced onion, 1 diced tomato, salt, and pepper, and 2 cups water. Cover and cook over medium heat, stirring occasionally, until meat is almost tender, about 1 hour. Arrange meat in the bottom of an earthenware casserole with a lid.

While meat is cooking prepare vegetables as follows:

Cut the stem off the eggplant. Then peel off a half inch wide strip of the black skin lengthwise, leaving the next half inch with the skin on. Repeat until you make a striped effect. Then cut the whole eggplant lengthwise into 4 equal pieces and each piece crosswise into 2 inch pieces.

Scrape zucchini. Cut each lengthwise into 2 equal parts and then crosswise into 2 inch pieces.

Cut each green pepper into 4 equal parts. Remove seeds.

Heat oil in a frying pan over high heat. Add eggplant pieces and sauté a few minutes on both sides. Remove with a perforated kitchen spoon, leaving oil in pan, and arrange over meat in the casserole.

If necessary more oil may be added to the pan to sauté vegetables. Sauté peppers, place one-third of them over eggplants with a few slices of onions. Keep rest of peppers in a bowl.

Sauté zucchini and arrange over eggplants. Again cover with one-third of the peppers and some onion slices.

Arrange beans over zucchini. Place the rest of peppers and onion slices over beans.

Last, arrange okra and cover with 2 peeled and sliced tomatoes. Add salt and pepper. Dot with 2 tablespoons butter. Cover and bake vegetables until tender, about 1 hour and 15 minutes.

Serve hot with Mashed Bean Salad*.

SERVES 8 PERSONS.

SUMMER VEGETABLE POT
Yaz Türlüsü

2 medium onions, chopped
¼ cup butter
1 pound lamb or beef, cut into 1 inch cubes
½ cup water
½ pound green beans or 1 package (10 ounce) frozen green beans, defrosted

2 medium zucchini
1 medium eggplant
2 large green peppers
¼ pound okra or 1 package (10 ounce) frozen okra, defrosted
3 medium tomatoes
Salt and pepper to taste

Sauté onions with butter in a saucepan until light brown. Add meat and sauté, stirring continually for about 10 minutes. Add ½ cup water, cover saucepan, and cook over medium heat until almost tender.

While meat is cooking prepare vegetables as follows:

Cut ends of beans, remove strings and cut into two crosswise.

Scrape zucchini and cut into 1 inch slices.

Cut the stem off eggplant. Then peel off a half inch wide strip of the black skin lengthwise, leaving the next inch with the skin on. Repeat until you make a striped effect. Then cut lengthwise into two and crosswise into 2 inch pieces.

Cut each green pepper into 4 equal parts. Remove seeds.

Trim okra by peeling the cone-shaped end without piercing the pod.

Peel and slice tomatoes.

When meat is nearly tender add beans, zucchini, eggplant, peppers, okra, and tomatoes in that order, piling them on top of each other, leaving the meat at the very bottom of the saucepan. Add salt and pepper to taste. Cover and cook over medium heat until vegetables are tender. If necessary, an additional ½ cup of water may be added.

Before serving invert into a deep dish so that the meat is on the top.

Serve hot with Tomato and Onion Salad*.

Makes a delicious summer luncheon dish.

SERVES 6 TO 8 PERSONS.

WINTER VEGETABLE POT
Kiş Türlüsü

2 pounds short ribs for	3 cups hot water
stewing, cut up into	Salt to taste
2 inch lengths	4 leeks
16 pearl onions, skinned	4 stalks celery
whole	2 medium carrots
5½ tablespoons butter	2 medium potatoes

Place meat into saucepan, add onions, 2 tablespoons butter. Cover and cook over medium heat for 20 minutes, shaking saucepan occasionally. Add 3 cups of hot water, salt, cover and cook over low heat until meat is almost tender, 1½ hours.

Cut the roots off the leeks, then cut them into 2 inch lengths, discarding coarse outer leaves. Wash well. Scrape celery stalks, cut into 2 inch lengths, including leaves, and wash. Place celery and leeks in a saucepan, add 1½ tablespoons butter and cook covered, stirring occasionally, for 15 minutes. Add to meat.

Scrape carrots, cut into 2 inch lengths, and wash. Place in the same saucepan in which leeks were cooked. Add 2 tablespoons butter and sauté for 5 minutes. Add to meat.

Peel and quarter potatoes. Fry in same butter as carrots for 5 minutes. Add to meat with the butter remaining in saucepan.

Continue to cook over medium heat until meat and vegetables are tender, 1 hour. If necessary, more water may be added.

Serve hot with Beet Salad*.

SERVES 4 TO 6 PERSONS.

ZUCCHINI WITH GROUND MEAT
Kabak Musakka

2 pounds zucchini
3 cups water
Salt to taste
½ pound ground beef
2 onions, grated
2 tablespoons butter
2 tomatoes, sliced
1 green pepper, seeded and
  chopped

¼ cup chopped dill
¼ cup chopped fresh mint
  leaves
Black pepper to taste
Dash cayenne
½ cup broth

Scrape and cut each zucchini crosswise into 4 pieces. Then cook them in 3 cups of boiling salted water for 3 minutes. Drain and place in one layer in a shallow cooking pan.

Sauté meat and onions in butter over medium heat for 5 minutes, stirring all the time. Add tomatoes and green peppers and sauté for another 5 minutes. Remove from heat and spread over the zucchini. Place dill and mint leaves on top, add salt, black pepper, and cayenne. Add ½ cup broth. Cover and cook over medium heat for 30 to 35 minutes.

Serve hot with egg noodles.

SERVES 4 TO 5 PERSONS.

ZUCCHINI WITH MEAT
Kabak Bastı

1 pound beef or lamb, cut
  into 1 inch cubes
2 onions, grated
4 tablespoons butter
2 tomatoes, sliced, or 1½
  tablespoons tomato paste
2 pounds zucchini
1½ cups chicken or beef
  broth

Salt to taste
1 green pepper, seeded and
  chopped
Black pepper to taste
Dash cayenne
¼ cup chopped dill
5 to 6 chopped fresh mint
  leaves

Cook meat, onions, and 2 tablespoons butter in covered saucepan over medium heat for 20 minutes, stirring occasionally. Add tomatoes or paste and cook for 10 minutes more.

While meat is cooking scrape and cut zucchini, first crosswise into two, then lengthwise into two, and place in a saucepan with 2 tablespoons butter and ½ cup broth. Cover and sauté on high heat for 10 minutes. Shake saucepan occasionally to keep zucchini from sticking to the bottom of the pot. Remove from heat.

Arrange half of the zucchini in a shallow saucepan that can be brought to the table. Put in the meat and add the rest of the zucchini over the meat. Add salt, green pepper, black pepper, cayenne, and 1 cup broth. Place wax paper on top and cover saucepan. Cook for 30 to 40 minutes over medium heat.

Garnish with dill and mint leaves.

Serve hot.

SERVES 5 TO 6 PERSONS.

BOILED CALF'S BRAINS

Beyin Haşlaması

2 sets calf's brains	6 black or green olives
2 tablespoons vinegar	2 scallions, chopped
4 cups water	2 tablespoons parsley, chopped
Salt to taste	Juice 1 lemon
Few large lettuce leaves	5 tablespoons salad or olive
2 tomatoes, sliced	oil
6 radishes	Pepper to taste
1 green pepper, sliced	

Wash brains under cold running water. Then soak in cold water to which 1 tablespoon of vinegar has been added. Let soak for 1 to 1½ hours. Again wash under cold running water and carefully remove membrane and veins that cover brain. Wash away all traces of blood.

Place 4 cups of water, 1 teaspoon salt, and 1 tablespoon vinegar in a saucepan and bring to a boil. Add brains and simmer uncovered over medium heat for 20 minutes. Remove from heat and cool for ½ hour. Drain. Dry with paper towels.

Place lettuce leaves on serving platter. Slice brains ½ inch thick crosswise and arrange on lettuce leaves. Garnish platter with tomatoes, radishes, green peppers, and olives. Sprinkle with scallions and parsley. Beat lemon juice and oil together and add salt and pepper. Pour over the brains.

Serve cold as an appetizer with buttered pumpernickel bread.

SERVES 4 TO 5 PERSONS.

FRIED CALF'S BRAINS
Beyin Kızartması

2 sets calf's brains	1 tablespoon flour
2 tablespoons vinegar	Pepper to taste
4 cups water	1½ cups frying oil
Salt to taste	2 tablespoons chopped
1 cup bread crumbs or	parsley
cornstarch	1 lemon, cut lenthwise into
3 eggs	6 wedges

Wash brains under cold running water, then soak in cold water to which 1 tablespoon of vinegar has been added. Let soak for 1 to 1½ hours. Again wash under cold running water and carefully remove membrane and veins that cover brain. Wash away all traces of blood.

Place 4 cups of water, 1 teaspoon salt, and 1 tablespoon vinegar in a saucepan and bring to a boil. Add brains and simmer uncovered over medium heat for 20 minutes. Remove from heat and cool for ½ hour. Drain and dry with paper towels.

Slice into ½ inch thick pieces crosswise. Lay on paper towels and dredge each piece well in bread crumbs or cornstarch.

Break eggs into a shallow bowl. Add 1 tablespoon flour, salt, and pepper. Beat lightly with a fork.

Heat oil in frying pan on high heat. Dip each piece of brain into egg, coating with as much egg mixture as possible. Fry until light golden on both sides, about 2 minutes on each side.

Heap pieces on platter and sprinkle parsley on top. Arrange lemon wedges around and serve immediately with either boiled

green peas or green beans, or with White Pilav* as an appetizer.
The brains can be served with both green peas and White Pilav
as a main course.

SERVES 4 TO 5 PERSONS
AS APPETIZER OR MAIN COURSE.

FRIED CALF'S OR LAMB'S LIVER
Ciğer Kızartması

1 pound calf's or lamb's liver	*6 scallions with green tops,*
½ cup flour	*chopped*
1 cup salad oil	*3 tablespoons chopped dill*
Salt and pepper to taste	*1 lemon, sliced*

Have your butcher skin off the membrane that covers the liver
and slice it into half inch thick pieces.

Spread flour on wax paper. Coat liver slices with flour on both
sides.

In frying pan heat oil very hot. Fry each slice on both sides,
about 4 or 5 minutes.

Arrange slices on platter, sprinkle with salt and pepper. Mix
scallions with dill and spread over liver. Garnish with lemon slices.

Serve with baked or fried potatoes.

SERVES 4 PERSONS.

LAMB OR PIG'S KNUCKLES WITH CHICK-PEAS
Nohutlu Kuzu Paçası

1 cup uncooked chick-peas	*½ lemon*
or 2 cups canned cooked	*2 sprigs parsley*
chick-peas, drained	*1 celery stalk*
4 medium onions	*1 teaspoon thyme*
8 quarts water	*1 bay leaf*
4 to 5 lamb's or pig's	*2 tablespoons tomato paste*
knuckles	*Salt and pepper to taste*
2 tablespoons butter	*Dash cayenne*
2 to 3 cloves garlic	

If using uncooked chick-peas, soak them overnight in cold water. Drain and place in a saucepan with 1 onion and 3 quarts of water. Boil until tender. Drain and set aside.

Have your butcher clean the knuckles for you. Then burn the unwanted hair by holding each knuckle over a flame. Wash several times.

Cook knuckles in a saucepan with 5 quarts of water, 1 tablespoon butter, garlic, 1 onion cut into halves, the lemon, quartered, parsley, celery, thyme, and bay leaf. Make sure that about 2 cups of broth remain after the knuckles are cooked, about 3 hours.

Drain knuckles and save stock. Separate knuckle meat from the bones and cut into small pieces. Set aside and discard bones.

Grate 2 onions into a saucepan. Add 1 tablespoon butter. Sauté about 5 to 8 minutes. Add tomato paste and continue to sauté 5 minutes more. Add chick-peas, knuckle meat, and 2 cups knuckle stock. Add salt, pepper, and cayenne. Cover and cook for 30 minutes over medium heat.

Serve hot with Cracked Wheat Pilav* and dill pickles.

This is a very hearty dish, good on cold winter days, especially after skiing or hard winter sports.

SERVES 6 TO 8 PERSONS.

KNUCKLE MOUSSE

Paça

6 lamb's or pig's knuckles	1 cup chicken stock
6½ cups water	8 tablespoons lemon juice
1 teaspoon olive oil	1 envelope 1½ ounces instant
1½ teaspoons salt	beef broth
1 small pickled cucumber,	2 egg whites, lightly beaten
diced	3 envelopes gelatin
1 small pickled carrot,	Parsley sprigs
diced	4 tablespoons ground
1 tablespoon capers	mustard
2 cloves garlic, minced	

Have your butcher clean the knuckles for you. Then burn the unwanted hair by holding each knuckle over a flame.

Place knuckles in a large saucepan with 6 cups of water, 1

teaspoon oil, and 1 teaspoon salt. Bring to a boil over medium heat. Skim off foam. Cover saucepan and turn heat to low. Cook knuckles until they are tender, about 3 hours.

Drain knuckles and save the stock. Separate knuckle meat from bones and discard bones. Dice meat and place in a bowl. Add cucumber, carrot, capers, garlic, and ½ teaspoon salt. Mix well and set aside.

Skim off all the fat from the stock and put stock in a saucepan. If there is more than 1½ cups stock, boil it uncovered until it is reduced to 1½ cups. Add 1 cup chicken stock, 2 tablespoons lemon juice, beef broth, and egg whites. Mix well. Place saucepan over low heat and simmer uncovered for 20 minutes.

Soak gelatin in ½ cup of cold water for 10 minutes. Then add to stock over heat. Stir well. Remove from heat. Strain through doubled cheesecloth. Stir in 2 tablespoons lemon juice.

Pour this mixture into a mold, filling only two-thirds of it. Place mold in refrigerator until it starts to set, about 30 minutes. Then add the diced knuckles. Stir and leave mold in refrigerator until it sets firmly, about 4 to 5 hours.

To unmold put mold in lukewarm water for a few minutes. Invert on a serving platter. Decorate with parsley sprigs.

Combine mustard with 4 tablespoons lemon juice. Beat well. Serve as a sauce.

Good as an appetizer or for buffet suppers.

SERVES 6 TO 8 PERSONS.

TRIPE CHICK-PEAS

Nohutlu Işkembe

1 pound dried chick-peas or 1 can (1 pound, 4 ounce) ready-cooked	*2 cloves garlic, whole and unskinned*
Salt	*3 tablespoons butter*
1 pound frozen tripe, defrosted and cut into 1 inch cubes	*2 medium onions, diced*
8 cups water	*4 tablespoons tomato paste*
Peel ½ lemon	*Pepper to taste*
	Dash cayenne

If using dried chick-peas, soak them overnight. Drain. Boil in salted water until almost tender, about 1 hour. Remove from heat and drain.

Put tripe in a saucepan with 8 cups water, lemon peel, garlic, and salt. Cook over medium heat until tripe is tender, about 3 hours. Drain, set aside, and save stock.

Put butter with onions in saucepan and sauté for 5 minutes. Add tomato paste, salt, pepper, and cayenne. Pour in 1 cup of tripe stock and stir. Add chick-peas, tripe, and cook over medium heat for 30 minutes or until tripe and chick-peas are tender. A little more stock may be added if necessary. If cooked canned chick-peas are used, reduce the cooking time.

This is a hearty dish good on cold winter days, especially after vigorous exercise.

Serve with dill pickles and Mashed Potato Salad* and fresh homemade-type bread.

SERVES 4 TO 5 PERSONS.

9. *Vegetables*

The Ottoman Empire stretched across vast territories in Europe, Asia, and Africa, which yielded a variety of vegetables including many subtropical crops. Likewise, republican Turkey enjoys different climates, which provide a very rich variety and abundance of products.

Also, Turkey has been part of the olive oil belt of the world. This combination of abundance with variety led to an extremely varied and interesting treatment of vegetables. The same vegetable can be prepared in many different ways. The story is told of a foreign visitor who was served dish after dish of different eggplant recipes; finally he asked for a glass of water and added, "Make it without eggplant, please."

There are three principal ways of cooking vegetables in the Turkish style. First, there are the meat dishes. Some are stewed with different vegetables. Others are cooked with chopped meat like *Musakka.* These are served as main courses.

Then we have the vegetables cooked with butter, which make excellent side dishes. Those can be served with meat, chicken, or fish dishes. *Güveç,* the casserole with mixed vegetables, keeps delectable company with chicken or roast meats.

Finally, there are the numerous recipes for vegetables with olive oil. Among these the rice dolmas stand out as colorful appetizers for buffet dinners. They can also be served as first courses during the summer, for olive-oil dishes in the Turkish cuisine are served cold. Fried eggplants and fried zucchini may be served as side dishes.

Vegetables are covered with wax paper while they are cooking so they will keep their fresh colors. The paper, tucked around them, also keeps them tightly in shape.

Turkish cuisine provides a rich variety of possibilities for the use of vegetables. They can be made to serve as the *pièce de résistance* of a party or they can fit into any corner of any local or international menu.

Vegetables

AS APPETIZERS

RICE DOLMAS

Sakaz cult, Bostangis du Sérail.
Figure 5

ARTICHOKE A LA TURCA

Zeytinyağlı Enginar

3 medium onions, cut in half
  lengthwise, then finely sliced
¼ cup salad or olive oil
2 small carrots, sliced thin
2 stalks celery, diced
2½ cups water
1 potato, diced

½ cup peas, fresh or frozen
2 tablespoons flour
2 lemons
6 large artichokes
1 teaspoon sugar
Salt to taste
½ cup chopped dill

Place onions in a saucepan, add oil, and sauté over medium heat until transparent. Add carrots, celery, and ½ cup of water and cook over medium heat for 20 minutes. Add potatoes and peas and remove from heat.

Fill a large bowl with cold water, sprinkle with flour, and add the juice of 1 lemon; mix and set aside.

Prepare artichokes as in Artichoke Meat Dolma*.

Drain well and arrange in a large saucepan in one layer. Place the cooked vegetable mixture between the artichokes and pour over the juice of the remaining lemon. Add sugar, salt, and 2 cups of hot water. Place wax paper over the entire surface. Cover saucepan and cook over medium heat for about 40 minutes or until artichokes are tender. Remove from heat and allow to cool in the saucepan. Arrange artichokes on a serving platter and fill the hearts with the vegetable mixture. Decorate tops with dill.

Serve cold as an appetizer or after the main course as a salad.

SERVES 6 PERSONS.

JERUSALEM ARTICHOKES
Zeytinyağlı Yerelması

1 pound Jerusalem artichokes	Salt to taste
2 medium onions, cut in half	½ teaspoon sugar
lengthwise, then finely sliced	2 cups water
4 tablespoons salad or olive	2 tablespoons lemon juice
oil	1 teaspoon crushed dried
1 medium carrot, sliced thin	mint leaves
1 tablespoon rice	

Peel artichokes and cut each into 2 or 3 chunks, depending on the size of the artichokes, and place in cold water.

In a saucepan, sauté onion in oil over medium heat for 5 minutes. Add carrots and sauté the mixture another 3 minutes. Drain artichokes and add to the onion mixture. Add rice, salt, sugar, and 2 cups hot water. Cover and cook over medium heat for about 40 minutes or until artichokes are tender. Remove from heat, cool in saucepan. Transfer to a serving platter, pour lemon juice over all, and decorate with crushed mint leaves.

Serve cold as an appetizer or salad with chilled tomato juice or white wine.

SERVES 4 PERSONS.

GREEN BEANS ISTANBUL
Zeytinyağlı Fasulye

1 pound green beans or	2 cups water
2 packages (10 ounce)	2 medium tomatoes, halved
frozen French-beans,	¼ cup olive or salad oil
defrosted	½ teaspoon sugar
2 medium onions, coarsely	Salt to taste
grated	

If fresh beans are used, remove strings from them and wash. Then cut lengthwise in two. Place beans and onions in a saucepan. Add 1 cup of water, cover with wax paper, then cover the pot and cook for 30 minutes over medium heat.

Remove wax paper, place tomato halves on top of beans, and add oil, sugar, and salt. Add 1 cup of water. Replace wax paper, cover, and cook for another 30 minutes. If necessary a little more water may be added.

If frozen beans are used, place beans and onions in a saucepan. Place tomato halves on top of beans. Add oil, sugar, salt, and 1 cup of water. Cover beans with wax paper. Place lid on saucepan. Cook for 40 minutes over medium heat. If necessary a little more water may be added.

Remove from heat. Transfer tomato halves carefully into a dish. Empty beans into a serving platter, placing tomato halves on top of beans. Allow to cool.

Serve cold as an appetizer or salad.

SERVES 4 TO 5 PERSONS.

FRESH PINTO BEANS PLAKI
Zeytinyağlı Barbunya

2 pounds fresh pinto beans with shells	½ teaspoon sugar
¼ cup olive or salad oil	Salt and pepper to taste
2 onions, grated	2 cups water
4 large tomatoes or 3 tablespoons tomato paste	2 tablespoons lemon juice
2 cloves garlic, chopped, optional	2 tablespoons chopped parsley

Shell and wash beans and place in a saucepan with enough cold water to cover beans. Cover and boil for 15 minutes. Drain.

Add oil, onions, tomatoes, garlic, sugar, salt, pepper, and 2 cups of water. Cover and cook over medium heat for 1 hour or until beans are tender.

Add lemon juice, stir and cook for 2 minutes more. Add more water if necessary. Beans should be left with a little water. Remove from heat and allow to cool in the saucepan. Empty into a serving dish, and garnish with parsley.

This dish can be served as appetizer.

SERVES 8 TO 10 PERSONS.

FRESH PINTO BEANS TARATOR
Taratorlu Barbunya

1 pound fresh pinto beans	*1 cup Tarator Sauce**
with shells	*2 tablespoons chopped*
5 cups water	*parsley*
Dash salt	

Shell and wash beans. Bring 5 cups of water and a dash of salt to a boil in a saucepan. Add beans and cook over medium heat until beans are tender, 45 minutes. Drain.

Place on a serving platter and pour sauce over them. Decorate with parsley.

Serve cold as an appetizer with sliced tomatoes.

SERVES 4 PERSONS.

WHITE KIDNEY BEANS PLAKI
Fasulye Plakisi

1 cup dried white kidney	*1 medium carrot, diced*
beans or 1 can (1 pound)	*2 stalks celery, diced*
cooked white kidney beans,	*¼ cup olive or salad oil*
drained	*½ teaspoon sugar*
Salt to taste	*1 medium potato, diced*
3 cups water	*Dash cayenne*
4 medium onions, diced	*2 tablespoons lemon juice*
2 cloves garlic, diced	*1 tablespoon chopped parsley*
1 tablespoon tomato paste or	*½ lemon, sliced thin*
2 medium tomatoes, diced	

Soak beans in cold water overnight. Drain.

Cook beans with 1 teaspoon salt in 3 cups boiling water over medium heat for 15 minutes. Drain. Place beans in a saucepan. Add onions, garlic, tomato paste, carrots, celery, oil, and enough water to cover contents of the saucepan. Cover and cook over medium heat for 30 minutes. Add sugar, potatoes, salt, cayenne, and lemon juice. Cover and cook for 20 minutes more or until beans are tender. If necessary, more water may be added. This dish should not be too dry.

If canned beans are used, place onions, garlic, tomato paste, carrots, celery, oil, and 2 cups water in a saucepan. Cover and cook for 30 minutes over medium heat. Add sugar, potatoes, salt, cayenne, lemon juice, and cook for 15 minutes more. More water may be added as necessary. Add beans and cook over low heat for 10 minutes only.

Remove from heat, transfer to a serving platter, and decorate top with chopped parsley and lemon slices.

Serve cold as an appetizer or salad.

SERVES 6 PERSONS.

FRESH FAVA BEANS
Zeytinyağlı Bakla

1 pound fresh fava beans	*¼ cup olive or salad oil*
1 bunch scallions	*¼ tablespoon sugar*
Salt to taste	*1½ cups water*
2 tablespoons lemon juice	*Yogurt Sauce I**
½ cup chopped fresh dill	

Remove strings and put beans in a bowl of cold water. Wash well and drain. Place in a bowl.

Cut the scallions into 1 inch long pieces, add to the beans. Add salt, lemon juice, and dill. Mix well. Transfer to a saucepan, add oil and sugar. Cover with a small dish to press down. Add 1½ cups of cold water. Cover saucepan and cook over medium heat about 1½ or 2 hours or until beans are tender.

Remove from heat, allow to cool covered in the saucepan. Transfer to a serving dish and serve cold (room temperature) with yogurt sauce I*.

This is a summer dish. It has an unusual flavor and can be an original addition to your menu.

SERVES 4 PERSONS.

CARROT PLAKI
Havuç Plakisi

6 *medium carrots*	½ *teaspoon sugar*
2 *medium onions, cut in*	*Salt to taste*
half lengthwise, then finely	2½ *cups water*
sliced	2 *tablespoons chopped*
¼ *cup olive or salad oil*	*parsley*
½ *tablespoon rice*	1 *lemon, cut into wedges*

Scrape and wash carrots. Cut diagonally into quarter inch oval slices.

Sauté onions with oil in a saucepan over medium heat for 6 minutes. Add carrots and cook for 3 minutes more. Add rice, sugar, salt, and 2½ cups water. Cover and cook over medium heat for about 45 minutes or until carrots are tender. If necessary, more water may be added.

Remove from heat and allow to cool in saucepan. Transfer to a serving platter. Decorate with parsley and lemon wedges.

Serve cold (room temperature) as an appetizer.

SERVES 4 TO 5 PERSONS.

ROOT CELERY A LA TURCA
Zeytinyağlı Kereviz

3 *large celery roots*	½ *cup salad or olive oil*
10 *cups water*	1 *medium carrot, diced*
2 *lemons*	3 *tablespoons green peas*
Salt to taste	1 *medium potato, diced*
10 *whole pearl onions,*	½ *teaspoon sugar*
cleaned	

Peel the dark outer skin of the celery roots until you get to the white part. Cut in two lengthwise. Scrape off the soft pulp inside. Place these halves in a bowl of cold water.

To 8 cups of water in a saucepan add the juice and peel of half a lemon, and a dash of salt. Bring to a boil, then add celery roots. Cook 10 minutes, drain, and set aside.

Place onions and oil in a shallow saucepan and sauté over medium heat, stirring constantly for 5 minutes. Add carrots and sauté 5 minutes longer. Add 2 cups of water, cover, and cook for 10 minutes on high heat. Add celery roots. Place wax paper on top, replace cover, reduce heat, and cook for 10 minutes more. Uncover, add peas, potatoes, juice of ½ lemon, sugar, and salt. Replace wax paper, cover, and cook for another 20 minutes over medium heat.

If necessary, more water may be added. This dish should not be too dry. It must have a little sauce left. Remove from heat. Allow to cool in the saucepan.

Place celery halves, hollow parts up, in a serving dish. Fill with carrots, potatoes, and peas. Pour the leftover sauce on the celery halves. Garnish with lemon wedges.

Serve cold as an appetizer or salad.

SERVES 6 PERSONS.

FRIED EGGPLANT AEGEAN
Domatesli Patlican Kızartması

1 large eggplant	*1 teaspoon sugar*
3 green peppers	*1 clove garlic, crushed,*
1½ cups olive or salad oil	*optional*
4 medium fresh tomatoes or	*1 bay leaf*
1 can (16 ounce) whole	*Salt to taste*
tomatoes, with juice	*2 tablespoons vinegar*
1 cup water	*Few mint leaves*

Cut the stem off the eggplant. Then peel off a half inch wide strip of the black skin lengthwise, leaving the next half inch with the skin on. Repeat until you make a striped effect. Then slice the whole eggplant crosswise into ⅓ inch pieces.

Cut peppers into halves lengthwise and remove seeds. In a frying pan, heat oil to boiling point. Fry eggplant slices on both sides until golden brown. Then place on absorbent paper. After they

have drained, arrange on a serving platter. Fry peppers the same
way and arrange around eggplant slices.

Empty leftover oil from pan and reserve. Peel, seed, and slice
tomatoes and put in pan. If canned tomatoes are used, empty
the whole can into the pan. Add 1 cup water, 3 tablespoons of the
leftover oil, sugar, garlic, bay leaf, and salt. Cook over medium
heat, stirring occasionally, until tomatoes are well cooked, about
50 minutes.

Add vinegar, stir and cook for 2 minutes more. Pour over eggplants and peppers. Cool and decorate with mint leaves.

Serve cold as an appetizer, plain or on toasted white bread.

SERVES 6 PERSONS.

EGGPLANT IMAM BAYILDI
Patlıcan Iman Bayıldı

2 medium onions, cut in half lengthwise, then finely sliced	2 cloves garlic, chopped
	Salt to taste
¼ cup olive or salad oil	2 tablespoons lemon juice
2 medium tomatoes, diced	3 medium eggplants, or
2 tablespoons chopped parsley	6 very small long ones
½ teaspoon sugar	2 cups water

Sauté onions in oil in a large frying pan for 5 minutes. Leaving
all the oil in the pan, remove onions and place in a bowl. Add
tomatoes, parsley, sugar, garlic, salt, and lemon juice and mix. Set
aside.

Cut the stems off the eggplants. Then peel off a half inch wide
strip of the black skin lengthwise, leaving the next half inch with
the skin on. Repeat until you make a striped effect. Then cut
each eggplant into 2 equal parts lengthwise. Now slash the middle
lengthwise on the cut side without piercing the outside and leaving
1 inch unslashed on both ends. If small long eggplants are used,
the whole vegetable may be slashed without cutting it into 2 pieces.

Sauté prepared eggplant pieces very lightly on both sides in the
leftover oil. Arrange with slashed parts up in one layer in the
same pan. Open slash and fill with onion and tomato mixture, and
spread the rest on top. Add 2 cups of cold water, cover with wax

paper, and then cover pan with a lid. Cook over medium heat until eggplants are tender, about 45 minutes. If necessary, add a little more water. See that eggplants are not too dry.

Remove from heat and let cool. Transfer to a serving platter and serve cold (room temperature) as an appetizer or salad.

SERVES 6 PERSONS.

FRIED EGGPLANT ISTANBUL
Patlıcan Kızartması

1 large eggplant
1½ cups olive or salad oil
Yogurt Sauce I*

Cut the stem off the eggplant. Then peel off a half inch wide strip of the black skin lengthwise leaving the next half inch with the skin on. Repeat until you make a striped effect. Then slice the whole eggplant crosswise into ⅓ inch slices.

Heat oil to boiling point. Fry eggplant slices on both sides until golden brown. Place each piece on absorbent paper. After they have been drained arrange on a serving platter. Pour yogurt sauce over just before serving.

Serve cold (room temperature) as an appetizer.

SERVES 6 PERSONS.

LEEKS A LA TURCA
Zeytinyağlı Pırasa

2 pounds leeks
2 onions, grated
⅓ cup salad or olive oil
1 carrot, cut into ⅛ inch
   slices
1 tablespoon tomato paste

2 tablespoons rice
¼ teaspoon sugar
Juice ½ lemon and
   1 lemon, sliced
Salt to taste
1 cup water

To prepare leeks, cut off roots, then remove 2 or 3 outer skins. Then cut leeks into 1½ or 2 inch long pieces. Wash and drain.

Sauté onions in oil in a saucepan for 3 minutes, stirring constantly. Add leeks, carrots, and tomato paste. Cover and cook over low heat for 30 minutes. Shake saucepan frequently. Add rice, sugar, lemon juice, salt, and 1 cup of water. Cover and cook about 30 minutes or until leeks are tender.

Remove from heat and allow to cool. Transfer to a platter and garnish with lemon slices.

Serve cold at the end of the main course instead of salad, or at the beginning of the meal as an appetizer.

SERVES 6 PERSONS.

TOMATO PLAKI
Domates Plakisi

4 large onions, cut in half lengthwise, then finely sliced	*1 teaspoon sugar*
½ cup salad or olive oil	*½ teaspoon allspice, optional*
2 pounds half-ripe tomatoes (green tomatoes may be used)	*Salt and pepper to taste*
	1 cup water
	2 tablespoons chopped parsley
¼ cup rice	

Sauté onions very lightly in oil about 5 or 6 minutes.

Cut tomatoes into halves and place in a shallow saucepan in one layer. Spread onions over the tomatoes and rice over the onions. Add the oil that is left from the sautéed onions. Sprinkle sugar, allspice, salt, and pepper over all. Add cup of water, cover, and cook over medium heat about 30 minutes, or until tomatoes and rice are tender. Remove from heat, cool, and transfer to a serving dish. Garnish with parsley before serving. Serve cold (room temperature) as an appetizer or salad.

SERVES 6 TO 8 PERSONS.

ZUCCHINI IMAM BAYILDI

Kabak Iman Bayıldı

4 *medium zucchini*	*Salt to taste*
2 *medium onions, cut in half*	1 *teaspoon sugar*
lengthwise, then finely sliced	1 *small tomato, cut into*
1 *cup chopped parsley, dill,*	4 *slices crosswise*
and fresh mint leaves,	5 *tablespoons salad or olive*
mixed; save parsley and	*oil*
dill stems	1 *cup water*
2 *cloves garlic, sliced*	2 *tablespoons lemon juice*

Scrape the zucchini and wash. Cut carefully through the middle lengthwise to within an inch of each end on one side only, taking care not to cut through.

Place onions in a bowl. Add parsley, dill, mint leaves, garlic, salt, and sugar. Mix well.

Put parsley and dill stems at the bottom of a saucepan, arrange the zucchini on top, placing them side by side, the cut section up. Fill the cut with the onion mixture. Whatever is left can be spread over the zucchini. Place a slice of tomato on each zucchini, add oil, a cup of water, and lemon juice. Place a plate on top to give weight during cooking. Cover and cook over medium heat about 40 minutes or until tender.

Remove from heat and allow to cool. Serve cold as an appetizer or after the main course instead of a salad.

SERVES 4 PERSONS.

ARTICHOKE RICE DOLMA
Zeytinyağlı Enginar Dolması

½ cup rice
1½ teaspoons salt
½ cup olive or salad oil,
   and 2 tablespoons olive
   oil
1 bunch scallions, with
   green tops, chopped
2 teaspoons sugar

1 cup chicken stock or
   water
2 lemons
½ cup chopped dill, save
   stems
2 tablespoons flour
6 large artichokes

Place rice in a bowl, add 1 teaspoon salt, and cover with hot water. Stir and allow to cool. Drain.

Place ½ cup oil in frying pan, add rice and sauté over medium heat, stirring constantly for 8 minutes. Add scallions, sauté 2 minutes more. Add ½ teaspoon salt, sugar, and stock. Stir, cover, and cook over medium heat until all stock is absorbed, about 10 minutes. Add the juice of half a lemon and the dill. Stir, cover, and set aside.

Fill large bowl with cold water; sprinkle with flour, add the juice of 1 lemon. Mix well and set aside.

Prepare artichokes as in Artichoke Meat Dolma*. Shake off excess water but save 4 cups of this water. Stuff hearts with rice mixture. Pour any remaining oil in saucepan of rice mixture over artichokes.

Place a rack at the bottom of a heavy saucepan and put dill stems on rack.

Cut out 6 pieces of wax paper 12×12 inches.

Place an artichoke in the middle of a piece of the wax paper. Gather ends and twist. Place each wrapped artichoke, bottom down, in the saucepan over dill stems. Put 2 tablespoons oil into saucepan. Add 2 cups of the lemon and flour water. Place a plate on top to give weight during cooking. Cover and cook over medium heat until water is absorbed. Add 2 cups more of the flour water and continue to cook, about 1½ hours.

Remove from heat and cool, covered. Unwrap artichokes and arrange on a serving platter. Decorate with lemon slices.

Serve cold as an appetizer.

SERVES 6 PERSONS.

CABBAGE RICE DOLMA
Zeytinyağlı Lahana Dolması

1 cup rice	Black pepper to taste
3 tablespoons salt	1 tablespoon allspice
6 medium onions, coarsely grated	1 tablespoon sugar
¾ cup olive oil	2 tablespoons lemon juice
2 tablespoons pignolia nuts	11½ cups water
1 large tomato, diced	1 white cabbage, 3 to 3½ pounds
1 cup beef stock or water	2 lemons, cut into wedges
2 tablespoons black currants	

Place rice in a bowl, add 1 tablespoon salt, and cover with hot water. Stir and allow to cool. Drain and set aside.

Sauté onions in frying pan with oil and 1 tablespoon salt, over medium heat, stirring constantly for 15 to 20 minutes.

Add rice and nuts. Continue to sauté for 10 minutes more, stirring constantly.

Add the tomato, stock, currants, pepper, allspice, and sugar. Stir, cover, and cook on low heat until all stock is absorbed, 15 to 20 minutes. Remove from heat. Add lemon juice and stir. Cover and set aside.

Put 10 cups of water and 1 tablespoon salt in a large saucepan. Bring to a boil.

Wash cabbage. Cut around core where leaves join it by inserting a sharp knife deep enough to loosen the leaves from the core, but not to detach them. Place cabbage core up in the boiling water. Cover, boil for 3 minutes. Remove cover and take out a few of the outer leaves. Tilt cabbage with the aid of a spoon and take leaves out with tongs, taking care not to break them. Cover saucepan and boil 3 minutes more. Again take out a few leaves. Continue same process until you come to the heart of the cabbage. Pile leaves in a colander to drain and cool.

Cut leaves into palm-size sections, discarding the hard vein in the middle and the curled parts near the core. Reserve discarded leaves. Pile prepared leaf sections on a dish.

Place several layers of discarded cabbage leaves at the bottom of a heavy saucepan.

Take 1 leaf section from the prepared pile into your palm. Stir rice mixture so that oil and rice are mixed. Place 2 heaping table-spoons of the rice mixture on the thicker end of the leaf 1½ inches from the edge. Fold thick part over filling. Then fold sides over and roll toward the end of the leaf. Place in saucepan over the layers of leaves, placing loose end down so that it is securely tucked in. Repeat same process with each leaf, placing dolmas close to each other in rows. When one layer is finished, start next layer over the first, and so on, until all rice mixture and leaves are used up.

Cover top of dolmas with a layer of discarded leaves. Place a plate on top to give weight during cooking. Add 1½ cups water, cover, and place saucepan over high heat for 5 minutes. Then lower heat to medium and cook until all water is absorbed, about 50 to 60 minutes.

Remove saucepan from heat and cool covered. After dolmas are thoroughly cooled arrange on serving platter. Decorate with lemon wedges.

Serve cold as an appetizer or for buffet dinners. Also may be taken to picnics.

ALLOW 3 TO 4 PER PERSON.

EGGPLANT RICE DOLMA
Zeytinyağlı Patlıcan Dolması

⅔ cup rice
1½ tablespoons salt
6 medium onions, coarsely grated
¾ cup olive oil
2 tablespoons pignolia nuts
2 medium tomatoes, diced
¾ cup beef stock or water
2 tablespoons black currants
Black pepper to taste
1 tablespoon allspice
1 tablespoon sugar

2 tablespoons chopped parsley, save stems
2 tablespoons chopped mint leaves
2 tablespoons chopped dill, save stems
3 eggplants, 6 inches long, medium fat
¼ cup salad oil
1½ cups water
Few parsley sprigs

Place rice in a bowl, add 1 tablespoon salt, and cover with hot water. Stir and allow to cool. Drain and set aside.

Place onions in frying pan with olive oil and ¼ tablespoon salt. Sauté over medium heat, stirring constantly, for 15 to 20 minutes.

Add rice and nuts and continue to sauté, stirring constantly, for 10 minutes more.

Add the tomatoes, stock, currants, pepper, allspice, and sugar. Stir, cover, and cook over low heat until all stock is absorbed, about 15 to 20 minutes. Remove from heat, add parsley, mint, and dill. Stir, cover, and set aside.

Cut off stem end of eggplants and shape into a cover to be used later. If the stem end is too narrow, cut off ½ inch from the opposite end and start scooping the inside from here. Discard. Leave about ½ inch thick shell. To make scooping easier, press gently against outside of eggplants to loosen pulp.

Heat salad oil to boiling in a frying pan. Sauté eggplants on each side, about 2 minutes per side. Do not overcook and be careful not to break shells. Set aside to cool.

Place a rack in a heavy saucepan. Put dill and parsley stems over rack. Lay wax paper on stems to cover the bottom of the saucepan.

Stuff shells with rice mixture. Shake shells so that rice will settle down but do not overstuff. When shells are stuffed replace covers.

Lay eggplants side by side over wax paper. Sprinkle with ¼ tablespoon salt. Add 1½ cups water. Cover with another piece of wax paper. Place a plate on top to give weight during cooking. Cover and cook over medium heat until eggplants are soft, about 50 minutes. Remove from heat and cool, covered.

Arrange eggplants on a serving platter. Cut into 2 or 3 sections crosswise. Decorate with parsley sprigs.

Serve cold as an appetizer. Also for cold buffet dinners or luncheons with a salad.

SERVES 6 TO 8 PERSONS.

GREEN PEPPER RICE DOLMA
Zeytinyağlı Büber Dolması

1 cup rice	1 tablespoon sugar
2 tablespoons salt	2 tablespoons chopped
6 medium onions, coarsely	parsley, save stems
grated	2 tablespoons chopped mint
¾ cup olive oil	leaves
3 tablespoons pignolia nuts	2 tablespoons chopped dill,
1 large tomato, diced	save stems
1 cup beef stock or water	2 tablespoons lemon juice
2 tablespoons black currants	10 medium green peppers
Black pepper to taste	2 cups water
1 tablespoon allspice	2 lemons, cut into wedges

Place rice in a bowl, add 1 tablespoon salt and cover with hot water. Stir and allow to cool. Drain and set aside.

In a frying pan sauté onions with 1 tablespoon of salt and oil over medium heat, stirring constantly for 20 minutes. Add rice and nuts, continue to sauté, stirring constantly, for 10 minutes more.

Add the tomato, stock, currants, pepper, allspice, and sugar. Stir, cover, and cook over low heat until all stock is absorbed, about 15 to 20 minutes. Remove from heat. Add parsley, mint, dill, and lemon juice and stir. Cover and set aside.

Slice through tops of peppers but do not sever them for the tops serve as covers. Remove seeds.

Place a rack in a heavy saucepan. Put parsley and dill stems on rack.

Stuff peppers with rice mixture, pressing it down. Do not over-stuff. Adjust cover and arrange in saucepan over stems cover side up. Add 2 cups of water. Cover with wax paper. Place a plate on top to give weight during cooking. Cover and cook over medium heat until all the water is absorbed and the peppers are cooked, about 1 hour. If necessary, more water may be added.

Remove from heat and cool, covered.

Decorate with lemon wedges and serve cold as an appetizer for dinner. Also good for luncheons.

ALLOW 1 PER PERSON.

TOMATO RICE DOLMA
Zeytinyağlı Domates Dolması

½ cup rice	Black pepper to taste
1 tablespoon salt	1 tablespoon sugar
12 large half-ripened tomatoes	2 tablespoons chopped dill, save stems
6 medium onions, coarsely grated	2 tablespoons chopped mint leaves
¾ cup olive oil	¼ cup water
2 tablespoons pignolia nuts	½ bunch parsley
⅔ cup beef stock or water	
2 tablespoons black currants	

Place rice in a bowl, add ½ tablespoon salt, and cover with hot water. Stir and allow to cool. Drain and set aside.

Slice through side of tomatoes opposite the stem, but do not sever for the tops serve as covers. Scoop out inside with a teaspoon. Dice and set aside pulp from 5 tomatoes. Discard the rest of the pulp.

Place onions in frying pan, add oil, and ½ tablespoon salt. Sauté over medium heat, stirring constantly, for 15 to 20 minutes.

Add rice and nuts, continue to sauté, stirring constantly for 10 minutes more.

Add the diced tomato pulp, stock, currants, pepper, and sugar. Stir, cover, and cook over low heat until all stock is absorbed, about 15 to 20 minutes. Remove from heat, add dill, mint, and stir. Cover and set aside.

Place a rack in a heavy saucepan. Put dill stems on rack. Stuff tomatoes with rice mixture; press down but do not overstuff. Replace tops of tomatoes and place in saucepan over dill stems, top side up. Add ¼ cup water. Cover with wax paper. Place a plate on top to give weight during cooking. Cover and cook over medium heat until all the water is absorbed and the tomatoes are cooked, about 40 minutes.

Remove from heat and cool, covered.

Arrange tomatoes around a round serving platter. Place parsley in the center as a decoration.

Serve cold as an appetizer, also for cold buffet dinners and luncheons.

ALLOW 1 PER PERSON.

ZUCCHINI RICE DOLMA
Zeytinyağlı Kabak Dolması

½ cup rice	1 cup chicken stock or water
1½ teaspoons salt	2 tablespoons chopped dill,
½ cup olive or salad oil	save stems
1 bunch scallions with	2 tablespoons chopped mint
green tops, chopped	leaves
2 tomatoes, fresh or canned,	6 large fat zucchini
diced	1½ cups water
1 teaspoon sugar	Few sprigs parsley

Place rice in a bowl, add 1 teaspoon salt, cover with hot water. Stir and allow to cool. Drain.

Place oil in frying pan, add rice, sauté over medium heat, stirring constantly for 8 minutes. Add scallions and sauté 2 minutes more. Add tomatoes and continue to sauté, stirring constantly for 3 minutes. Add ½ teaspoon salt, sugar, and stock. Stir, cover, and cook over medium heat until all stock is absorbed, about 15 minutes.

Add dill and mint. Stir, cover, and set aside.

Scrape and wash zucchini. Cut off stem end and shape into a cover to be used later. Trim opposite end. Scoop out inside, leaving a ⅓ inch shell. If stem end is too narrow, cut off a half inch from opposite end and shape into a cover. Scoop out from cover end.

Fill shells with rice mixture a little at a time, pushing down with the handle of a spoon or shaking the zucchini. Do not overstuff. Leave 1 inch empty space at the mouth. Replace cover. Repeat until all the zucchini are stuffed.

Place a rack in a heavy saucepan. Put dill stems on rack. Arrange zucchini over stems. Add 1½ cups water. Place wax paper over zucchini and place a plate on top to give weight during cooking. Cover and cook over medium heat until zucchini are tender, about 1¼ hours.

Remove from heat and cool, covered.

Arrange zucchini on a serving platter. If any juice remains in saucepan, pour over zucchini. Decorate with parsley sprigs.

Serve cold or as an appetizer, or as a luncheon dish with Tomato and Cucumber Salad*.

ALLOW 1 PER PERSON.

GREEN BEANS A LA TURCA
Tereyağlı Taze Fasulye

1 medium onion, coarsely grated	*1 teaspoon sugar*
2 tablespoons butter	*Salt and pepper to taste*
3 medium tomatoes, fresh or canned, peeled and sliced	*½ cup water*
2 packages (9 ounce) frozen French-cut green beans, defrosted	

Sauté onion with butter in a saucepan over medium heat for 5 minutes, stirring all the time. Add tomatoes and continue to sauté for 5 minutes more, stirring occasionally.

Add beans, sugar, salt, pepper, and ½ cup water. Cover and cook over medium heat until beans are tender and all the water is absorbed, about 40 minutes. If necessary a little more water may be added.

Serve hot with all roasted meats and poultry.

SERVES 5 TO 6 PERSONS.

FRIED CARROTS
Havuç Kızartması

6 *large carrots*	1 *cup flour*
5 *cups water*	1½ *cups olive or salad oil*
1½ *teaspoons salt*	*Yogurt Sauce I**

Scrape and wash carrots, then cut diagonally into ⅙ inch thick oval slices.

In a saucepan bring to a boil 4 cups of water and 1 teaspoon salt. Add carrots and cook over high heat for 10 minutes or until carrots are tender, but not too soft. Drain, dry on paper towel, and cool.

Place flour in a mixing bowl. Gradually add 1 cup cold water, stirring constantly until smooth.

Place oil in frying pan over high heat. Dredge each carrot heavily in flour mixture and fry each side in hot oil for a few minutes, until a crust is formed around the carrots. Do not brown too much.

Remove to serving platter, making a neat pile. Sprinkle with remaining salt.

Serve hot as a side dish with meat or poultry courses, or as an appetizer with yogurt sauce.

SERVES 6 TO 8 PERSONS.

FRIED CAULIFLOWER
Karnıbahar Kızartması

4 cups water
2 tablespoons lemon juice
1 small cauliflower
4 eggs
1 cup grated Gruyère or
   Cheddar cheese

Salt and pepper to taste
1 cup bread crumbs
1 cup salad oil or shortening

Bring 4 cups of water and lemon juice to a boil in a saucepan. Add the whole cauliflower, cleaned and washed. Boil until tender but not too soft, about 10 to 15 minutes.

Remove cauliflower and separate branches into 3 inch long pieces. Press and flatten each piece in your palm and place carefully on wax paper.

Beat eggs, add cheese, salt, and pepper and mix well.

Coat cauliflower pieces with bread crumbs on both sides. Dip into egg mixture. Fry in hot oil on one side until golden brown, then turn and fry the other side. Serve hot.

Serve with any main dish, especially with beef dishes. May also be served with Yogurt Sauce I* as an appetizer.

SERVES 6 TO 8 PERSONS.

EGGPLANT PUREE
Beğendi

Juice 1 lemon
Salt to taste
5 cups cold water
6 medium eggplants
4 tablespoons butter

2 tablespoons flour
1 cup warm milk
½ cup grated Gruyère or
   Cheddar cheese

Mix lemon juice and 1 teaspoon salt with 5 cups of cold water in a bowl. Set aside.

Insert knife into whole eggplants about an inch deep at several places. Place them directly over a high gas flame and turn often to make cooking even. Allow skin to burn and turn black. If an electric stove is used, place the eggplant directly over the heating unit. When skin is all black and the eggplant is soft it is done. Skin eggplants with a knife while still hot. Remove seeds and drop eggplants into the bowl of cold water.

Place butter in a saucepan. Add flour and sauté over medium heat, stirring constantly until flour turns very light golden in color, about 5 minutes. Add warm milk and continue stirring until the mixture is smooth.

Quickly squeeze all the water out of the eggplants and chop them. Add to the milk mixture. Add cheese and salt. Mash with a potato masher into a smooth paste and cook, stirring constantly until the mixture bubbles, about 10 minutes.

Serve hot. To serve with Sultan's Delight* arrange meat in the middle of a round serving platter and eggplant paste in a circle around the meat. Decorate meat with chopped parsley.

See also Chicken with Eggplant Purée*.

Eggplant purée also makes an excellent side dish.

SERVES 6 PERSONS.

EGGPLANT BOEREKS
Patlıcan Böreği

¼ cup crumbled white or feta cheese	1 medium eggplant
	Salt and pepper to taste
2 tablespoons grated Cheddar cheese	1 cup salad oil
	4 radishes
¼ cup chopped parsley	8 black olives
2 eggs	

Place white cheese, Cheddar, parsley, and 1 egg in a bowl and mix well.

Cut the stem off the eggplant. Then peel off a half inch wide strip of the black skin lengthwise, leaving the next half inch with the skin on. Repeat until you make a striped effect. Slice into pieces 3 inches long and ½ inch thick. Slash each piece lengthwise without separating it at one end. Fill the inside with the cheese mixture.

Beat the other egg in a bowl and add pepper and salt. Dip filled eggplant slices into the egg batter and sauté in oil on both sides over medium heat until golden brown. Serve hot as a side dish with meat or poultry or as an appetizer with radishes and olives.

SERVES 4 PERSONS.

EGGPLANT FRIED IN EGGS
Yumurtalı Patlıcan Kızartması

1 medium eggplant	*2 eggs*
2 tablespoons salt	*¼ cup flour*
1 cup olive or salad oil	*Yogurt Sauce I*, optional*

Cut the stem off the eggplant. Then peel off a half inch wide strip of the black skin lengthwise, leaving the next half inch with the skin on. Repeat until you make a striped effect. Then cut into ½ inch thick slices crosswise. Place slices in bowl. Add 2 tablespoons salt, cover with water. Weight down with a heavy object so that the slices are kept in the water. Leave 2 hours.

Drain eggplants. Squeeze all the water out between palms of hands. Dry with paper towel.

Heat oil to boiling point in a medium-size saucepan over high heat.

Beat eggs in a small bowl until frothy. Coat eggplant slices lightly with flour. Dip into beaten eggs.

Fry on both sides in the oil until golden brown, 4 to 5 minutes on each side.

Serve warm as a side dish with roast meats or roast chicken.

Also may be served as an appetizer with yogurt sauce I poured on. If so, double the ingredients.

SERVES 4 TO 5 PERSONS.

EGGPLANT SOUFFLE
Patlıcan Suflesi

Juice 1 lemon	*5 tablespoons flour*
Salt to taste	*1 cup warm milk*
5 cups cold water	*Pepper to taste*
5 medium eggplants	*4 eggs*
3 tablespoons butter	*¾ cup grated Gruyère cheese*

Preheat oven to 400 degrees F.

Mix lemon juice and 1 teaspoon salt with 5 cups of cold water in a bowl. Set aside.

Follow directions in Eggplant Purée* to cook, skin, and seed eggplant. Drop eggplants into the bowl of cold water.

Place butter in a saucepan. Add flour and sauté over medium heat, stirring constantly until flour turns pinkish, about 5 minutes. Add warm milk and continue stirring until the mixture is smooth. Add salt and pepper and remove from heat. Quickly squeeze all the water out of the eggplants and chop them. Add to the milk mixture and return to the stove and cook for 5 minutes, stirring constantly. Remove from heat and cool.

Separate egg yolks; beat until light and fold into the cooled eggplant mixture, stirring constantly. Beat egg whites until stiff and fold into the eggplant mixture. Add cheese and stir.

Pour eggplant mixture into a buttered 8×8×3 inch oven-proof dish. Bake for about 20 to 25 minutes. Serve immediately.

SERVES 6 PERSONS.

OKRA STEW
Tereyağlı Bamya

1 pound tomatoes, sliced	*Salt to taste*
2 tablespoons butter	*2 tablespoons lemon juice*
2 cups broth or water	
1 pound fresh okra or	
* 2 packages (10 ounce)*	
frozen okra, defrosted	

Place tomatoes, butter, and broth in a saucepan. Simmer over medium heat for 45 minutes or until tomatoes are thoroughly cooked and the broth is reduced to half its original amount.

Trim okra by only peeling the cone-shaped end without piercing the pot. Wash and add to the tomatoes. Cook covered for 30 minutes over high heat. Add salt and lemon juice and cook 5 minutes longer. Remove from heat and serve hot with a meat dish and Mashed Rice*.

SERVES 8 PERSONS.

SPINACH STEW
Borani

2 pounds fresh spinach	2 tablespoons rice
1 large onion, grated	Pinch sugar
2 tablespoons butter	Salt and pepper to taste
1 tablespoon tomato paste diluted with ¼ cup water	

Wash spinach several times. Cut into two.

Sauté onion in a saucepan with butter, stirring constantly for 5 minutes. Add spinach and tomato paste. Place rice on top. Add sugar, salt, and pepper. Cover and cook on medium heat for 25 minutes or until spinach is cooked.

If necessary a little more water may be added.

Serve with meat as a vegetable side dish.

SERVES 6 PERSONS.

FRIED SPINACH
Ispanak Kavurması

2 pounds fresh spinach or 3 packages (10 ounce) frozen chopped spinach	2 medium onions, grated
	2 tablespoons butter
	¼ teaspoon sugar
Salt to taste	Pepper to taste
6 cups water	

When fresh spinach is used, discard damaged stems and leaves. Cut off and discard very carefully roots that come from under the soil. Do not separate stems from the pinkish roots and cut them about 2 or 3 inches long. They can be used for different dishes. (See Spinach Root Salad* or Cultured Spinach Roots*.)

Wash leaves several times in cold water. Drop leaves in 6 cups of salted boiling water and boil for 5 minutes. Drain and chop. Set aside.

When frozen spinach is used, defrost, squeeze the water out, and set aside.

Sauté onions very lightly in butter for 3 minutes. Add spinach, sugar, salt, and pepper. Fry, stirring constantly 15 to 20 minutes.

Serve with lamb chops or other meat dishes; also with fried fish.

SERVES 6 PERSONS.

VEGETABLE CASSEROLE
Güveç

1 medium eggplant
2 medium zucchini
3 green peppers
⅓ cup olive or salad oil
2 medium onions, cut into
   round slices
1 package (10 ounce)
   frozen French-cut green
   beans, defrosted

1 package (10 ounce)
   frozen okra, defrosted
3 medium tomatoes, fresh or
   canned, peeled and sliced
Salt and pepper to taste
2 tablespoons butter

Preheat oven to 350 degrees F. after the vegetables have been prepared.

Prepare vegetables as follows: Cut the stems off eggplant. Then peel off a half inch wide strip of the black skin lengthwise, leaving the next half inch with the skin on. Repeat until you make a striped effect. Then cut the whole eggplant lengthwise into 4 equal parts and then cut each piece crosswise into 2 inch pieces.

Scrape zucchini. Cut the whole zucchini lengthwise into 2 equal parts and each piece crosswise into 2 inch pieces.

Cut green peppers into 4 equal parts and remove seeds.

Dry all vegetables with paper towel.

Heat oil very hot in a frying pan; add eggplants and sauté a few minutes on both sides. Remove with a perforated kitchen spoon and arrange in the bottom of an earthenware casserole.

In the same oil sauté peppers and place a few pieces over eggplant with a few slices of onions.

Sauté zucchini and arrange over eggplant. Again cover with a few peppers and onion slices.

Make next layer of beans, followed by the rest of the pepper and onion slices.

Last, add okra and cover with tomatoes. Add salt and pepper. Dot with 2 tablespoons butter. Cover and bake until tender, about 1¼ hours.

Serve with roast chicken or roast meat dishes.

SERVES 8 PERSONS.

FRIED ZUCCHINI AEGEAN
Kabak Kızartması

1 pound zucchini	*2 cups salad oil*
1 cup flour	*Salt to taste*
1 can beer	

Scrape, wash, and dry zucchini. Cut lengthwise into slices about ⅜ inch thick. Coat with flour, then dip into beer. Fry in hot oil on both sides, about 3 minutes on each side. The slices should be crisp.

Pile zucchini in a mound on a serving dish and sprinkle salt on top.

Serve hot as a side dish with meat or poultry or as an appetizer or salad with Yogurt Sauce I*.

SERVES 5 TO 6 PERSONS.

BAKED ZUCCHINI
Fırında Kabak

6 small zucchini
3 eggs
5 scallions with green tops,
  chopped
½ cup chopped dill
½ cup chopped fresh mint
  leaves
½ cup chopped parsley

1 cup grated Gruyère cheese
½ cup grated feta or white
  cheese
1½ cups flour
Salt and pepper to taste
Dash cayenne
4 tablespoons butter
10 black olives, optional

Preheat oven to 350 degrees F.

Scrape, wash, and dry zucchini. Grate coarsely into a large bowl.
Add eggs, scallions, dill, mint, parsley, both cheeses. Add flour a
little at a time, mixing continually. Add salt, pepper, and cayenne.

Grease a 9×9 inch oven-proof dish with 2 tablespoons butter.
Pour in the mixture evenly. Decorate with olives. Dot top with the
rest of the butter.

Bake for 45 to 55 minutes until well browned. Cut into squares
and serve hot or cold as a side dish with meat, poultry, or fish.

SERVES 10 TO 12 PERSONS.

ZUCCHINI ROUNDS
Mücver

6 small zucchini
3 eggs
5 scallions with green tops,
  chopped
½ cup chopped dill
½ cup chopped fresh mint
  leaves

½ cup chopped parsley
1 cup grated Gruyère cheese
1½ cups flour
Salt and pepper to taste
Dash cayenne
1 to 1½ cups salad oil

Scrape, wash, and dry zucchini. Grate coarsely into a large bowl. Add eggs, scallions, dill, mint leaves, parsley, and cheese. Add flour a little at a time, mixing continually. Add salt, pepper, and cayenne.

Heat oil very hot in a frying pan. Drop zucchini mixture by tablespoonfuls one at a time into the oil. Fry first on one side, then turn and fry on the other side until golden brown.

Serve hot as a side dish with meat, poultry, or fish. Smaller rounds may be made and served as hot hors d'oeuvres.

SERVES 10 TO 12 PERSONS.

ZUCCHINI WITH CHEESE
Peynirli Kabak

3 medium zucchini	1 tablespoon chopped parsley
Salt to taste	1 tablespoon chopped dill
½ cup grated Gruyère cheese	1 teaspoon flour
¼ cup mashed feta or white cheese	Pepper to taste
	2 tablespoons butter
2 eggs	Paprika

Preheat broiler after the zucchini have been filled.

Scrape and wash zucchini and cut into halves lengthwise. Scoop out the inside and discard, leaving a half inch thick shell. Take care not to pierce the shell. Boil zucchini in salted water for 15 minutes and drain. To make handling easy, do not overcook them. Arrange zucchini side by side in an oven-proof dish.

In a bowl place Gruyère and white cheese; add eggs, parsley, dill, flour, salt, and pepper and mix with a fork.

Fill the inside of each zucchini with this mixture and dot with butter. Sprinkle on a little paprika. Broil until cheese melts and browns evenly. Serve hot as an appetizer or as a side dish with meat or poultry.

SERVES 6 PERSONS.

ZUCCHINI A LA TURCA
Kalye

2 *pounds fresh, tender* *zucchini*	4 *ounces canned tomato* *sauce*
1 *large onion, cut in half* *lengthwise, then finely* *sliced*	*Salt and pepper to taste* 4 *tablespoons butter* 1 *cup water*

Scrape, wash, and cut the zucchini in half lengthwise and then into 2 inch long pieces crosswise and place in a saucepan. Add onions, pour the tomato sauce over them, and add salt, pepper, and butter. Add 1 cup of water, cover, and cook over medium heat until the zucchini is tender, about 40 minutes.

This is an appetizing and light side dish served with grilled or broiled fish, poultry, or meat.

SERVES 6 PERSONS.

10. Rice—Macaroni—Boereks

Rice is extensively used in Turkish cuisine and in food value it serves the same purpose as potatoes. It is used more diversely by the Turks. It is served as a side dish, as several pilav dishes, it is used as an ingredient in dolmas, and becomes an excellent entrée in Pilav Pie.

In the traditional Turkish menu pilav was an indispensable last course before dessert. The great chefs earned their reputation by the quality of the pilav they served. Even today a Turkish housewife's cooking ability is often judged by her pilav. The Turkish standard requires that the rice be well cooked and fluffy and that each grain stands out individually and not stick together. Rice should always be handled carefully in order not to break or mash it.

Actually this is an art easily acquired. It depends largely on testing and learning the absorbing capacity of the rice used. The fluffiness depends on the amount of broth used in cooking. Although there is a general proportion, different kinds of rice require slightly varying amounts of liquid. The art of good pilav making depends to a large extent in determining this slight variation. Usually rice dishes are covered with a napkin after cooking in order to allow the absorption of excess steam.

For pilav long grain rice yields the best result. On the other hand, for stuffing and as an ingredient for meat and soups, short grain is recommended. If cooking is required before stuffing, as with some dolmas, then long grain should be used.

Rice, in some form or other, must be present in a menu with a Turkish accent.

Boerek is a Turkish specialty. It appeals to every palate. Based on ready-made Phyllo pastry* dough, called *yufka* in Turkish, it can be prepared with every kind of filling from cheese to chicken and spinach.

The ready-made dough comes in 1 pound packages, consisting of paper-thin sheets of pastry approximately 18 inches long and 16 inches wide. In 1 pound there are about 25 sheets of pastry. However, some pastries are made very thin, so the number of sheets goes up to 50. The pastry can be kept in the refrigerator in its wax paper box for a few days. But best results are obtained when used immediately. The paper-thin sheets are very delicate and dry up easily and break, making handling very difficult. Handle with care and work quickly to avoid drying.

Boereks can be served as appetizers as well as main courses. Spinach and Cheese Boerek make a wonderful first course. Spinach Boerek may be served with yogurt sauce. Puff and Cigarette Boerek can be served with light soups such as chicken soup or hot bouillons. On the other hand Chicken Boerek, Meat Boerek, and Tatar Boerek make a substantial main course. In that case they can be preceded with smoked salmon or with artichokes or some other similar appetizer.

Rice—Macaroni—Boereks

RICE

MACARONI

BOEREKS

CHICKEN LIVER PILAV
Iç Pilav

1½ cups long grain rice
Salt to taste
6 tablespoons butter
¼ cup pignolia nuts
¼ pound chicken livers, diced
¼ cup black currants

2½ cups chicken broth
Pepper to taste
1 bunch scallions, whites
*   only, finely chopped*
¼ cup chopped dill

Place rice in a bowl, add 1 tablespoon salt, and cover with hot water. Stir and allow to cool. Drain and set aside.

Melt 2 tablespoons butter in a small saucepan, add nuts, and sauté golden brown. Remove. Add livers and sauté in the same butter.

In a heavy saucepan place nuts, currants, the remaining butter, broth, salt, and pepper and bring to a boil. Add rice while the broth is still boiling. Stir once only, cover and cook on high heat without stirring for 5 minutes. Lower heat and cook until rice absorbs all the broth, about 15 minutes. Fold scallions into rice together with dill and sautéed chicken livers. Remove from heat. Take off cover, put a napkin over the pot, and replace cover. Leave for 40 minutes in a warm place. With a large spoon, gently transfer rice to a serving dish, taking care not to mash or break rice.

This is a rich dish and can be served with roast chicken, roast turkey, roast leg of lamb, or roast veal.

SERVES 8 PERSONS.

PILAV WITH CALF'S BRAINS
Beyinli Pilav

*White Pilav**
*Fried Calf's Brains**
Few parsley sprigs

Fill a large ring mold with hot pilav pressed down tightly so that rice stays in shape. Invert into a round serving platter. Pile fried brain pieces into the middle of the rice ring and decorate with parsley.

Serve as an appetizer or after fish or chicken as a second course.

SERVES 6 PERSONS.

PILAV CHICK-PEAS
Nohutlu Pilav

1 can (1 pound 4 ounce)	*2 tablespoons butter*
cooked chick-peas, or 1 cup	*Tomato Pilav**
uncooked chick-peas	*Salt to taste*

If you use canned cooked chick-peas, drain them and sauté in butter. Stir them into the rice just before serving.

If you use uncooked chick-peas, soak peas overnight and boil in salted water until soft. Drain and sauté in butter. Stir them into the rice just before serving.

SERVES 6 TO 8 PERSONS.

EGGPLANT PILAV
Patlıcanli Pilav

1 cup long grain rice
1¼ tablespoons salt
1 large eggplant
1 cup salad oil
⅓ cup olive or salad oil
2 large onions, coarsely grated
4 medium tomatoes, fresh
  or canned, diced

2 cups beef stock
1 teaspoon allspice
1 teaspoon sugar
2 tablespoons chopped mint
  leaves

Place rice in a bowl, add 1 tablespoon salt, and cover with hot water. Stir and allow to cool. Drain and set aside.

Cut the stem off the eggplant. Then peel off a half inch wide strip of the black skin lengthwise, leaving the next half inch with the skin on. Repeat until you make a striped effect. Then cut eggplant lengthwise into 4 equal parts, and each of these pieces into 1½ inch pieces.

In hot oil in a medium saucepan, deep-fry eggplant pieces golden brown on all sides. Drain off excess oil, place in a bowl, and set aside.

Place 2 tablespoons of the olive oil in a saucepan with the onions. Sauté over medium heat, stirring constantly, until onions are light golden, about 10 minutes.

Place tomatoes in a medium-size heavy saucepan where the final cooking will take place. Cook over medium heat, stirring occasionally until soft and well cooked, about 20 minutes.

Add stock, the rest of the olive oil, onions, allspice, sugar, and remaining salt. Bring to a boil. Add eggplant and mint, and keep boiling. Add rice, stir once, cover, and cook over high heat for 5 minutes. Turn heat to low and cook until rice absorbs all the stock, about 15 minutes.

Remove from heat, uncover, place a napkin over saucepan. Replace cover and leave for 40 minutes in a warm place.

When transferring to a serving platter, stir gently with a large spoon, taking care not to mash or break rice.

Serve cold as an appetizer and at buffet suppers.

SERVES 8 TO 10 PERSONS.

KEBAB PILAV
Pilavlı Kebab

Tomato Pilav*
Shish Kebab*

Arrange pilav on a round or oblong serving platter. Flatten top.
Take meat and vegetables off the skewers. Arrange meat on the
top of pilav. Arrange vegetables, alternating onions, peppers, tomatoes, and mushrooms, around the pilav.
Serve immediately.

SERVES 6 PERSONS.

At table keep a short hand, in company keep a short tongue.

MASHED RICE
Lapa

1 small onion, grated	3⅓ cups chicken broth
2 tablespoons butter	Salt and pepper to taste
2 small tomatoes, diced	1 cup short round grain rice
½ green pepper, seeded and diced	

Sauté onion for 5 minutes in butter, stirring all the time. Add tomatoes and green pepper, and continue to sauté for another 5 minutes.
Add broth, bring to a boil. Add salt and pepper and simmer for a
few minutes. Add rice, stir once, cover, and cook over low heat,
stirring occasionally until all broth is absorbed and rice is well
cooked and mushy in texture.
Remove from heat and keep covered in a warm place for 30
minutes.
Serve warm as a side dish with stewed vegetable dishes. Especially
good with Meat with Okra*.

SERVES 6 PERSONS.

PILAV PIE
Yufkalı Pilav

2 cups long grain rice
Salt to taste
1 small chicken, 2½ pounds
5 cups water
2 carrots, scraped, 1 quartered,
   1 grated coarsely
2 onions, skinned, 1 quartered,
   1 grated coarsely

2 sprigs parsley
6 peppercorns
12 tablespoons butter
2 ounces slivered almonds
Pepper to taste
8 sheets Phyllo pastry*

Preheat oven to 350 degrees F. after the rice mixture has been prepared.

Place rice in a bowl, add 1 tablespoon salt, and cover with hot water. Stir and allow to cool. Drain and set aside.

Clean and wash chicken, place in a saucepan with 5 cups of water and cut up carrot, onion, parsley, salt, and peppercorns. Bring to a boil, cover, and cook over medium heat until chicken is tender, about 45 minutes. Remove chicken from saucepan. Cool, take off skin and remove bones. Separate meat into 2 or 3 inch long pieces. Set aside. Strain stock and save.

In a heavy saucepan sauté grated onion with 9 tablespoons of butter over medium heat for 5 minutes, stirring constantly. Add grated carrot and sauté for 5 minutes more. Add almonds and continue to sauté another 3 minutes. Add chicken pieces and cook 5 minutes, stirring occasionally. Add pepper.

Bring 3 cups of the chicken stock to a boil in a saucepan. Add the chicken mixture and bring to a boil again. Add the rice, stirring carefully not to break it. Cover and cook without stirring over high heat for 5 minutes. Turn heat to medium and cook until small holes appear on the surface of rice, but not all the broth is absorbed, about 10 minutes.

While rice is cooking, grease a 4 quart casserole with half the remaining butter. Line it with pastry sheets, covering the bottom with one end and leaving the other end hanging out over the rim of the casserole. The sheets should overlap so that the entire casserole, bottom and sides, is covered with pastry sheets.

Place half-cooked rice mixture in the casserole. Fold pastry sheets over rice, like a package. Butter top with remaining butter. Bake until top is golden brown, about 25 to 30 minutes.

Remove from oven. Invert on a round serving platter. Cut through the crust with a sharp knife, and serve together with the rice.

Serve warm as an appetizer for formal dinners or as a luncheon course with Romaine Lettuce Salad*.

SERVES 8 TO 10 PERSONS.

PILAV QUAIL
Bıldırcınlı Pilav

6 quail   Tomato Pilav*
Salt and pepper to taste
3 tablespoons butter, if
  necessary

Preheat broiler or have charcoal fire ready.

Split quail down back. Carefully remove breast bones and back-bones. Flatten birds by pounding with a mallet.

Rub with salt and pepper.

Place a wire rack over charcoal fire, 3 or 4 inches above the coals, which should be hot but not flaming. Broil birds 8 to 10 minutes on each side. Turn only once. Do not overbroil. If birds are dry, baste with melted butter before broiling.

Place pilav on a platter, cover top with broiled birds, and serve with Romaine Lettuce Salad*.

SERVES 6 PERSONS.

SULTANA PILAV
Üzümlü Pilav

2 cups seedless fresh white grapes
Tomato Pilav*

Wash and detach, one by one, 2 cups of grapes. Set aside.

Fill a 10×2 inch ring mold with the hot pilav, pressing down with a spoon. Invert mold into a round platter and fill center with grapes.

Serve after fish or poultry as a second course.

SERVES 6 TO 8 PERSONS.

TOMATO PILAV

Domatesli Pilav

1½ cups long grain rice	*2½ cups beef or chicken*
Salt to taste	*broth*
4 medium tomatoes, cubed	*Pepper to taste*
6 tablespoons butter	

Place rice in a bowl, add 1 teaspoon salt, and cover with hot water. Stir and allow to cool. Drain and set aside.

Cook tomatoes in butter over medium heat in a heavy saucepan, stirring constantly until it forms a paste, about 30 minutes. Add the broth, salt, and pepper, and boil for 2 minutes. Add rice while the broth is still boiling. Stir it once only, cover and cook on high heat without stirring for 5 minutes. Turn heat low and cook until rice absorbs all the broth, about 15 minutes. Remove from heat. Remove cover, place a napkin over the saucepan, and replace cover. Leave covered for 40 minutes in a warm place. Transfer rice gently to a serving dish with a spoon.

SERVES 6 TO 8 PERSONS.

VERMICELLI PILAV

Şehriyeli Pilav

1½ cups long grain rice	*2½ cups chicken broth*
Salt to taste	*Pepper to taste*
¾ cup broken vermicelli	*1 bunch scallions, white only,*
pieces	*finely chopped*
8 tablespoons butter	

Place rice in a bowl, add 1 tablespoon salt, and cover with hot water. Stir and allow to cool. Drain and set aside.

Sauté vermicelli in a saucepan with 2 tablespoons butter until light brown.

Remove vermicelli to a heavy saucepan, add broth, 6 tablespoons butter, salt, and pepper and boil for 2 minutes. Add rice to vermicelli while it is still boiling. Stir once only. Cover and cook over high heat without stirring for 5 minutes. Lower heat and cook until rice absorbs all the broth, about 10 minutes.

Fold scallions into rice and vermicelli. Remove from heat. Remove the cover, put a napkin over the saucepan, and replace cover. Leave covered for 40 minutes in a warm place. Transfer rice gently to a serving dish with a spoon.

When served with Chicken Stew* and Shepherds' Salad* it makes a good, balanced meal.

SERVES 6 TO 8 PERSONS.

WHITE PILAV
Beyaz Pilav

1½ cups long grain rice	*2½ cups chicken broth*
Salt to taste	*White pepper to taste*
6 tablespoons butter	

Place rice in a bowl, add 1 teaspoon salt, and cover with hot water. Stir and allow to cool. Drain and set aside.

Boil butter and broth for 2 minutes in a heavy saucepan. Add salt and pepper. Add rice while the broth is still boiling, stir once only. Cover and cook over high heat without stirring for 5 minutes. Turn heat on low and cook until rice absorbs all the broth, about 15 minutes. Remove from heat, remove cover, place a napkin over the saucepan, and replace the cover. Leave covered for 40 minutes in a warm place. Transfer rice gently to a serving dish with a spoon.

SERVES 6 TO 8 PERSONS.

CRACKED WHEAT PILAV
Bulgur Pilavı

1 cup large grain bulgur[1]
5 tablespoons butter
1 large onion, coarsely grated
1 tablespoon tomato sauce
   or 1 small tomato

1½ cups beef or chicken
   broth
Salt and pepper to taste

Wash bulgur with cold water. Drain and set aside.

Place 2 tablespoons butter in a heavy saucepan, add onion and sauté golden brown, stirring constantly, about 6 minutes. Add tomato sauce or diced tomato and cook another 5 minutes. Add broth, the rest of the butter, salt, and pepper and bring to a boil. Add bulgur, stir once, cover, and boil for 5 minutes on high heat. Then reduce heat and cook until bulgur absorbs all the broth, about 25 minutes.

Remove from heat, remove cover, place a napkin over the saucepan, and replace cover. Leave in a warm place for 40 minutes. The bulgur should be flaky and not mushy like oatmeal.

This makes an excellent side dish with all kinds of meat dishes.

SERVES 6 PERSONS.

MACARONI A LA TURCA
Kıymalı Makarna

1 medium onion, grated
3 tablespoons butter
½ pound ground beef
1 tablespoon tomato paste
   or 2 medium fresh
   tomatoes, diced

Salt and pepper to taste
½ pound bow-type macaroni
2 quarts water
2 cups Yogurt Sauce I*

Sauté onion in a saucepan with butter over medium heat until light brown, stirring constantly for 5 minutes. Add meat, continue to

[1] Bulgur is cracked wheat. It may be obtained from Near Eastern specialty stores. For a list of such shops see the Appendix.

sauté and stir until meat is browned, 10 minutes. Add tomato paste and cook 5 minutes more. Add salt and pepper and keep hot over very low heat.

Cook macaroni in boiling salted water 10 to 12 minutes. Drain. Add to beef sauce in saucepan, mixing well. Reheat over medium heat.

When serving individual dishes, top each serving with 2 or 3 tablespoons of yogurt sauce.

SERVES 5 TO 6 PERSONS.

MACARONI WITH WHITE CHEESE OR FETA
Beyaz Peynirli Makarna

1 package (8 ounce) egg noodles, homemade type	*½ pound diced feta or white cheese*
4 tablespoons butter	*Dash paprika*

Cook noodles according to directions on package. Drain and leave noodles in colander.

Melt butter in saucepan over medium heat. Add cheese and sauté for 2 minutes, stirring with a perforated kitchen spoon. Add noodles and paprika and stir carefully several times so that cheese blends with the noodles. Empty into a serving platter. This dish does not need any extra salt because the cheese has enough salt.

Serve hot as an appetizer with Tomato and Onion Salad*. Or serve after a cold vegetable appetizer.

SERVES 6 PERSONS.

MUFFINS A LA TURCA
Kıymalı Pide

1 pound ground beef
1 green pepper, seeded and
  chopped
1 medium onion, grated
2 medium tomatoes, cubed
Salt and black pepper to taste
1 tablespoon wine vinegar
½ cup chopped parsley
½ cup chopped dill
4 English muffins
2 cups hot beef broth
2 cups Yogurt Sauce I*
2 tablespoons butter
Dash cayenne
1 teaspoon paprika

Cook meat in frying pan with green pepper, onion, and to-matoes over medium heat for 30 minutes, stirring occasionally. Add salt, black pepper, vinegar, parsley, and dill. Mix well and cook for 5 minutes more, stirring occasionally. Remove from heat.

Cut muffins in two and toast each half on both sides. Put halves together again. Place muffins in a pan that can be brought to the table. Put pan over very low heat. Pour hot broth over muffins a little at a time, allowing each piece to soften and swell. Remove top part of each muffin with a spatula and spread the meat mixture on the bottom one. Replace top and keep warm.

Pour yogurt sauce on muffins.

Heat butter, add cayenne and paprika, pour over the yogurt and serve immediately.

ALLOW 1 MUFFIN FOR EACH PERSON.

BEEF BOEREK
Kıymalı Börek

FILLING:

1 pound ground beef or lamb	1 cup chopped parsley
4 tablespoons butter	2 tablespoons pignolia nuts
1 large onion, grated	2 tablespoons black currants
1 green pepper, seeded and	½ teaspoon sugar
diced	Salt and pepper to taste
1 medium tomato, diced	3 eggs

1 pound Phyllo pastry* sheets
12 tablespoons butter, melted
¼ cup milk

Preheat oven to 350 degrees F. after the filling has been prepared.

Filling: Sauté meat in frying pan with butter, onions, pepper, and tomatoes over medium heat. Stir occasionally, and cook for 30 minutes. Remove from heat, add parsley, nuts, currants, sugar, salt, pepper, and the eggs. Mix well.

Lay 1 sheet of pastry on a well-buttered 12×15 inch baking pan. Brush pastry with melted butter and sprinkle with a few drops of milk. Place second sheet on top of the first, butter and sprinkle with milk. Repeat until half of the pastry sheets have been used up. Then spread meat mixture over the entire surface. Build up the remaining half of the sheets over meat mixture, one over the other, buttering each and sprinkling with milk. Butter top generously and cut into 16 squares. Bake for 30 minutes or until boerek is golden brown.

Serve warm as an appetizer or main course for lunch.

ALLOW 1 PER PERSON FOR APPETIZER, 2 FOR MAIN COURSE.

CHEESE BOEREK
Peynirli Börek

FILLING:

½ pound feta or white cheese, soaked in water and refrigerated for 1 day, then drained before using

1 package (8 ounce) cream cheese

¼ pound Cheddar cheese, grated

4 eggs

2 tablespoons butter

2 tablespoons milk

1 cup chopped parsley

1 pound Phyllo pastry* sheets
¼ pound butter, melted
¼ cup milk

Preheat oven to 350 degrees F.

Filling: Place feta and cream cheese in mixing bowl and mash with a fork. Add Cheddar, eggs, butter, milk, and parsley and mix well.

Divide pastry sheets into 3 equal parts. Lay 1 sheet on a greased 12×15 inch baking pan. Brush surface with melted butter. Sprinkle with a few drops of milk. Place second sheet on top of the first, butter, and sprinkle with milk. Repeat until one-third of the pastry sheets have been used up. Then spread half of the filling over the entire surface.

Build up the second third of pastry sheets in the same way. Then spread the remaining half of the filling over the entire surface. Again, build up the last third of the pastry sheets in the same way. Butter top generously and cut into 16 squares.

Bake for 30 minutes, or until golden brown.

Serve warm as an appetizer or main course for lunch.

ALLOW 1 PER PERSON FOR APPETIZER, 2 FOR MAIN COURSE.

CHICKEN BOEREK
Tavuklu Börek

FILLING:

1 chicken (3 pounds), cut
into 6 portions
3 tablespoons butter
4 large onions, cut in half
lengthwise, then finely sliced
1 large tomato, diced

½ cup water
Few rosemary leaves
Salt and pepper to taste
1 can (10 ounce) cooked
mixed carrots and peas

12 Phyllo pastry sheets*
¼ pound butter, melted
2 cups clear chicken broth

Preheat oven to 350 degrees F. after the filling has been prepared.

Filling: In a frying pan, sauté chicken pieces in butter over high heat for 10 minutes, stirring occasionally. Add onions and continue to sauté until onions are wilted, about 10 to 14 minutes. Add tomato and ½ cup water, rosemary, salt, and pepper. Cover and cook until chicken is tender and no water is left, about 30 minutes. Allow to cool.

Take chicken pieces out and discard bones and skin. Divide chicken meat into small 2 or 3 inch long pieces. Return to pan, add carrots and peas. Mix well. Divide filling into 6 equal portions.

Lay 1 sheet of pastry on table. Brush surface with melted butter. Lay second sheet over the first. Butter surface. Place 1 portion of filling in the middle, making a 3 inch square pile. Fold just 1 side vertically over filling, butter it, then fold the other side over the first side and butter. Then fold again, horizontally from the opposite ends, making a square package 3 to 3½ inches large. Butter between folds.

Place each square on greased baking pan. When all 6 squares are finished and placed on pan, butter the tops.

Bake for 25 to 30 minutes, or until golden brown. Do not overbake. Remove to a serving platter. Heat chicken broth and empty into a sauceboat.

Serve warm with chicken broth on the side. Makes a delicious luncheon course. Place 1 boerek on dinner plate. Pour a few spoonfuls of broth to soften crust. Serve with Tomato and Cucumber Salad*.

SERVES 6 PERSONS.

CIGARETTE BOEREK
Sigara Böreği

CHEESE FILLING:
  ½ pound white or feta cheese
  1 egg
  1 cup chopped parsley

MEAT FILLING:
  ½ pound ground beef   *1 cup chopped parsley*
  1½ tablespoons butter   *Salt and pepper to taste*
  1 medium onion, grated

  ½ pound Phyllo pastry*
    sheets
  1 cup salad oil

Cheese filling: Break cheese into small crumbs and place in a bowl. Add the eggs and parsley. Mix well.

Meat filling: Place meat in frying pan, add butter and onion. Sauté over medium heat, stirring constantly, for 10 minutes. Remove from heat. Add parsley, salt, and pepper. Mix well.

Put the pastry sheets, which come in a block piled on top of each other like sheets of paper, on a cutting board. Cut the block crosswise into 2 equal parts as in Figure 1. Place the two parts on top of each other, making an orderly pile. Now the cut pastry sheets are ready to use as in Figure 2.

Take 1 sheet from the pile. Place it in front of you. Place 1 tablespoon filling, cheese or meat, in a ½ inch thick strip about 4 inches long as in Figure 3. Roll a few times like a cigarette as in Figure 4. Fold both ends of pastry over filling as in Figure 5. Now roll until the end. Paste ends with water as in Figure 6. Roll all pastry sheets and place on wax paper.

Place oil in frying pan over high heat. When oil is very hot, fry cigarettes golden brown on both sides, a few minutes on each side. Do not overcook. Lower heat as necessary.

Serve hot as appetizers, or to accompany soups.

MAKES ABOUT 24 TO 26 CIGARETTES.
ALLOW 2 OR 3 PER PERSON.

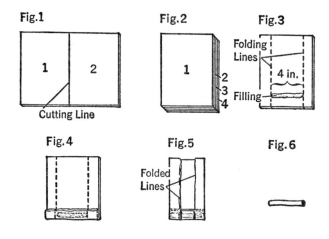

MEAT BOEREK
Talaş Böreği

FILLING:

2½ pounds boneless lamb or
    beef, cut into ½ inch cubes
4 tablespoons butter
1 large onion, grated
1 medium tomato, diced
1 medium green pepper,
    seeded and diced

½ teaspoon thyme leaves
3 cups water
½ cup chopped dill
½ cup chopped parsley
Salt and pepper to taste

1 pound Phyllo pastry* sheets
½ pound butter, melted
2 cups broth, taken from meat
    filling

Preheat oven to 350 degrees F. after the filling has been prepared.

Filling: Put beef in a saucepan and add butter, onion, tomato, green pepper, thyme, and 2 cups water. Cover and cook over medium heat for about 1 hour. Add dill, parsley, salt, and pepper and 1 cup warm water and continue to cook covered 30 minutes more or until meat is tender. At this time there should be plenty of broth in the saucepan. Remove the broth, which should be at least 2 cups, with a large kitchen spoon to a saucepan. Bits of thyme leaves, parsley, and dill flakes may be seen in this thin meat broth. Set aside. This is the sauce to be poured over boereks at the dinner table.

Cook meat a few minutes more so that all the juices are absorbed, and remove from heat.

When cool, divide into 8 equal portions.

Lay 1 sheet of pastry on table. Brush surface with melted butter. Lay second sheet over the first. Butter the surface. Lay a third sheet over the second and butter again. Place 1 portion of filling in the middle, making a 3 to 3½ inch square pile. Fold first one side vertically over filling, butter it, then fold the other side over the first side, butter again. Then fold again horizontally from the opposite ends making a package 3 to 3½ inches square. Butter between the folds.

Place all 8 squares on a greased baking pan and butter the tops. Bake for 25 to 30 minutes or until golden brown. Do not overbake. Remove to a serving platter. Heat the saved broth and empty into a sauceboat.

Place 1 boerek on dinner plate. Pour a few spoonfuls of broth over to soften crust. Serve warm with Romaine Lettuce Salad* as main course.

SERVES 8 PERSONS.

MUSHROOM BOEREK
Mantarlı Börek

FILLING:

Preparation of cream sauce:
  2 *tablespoons butter*   *Salt and pepper to taste*
  2 *tablespoons flour*
  1 *cup milk*
  2 *tablespoons diced hard*
    Turkish cheese, Kasar or*
    Cheddar

Preparation of mushrooms:
  1 *pound large mushrooms*   1 *tablespoon onion flakes*
  3 *tablespoons butter*   1 *tablespoon chopped dill*

  12 *sheets Phyllo pastry* sheets*
  ¼ *pound butter, melted*
  2 *cups clear beef broth, optional*

Preheat oven to 350 degrees F. after the filling has been prepared.

Filling: Melt 2 tablespoons butter in a saucepan. Add 2 tablespoons flour, stir. Sauté over low heat for 2 minutes. Add 1 cup milk slowly, stirring all the time. Continue stirring and cooking until mixture thickens. Add cheese and cook another 3 minutes. The cheese does not have to melt. Add salt and pepper, stir, and set in a warm place.

Clean whole mushrooms and slice into thick pieces. Melt 3 tablespoons butter in a frying pan. Add onion flakes and mushrooms. Sauté over high heat for 1 minute, shaking and stirring pan. Add dill. Add mushrooms to cream sauce and stir. Now the filling is ready. Divide filling into 6 equal portions.

Lay 1 sheet of pastry on table. Brush surface with melted butter. Lay a second sheet over the first and butter. Place 1 portion of filling in the middle making a 3 inch square pile. Fold first one side vertically over filling; butter it. Then fold the other side over the first side; butter again. Fold again horizontally from the opposite ends, making a package 3 to 3½ inches square. Butter between folds. Do the other 5 packages the same way as the first. Place all six squares on greased baking pan and butter the tops.

Bake for 25 to 30 minutes or until golden brown. Do not overbake. Remove to a serving platter. Heat beef broth and empty into a sauceboat.

Place 1 boerek on a dinner plate. Pour a few spoonfuls of broth over to soften crust. Serve warm with Tomato and Onion Salad* as a luncheon dish. Also makes a delicious appetizer.

SERVES 6 PERSONS.

PUFF BOEREK
Puf Böreği

FILLING:
¼ pound feta or white cheese
1 egg white
½ cup chopped parsley

1¾ cups all-purpose flour   *½ cup all-purpose flour for*
1 egg yolk   *rolling dough*
3 tablespoons melted butter   *1½ cups salad oil*
½ cup water with 1 teaspoon
salt added

Filling: Break cheese into small crumbs and place in a bowl with egg white and parsley. Mix well and set aside.

Sift flour into a bowl and make a hole in the middle. Put egg yolk and 1 tablespoon melted butter into the hole. Slowly add the salted water and work into a springy dough. Knead well for 5 minutes. Shape into a ball, cover with a wet cloth, and let stand for 20 minutes.

Use kitchen table or other large wooden surface for rolling dough. Sprinkle flour on the table, place dough on it, and shape into a round roll 12×2 inches. Cut this into 12 equal parts. Flatten each by hand and butter each on one side only. Then stick 2 buttered sides together, making 6 pairs. Place under wet cloth and let stand for 5 minutes.

Flour and roll each buttered pair with a rolling pin into flat rounds 5 inches in diameter. Butter top of one, place next one on top of it, butter the top and place the third one on the pile. Cover with a wet cloth. Repeat the same process with the remaining 3 pairs. Let stand under the wet cloth for 5 minutes.

Take one of the triple pieces and place it on the floured surface. Roll out with rolling pin until it is 8 or 9 inches in diameter. Now change to a long, thin rolling pin about ⅓ inch in diameter and 25 inches long. An old wooden curtain rod will do. Roll up the pastry around the pin, pressing down gently and continually toward the ends of the pin. Unroll and roll from the opposite side, dusting table and dough with flour at each rolling. Roll until dough is 16 or 17 inches in diameter.

When the proper size is reached, place half teaspoonfuls of filling 2 inches away from the edge at 3 inch intervals around one half of the dough. Fold edge over 1 inch beyond filling and press down with fingers along the edge. Cut into elongated quarter moons with a demitasse saucer, pressing down so that the edges are sealed. Remove moons to a tray. Repeat again, starting from cut edge. Discard any small leftover pieces of the dough. Repeat same process until all dough is used and placed on the tray. Place wax paper over the boereks and cover with a kitchen towel.

Half an hour before serving fry boereks in very hot oil in a frying pan until they puff up and become a light golden brown on both sides. This takes 2 minutes on each side.

Serve hot as an appetizer or with light soups.

MAKES 30 TO 40 BOEREKS.
ALLOW 3 TO 4 PER PERSON.

SPINACH BOEREK
Ispanaklı Börek

FILLING:

4 packages (10 ounce) chopped frozen spinach
1 large onion, grated
3 tablespoons salad or olive oil
4 tablespoons grated Parmesan cheese

2 tablespoons crumbled feta or white cheese
½ tablespoon sugar
4 tablespoons milk
Salt and pepper to taste
3 eggs

1 pound Phyllo pastry* sheets
12 tablespoons butter, melted
1 pint yogurt

Preheat oven to 350 degrees F. after the filling has been prepared.

Filling: Defrost spinach, squeeze out all the juice, and set aside.

Put onion into frying pan, add oil, and sauté for 8 minutes over medium heat, stirring occasionally. Remove from heat. Add the spinach, cheeses, sugar, milk, salt, pepper, and eggs. Mix well. Divide filling into 4 or 5 equal portions, depending on the number of pastry sheets.

Butter an 18×12 baking pan.

Divide pastry sheets into 4 or 5 portions. Each portion should not have more than 6 or 7 pastry sheets. Read instructions for Boereks*. Lay 1 sheet of pastry on a smooth surface, brush surface with a little butter, but do not over-butter. Take a second sheet, lay it on top of the first, and butter it in the same manner. Do this until one-fourth or one-fifth of the pastry sheets have been used.

Then arrange 1 portion of the spinach along the longer edge of the pastry in a straight line 5 inches away from the edge. Fold the edge over the spinach and roll like strudel pastry. Place in the baking pan.

Repeat process until 4 or 5 rolls have been completed and placed in the pan. Brush the tops with butter and bake for 30 minutes, or until the boereks are golden brown.

Cut boereks 2 or 3 inches long, making about 25 pieces. This is
an excellent appetizer for large parties. It may be prepared a day in
advance, kept in the refrigerator, and baked before serving. Serve
with plain yogurt on the side.

SERVES 10 TO 12 PERSONS.

TATAR BOEREK
Tatar Böreği

FILLING:

½ pound ground beef	Pepper to taste
½ cup chopped parsley	¼ teaspoon salt

1¼ cups all-purpose flour	4 tablespoons butter
1 egg	3 cups beef stock
¼ teaspoon salt	1 teaspoon paprika
3 tablespoons water	2 cups Yogurt Sauce I*

Preheat oven to 350 degrees F. after the boereks have been prepared.
  Filling: Mix meat well in a bowl with parsley, pepper, and salt.
Set aside.
  Sift 1 cup flour into a bowl. Make a hole in the middle. Put
egg, salt, and water into the opening and work into a dough. Knead
well for 3 minutes. Shape into a ball, cover with wet cloth, and let
stand for 20 minutes. Use kitchen table, preferably a wooden one,
for rolling dough. Use ¼ cup flour for dusting dough. Sprinkle flour
on table. Take only half of dough, keeping other half under the wet
cloth. Roll with rolling pin until dough is about 7 inches in diameter.
Then use a long, thin rolling pin, about ⅓ inch in diameter and 25
inches long. An old wooden curtain rod will do. Roll up the pastry
around the pin, pressing down gently and continually toward the ends
of the pin. Unroll and roll from the opposite side, dusting table and
dough with flour at each rolling. Roll until dough is about 15 inches
in diameter and about $\frac{1}{16}$ inch thick.
  Now cut dough into long strips 2 inches wide. Then cut strips
into 2½ inch pieces. Trim off irregular edges and discard.
  Grease a 10×14 inch baking pan with 2 tablespoons butter.
Form each piece into a small canoe by pressing the two ends

together. When all the canoes are in the pan, fill each with a small ball of the beef mixture.

Heat stock. Ladle about 1 cup over canoes. Place pan in oven and bake 10 minutes. Again ladle a cup of stock over the canoes and bake 10 minutes more. Then ladle in the rest of stock and bake 20 minutes.

Melt 2 tablespoons butter but do not burn. Add paprika and stir. Keep hot.

Remove canoes to a large serving platter and pour over them the yogurt sauce. Decorate top with hot paprika and butter mixture. Serve hot as a luncheon course.

SERVES 4 PERSONS.

WATER BOEREK
Su Böreği

CHEESE FILLING:

½ pound feta or white   *1 egg*
cheese, soaked in water   *1 cup chopped parsley*
and refrigerated for 1 day   *4 tablespoons milk*
and drained before using

MEAT FILLING:

¼ pound ground beef   *1 cup chopped parsley*
1½ tablespoons butter   *Salt and pepper to taste*
1 medium onion, grated

2¾ cups flour   *1 cup extra flour or*
3 eggs   *cornstarch to be used for*
1 teaspoon salt   *rolling dough*
5 tablespoons water   *8 tablespoons butter, melted*

Preheat oven to 350 degrees F. after the boereks have been prepared.

Cheese filling: Break cheese into small crumbs and put in a bowl. Add egg, parsley, milk, and mix well.

Meat filling: Sauté meat in frying pan with butter and onion over medium heat, stirring constantly for 10 minutes. Remove from heat and add parsley, salt, and pepper. Mix well.

Sift flour into a bowl. Add eggs and salt and enough water to make a springy dough, about 5 tablespoons. Knead dough well. Cover with a wet cloth and let stand for ½ hour.

Use a large kitchen table, preferably a wooden one, for rolling dough. Sprinkle flour on the table and place dough on it. Shape into a round roll 18 inches long and about 2 inches in diameter. Cut this into 9 equal parts. Knead each piece well and shape it into a round ball. Flour and place under wet cloth.

Flour the table again and roll out a ball with a rolling pin until dough is as large as a dinner plate. Then use a long, thin rolling pin about ⅓ inch in diameter and 25 inches long. An old wooden curtain rod will do. Roll up the pastry around the pin, pressing down gently and continually toward the end of the pin. Unroll and roll from the opposite side, dusting table and dough at each rolling. Roll until dough is about 12 inches in diameter. Repeat the same process with each ball of dough. Pile rolled sheets one over the other, placing wax paper in between.

Grease a round baking pan about 12 inches in diameter and 1½ inches high. Lay the largest sheet on it. Butter the top.

Place a large saucepan of water over stove to boil. Fill another large saucepan with cold water and place it near the first saucepan of boiling water.

Take one of the pastry sheets and drop it into the boiling water. Ladle water over it so that the top also is soaked. Allow it to remain 1 or 1½ minutes. Scoop sheet out gently with a large strainer and a perforated kitchen spoon. Drop sheet into the saucepan of cold water and leave 2 minutes. Scoop sheet out gently, again using a strainer and perforated spoon. Squeeze out all water carefully by hand. Then lay it over the first uncooked sheet. If a sheet breaks when you squeeze out the water, you can still use it. Brush with a little melted butter. Follow the same process with each sheet until 5 sheets are used. Then lay filling, either cheese or meat, over the entire surface.

Continue the same process over filling until all sheets are used. Butter surface. Bake until surface is golden brown and crisp and the inside layers are soft, about 1½ hours.

Invert onto a round serving platter and cut into slices.

Serve as an appetizer or as main dish for luncheon with a salad.

SERVES 12 PERSONS AS APPETIZER,
8 TO 10 AS MAIN COURSE.

A kettle will not boil without its lid.

THE TAX RECORDS

Nasrettin Hoca lived in Akşehir, a small town in central Turkey. During his time the city was occupied by Tamerlane, who acted as a merciless conqueror. One day Nasrettin Hoca was caught in the audience as Tamerlane thundered to punish the tax collector for alleged fraud, looking at his piles of tax receipts, he shouted, "Fraud! And you expected me to swallow all these falsifications. Not I! You will swallow them. Eat them or you lose your neck."

Then, looking at his audience, he picked Nasrettin Hoca as his new tax collector.

"In three months we meet here again," he told him, "with your records and the money."

On the prescribed date Nasrettin Hoca appeared before the hard conqueror with a wheelbarrow covered with a clean white cloth. He bowed and handed Tamerlane two bags of gold.

"The records," commanded Tamerlane. Hoca turned confidently to the wheelbarrow and with deliberate care removed the white cloth, revealing two rows of baked dough sheets.

"What is this?" thundered the conqueror in surprised anger.

Hoca, picking up the topmost sheet carefully, approached Tamerlane and read the inscription that had been meticulously inscribed before the dough was baked.

"Sire," he said, "I reckoned that one of us had to swallow them. So I wanted to make it easy on whoever had to eat them."

11. Desserts

Anyone with an adventurous palate has heard of Baklava or *Kadayif*. They are enjoyed in all Eastern Mediterranean countries but they are essentially of Turkish origin. They vary albeit slightly from region to region. The Turkish variety tends to be more flaky and less sweet. This pastry type dominates the Turkish dessert field in which such varieties as Harem Navels and Belle Lips match the attractiveness of their names with the pleasantness of their taste.

Baklava is not as difficult to prepare as it appears. Once you have acquired the knack of using *yufka*, the layers of paper-thin pastry used for baklava or boerek, the rest comes within easy reach of your competence.

The pastry types of Turkish desserts are especially recommended for buffet dinners or for afternoon or late evening coffee snacks.

The puddings, which have a special flavor of their own as distinct from those of other countries, help to end a full course dinner with a light touch.

Classifying Turkish desserts according to their heaviness, the pastry types rank on top of the list. The puddings come in the middle and the fruit desserts are the lightest.

Turkey is a fruit paradise, growing every kind distinquished by flavor, aroma, and even size and color. The Izmir figs and melons, the Sultana grapes have been coveted since the days of antiquity. Cherries have their origin in ancient Cerasus, modern Giresun. From the foot of Mt. Olympus in Bursa, the peach capital of the world, the Romans took the first kernels for their orchards in Italy.

The Turks have always enjoyed eating their fruit fresh and have never suffered from vitamin deficiencies. But Turkish cuisine has also developed a variety of cooked fruit desserts. The Creamed Apricot Bowl, the Stuffed Apricots, and the Quince Compote are recommended after a menu that includes pilav. Melon Dolma provides a cool and refreshing dessert on a hot summer evening. Rose Jam also offers many possibilities as an exotic dessert sauce.

Desserts

PUDDINGS

FLOUR CAKES AND HELVAS

MILK PUDDING ALMONDS
Bademli Muhallebi

6 ounces finely ground
    blanched almonds
2 heaping tablespoons
    cornstarch
2 heaping tablespoons rice
    flour

½ cup cold water
2 quarts milk
1 cup sugar
Dash salt
1 tablespoon almond extract

Place almonds in a bowl. Cover with boiling water and soak for ½ hour. Rub skins off. Dry almonds in a towel and grind with nut grinder. Set aside.

Place cornstarch and rice flour in a bowl; add half a cup of cold water, stir, and set aside.

Place milk in a saucepan, add sugar and salt and bring to a boil over medium heat. Slowly pour in the cornstarch and rice flour mixture, stirring constantly. Cook about 30 minutes, stirring constantly. Add the ground almonds and stir well. Then let simmer, stirring occasionally until mixture is the consistency of a thick pudding, about 15 minutes. Remove from heat and stir in almond extract. Then pour pudding into bowls for individual helpings or into 1 large bowl. Brown surface under the broiler if desired. In that case an oven-proof dish should be used.

Cool for 2 or 3 hours.

This pudding may be prepared a day in advance and kept in the refrigerator.

Serve with your favorite cookies.

SERVES 8 TO 10 PERSONS.

MILK PUDDING COCONUT
Hindistancevizli Muhallebi

2 *heaping tablespoons*	2 *quarts milk*
cornstarch	1 *cup sugar*
2 *heaping tablespoons rice*	4 *ounces shredded coconut*
flour	*Dash salt*
½ *cup cold water*	

Place cornstarch and rice flour in a bowl; add half cup of cold water, stir and set aside.

Place milk in a saucepan, add sugar, coconut, and salt and bring to a boil over medium heat. Slowly pour in the cornstarch and rice flour mixture, stirring constantly. Cook about 30 minutes, stirring constantly. Then let simmer, stirring occasionally until mixture is the consistency of a thick pudding, about 15 minutes. Remove from heat, pour into bowls for individual helpings or into 1 large bowl. Brown surface under the broiler if desired. In that case an oven-proof dish should be used. Cool for 2 or 3 hours.

This pudding may be prepared a day in advance and kept in the refrigerator.

Serve with your favorite cookies.

SERVES 8 TO 10 PERSONS.

MILK PUDDING PISTACHIO NUTS
Fıstıklı Muhallebi

½ *cup shelled pistachio nuts*	½ *cup cold water*
2 *heaping tablespoons*	2 *quarts milk*
cornstarch	1 *cup sugar*
2 *heaping tablespoons rice*	*Dash salt*
flour	1 *teaspoon vanilla extract*

Place whole nuts in a saucepan, cover with water, and boil for 5 minutes. Remove from heat, pour 2 cups of cold water over them, and remove the dark skins of the nuts. Dry in a towel and grind with nut grinder. Set aside.

Place cornstarch and rice flour in a bowl, add half a cup of cold water, stir and set aside.

Place milk in a saucepan, add sugar and salt, and bring to a boil over medium heat. Slowly pour in the cornstarch and rice flour mixture, stirring constantly. Cook about 35 minutes, stirring constantly, until mixture is the consistency of a thick pudding. Add half of the pistachios and the vanilla; mix well. Remove from heat, pour into bowls for individual helpings or into 1 large bowl. Decorate top with the remaining half of the pistachio nuts.

Cool for 2 or 3 hours.

This pudding may be prepared a day in advance and kept in the refrigerator. Serve with lemon cookies.

SERVES 6 TO 8 PERSONS.

MILK PUDDING ROSE WATER
Gül Sulu Muhallebi

1 tablespoon sugar	*¼ cup confectioners' sugar*
¼ teaspoon salt	*2 tablespoons Rose Water*
3½ cups milk	*or Orange Flower Water**
2 tablespoons cornstarch	*Strawberries or raspberries, if*
3 tablespoons rice flour	*available*
¾ cup cold water	

Add 1 tablespoon sugar and ¼ teaspoon salt to milk in a saucepan. Bring to a boil over medium heat.

Place cornstarch and rice flour in a bowl. Slowly add ¾ cup cold water, stirring constantly until smooth.

Just as the milk is almost boiling, begin pouring the flour mixture very slowly into milk while stirring constantly and vigorously. Keep stirring constantly for 30 to 40 minutes until pudding thickens and starts to bubble. Let bubble for 2 or 3 minutes, then stir again. While still cooking, test by placing a teaspoonful of the pudding on a small dish. Let it cool in the refrigerator for a few minutes. When moved with a finger, if it does not stick to the dish, it is ready. If it sticks, test again after cooking a few minutes more.

Empty mixture into a flat round or square tray or a Pyrex dish. The height of the pudding should not be more than 1 inch.

Cool for 6 hours or overnight. Invert onto a serving dish by placing the dish over the pudding and turning it very quickly upside down. Or cut into serving portions and place on the dish. Cover with confectioners' sugar and sprinkle with rose water just before serving. Decorate with strawberries or raspberries, if available.

SERVES 4 TO 6 PERSONS.

GRAPEFRUIT AND ORANGE PUDDING
Portakal Peltesi

1 cup cold water
4 level tablespoons cornstarch
2 grapefruits
1 large orange
2 cups orange juice
2 cups grapefruit juice

1½ cups sugar
1 cup diced blanched almonds
1 cup pomegranate seeds, optional
1 cup whipped cream

Add 1 cup cold water to cornstarch in a bowl to soften it.

Pare grapefruits and the orange and separate them into segments. Take off white inner skins, remove the seeds, and reserve segments.

Pour orange and grapefruit juice in a saucepan with the sugar. Mix the softened cornstarch well with the water and add to the saucepan. Cook over medium heat, stirring constantly until pudding thickens and starts to bubble, about 20 minutes. Add the orange and grapefruit segments; stir carefully to avoid breaking of the segments. Cook for 2 minutes more. Remove from heat. Stir in the almonds. Pour into bowls for individual helpings or into 1 large bowl. Cool and refrigerate for 2 or 3 hours or overnight.

Decorate with pomegranate seeds and serve with whipped cream.

SERVES 8 PERSONS.

NOAH'S PUDDING
Aşüre

⅓ cup chick-peas	¼ cup chopped figs, optional
⅓ cup dried fava beans	¼ cup chopped dates,
⅓ cup white kidney beans	optional
1 cup whole wheat, special	3 tablespoons Rose Water
for aşüre*	or Orange Flower Water*
1 tablespoon rice	½ cup chopped walnuts
⅓ cup Sultana raisins	½ cup blanched almonds
8 quarts water	¼ cup black currants
1½ cups sugar	½ cup pomegranate seeds,
1 cup milk	optional

Soak chick-peas, fava beans, and white kidney beans overnight. Wash wheat and rice with cold water and drain. Soak wheat and rice in a large saucepan with 5 quarts of water overnight.

Next morning cook chick-peas, fava beans, and white kidney beans in boiling water until barely tender. Drain and set aside. Soak raisins. Cook wheat and rice over low heat until the water is reduced to 2 quarts. Stir frequently to prevent scorching. Add 3 more quarts of water. Add chick-peas, fava beans, and the white beans and cook until liquid is reduced to 4 quarts. Add sugar. Continue cooking and stirring constantly until sugar melts and the pudding thickens. The pudding should not be too thick. If this happens, always add a little more water. Add milk, drained raisins, figs, and dates and cook for 15 minutes more. Remove from heat. Add rose water and stir. Pour into bowls for individual helpings or into 1 large bowl. Cool and refrigerate for 2 or 3 hours or overnight. Decorate with walnuts, almonds, currants, and pomegranates.

SERVES 12 TO 14 PERSONS.

RICE PUDDING
Sütlaç

1 heaping tablespoon rice	*½ tablespoon rice flour*
1⅛ cups water	*½ cup sugar*
4 cups milk	*1 teaspoon cinnamon,*
Dash salt	*optional*
1 tablespoon cornstarch	

Place rice in a small saucepan. Add ⅔ cup water. Cook over medium heat, stirring occasionally until rice is tender and all the water is absorbed. Remove from heat.

Place milk in a saucepan, add the cooked rice and salt. Bring to a boil over medium heat.

Place cornstarch and rice flour in bowl, add ½ cup cold water, stirring constantly until smooth. Add gradually to the boiling milk and stir constantly for 10 minutes. Add sugar and continue to stir until mixture thickens, about 20 minutes. Remove from heat. Pour into 6 earthenware bowls for individual helpings or into 1 large bowl. Brown surface under the broiler if desired. In that case an oven-proof dish should be used. Cool and refrigerate for 2 or 3 hours or overnight. Remove from refrigerator 1 hour before serving.

Before serving, sprinkle cinnamon on top if desired.

SERVES 6 PERSONS.

Who is fond of cream should take the cow round with him.

ALMOND ROLLS
Tulumba Tatlısı

SYRUP:

3 cups sugar
2½ cups water
2 tablespoons lemon juice

4 tablespoons butter
1⅓ cups water
2 tablespoons almond extract
1½ cups flour
1 teaspoon salt
4 eggs

1½ cups vegetable shortening
4 tablespoons ground
  almonds
½ pint heavy cream,
  whipped

Syrup: Place sugar, 2½ cups water, and lemon juice in a saucepan. Cook over medium heat, stirring constantly until sugar is dissolved. Bring to a boil and simmer for 15 minutes without stirring. Remove from heat and allow to cool.

Place butter in a saucepan and melt over medium heat. Add 1⅓ cups water, less 2 tablespoons, and the almond extract and bring to a boil. Reduce heat to low. Add all the flour at once. Sprinkle salt over and continue cooking for 6 minutes, stirring constantly with a wooden spoon. Remove from heat and cool. When thoroughly cooled, add eggs, one at a time, beating each into flour mixture. Then knead well until no lumps remain, about 10 minutes.

Heat half of the oil in a frying pan over low heat until lukewarm.

Fill cooky tube or a pastry bag with the dough, using a round nozzle, preferably with a sharp tooth edge. Press into pan in 2 inch long pieces. Wait until the pieces start to swell, then increase heat to high and fry on each side to light golden. Do not crowd the frying pan. Allow enough space to take care of enlarged dough. When 1 or 2 panfuls are done add the rest of the shortening. Cool the pan after each panful is finished. Place fried pieces in cold syrup and leave until next panful is ready. Remove pieces from syrup to a serving platter. Allow to cool.

Sprinkle with almonds and serve with whipped cream.

MAKES ABOUT 55 TO 60 PIECES.
ALLOW 4 TO 5 PER PERSON.

BAKLAVA

SYRUP:
3 cups sugar
2½ cups water
1 tablespoon lemon juice

½ pound sweet butter
1 pound Phyllo pastry* sheets
2 cups ground walnut meats
  or

1 cup ground walnut meats
and 1 cup ground almonds
1 pint heavy cream, whipped,
  optional

Preheat oven to 200 degrees F.

Melt butter and grease in 11×16 inch baking pan. Lay 1 sheet of pastry in the pan, then brush surface generously with melted butter. Lay a second sheet on top of the first and butter. Repeat until half of the pastry sheets have been used. Then spread walnuts evenly over the entire surface. Build up the remaining half of the pastry sheets, buttering each generously. Pour any remaining butter over the top.

Cut into diagonal strips, 2 inches wide, across the pan and cut intersecting diagonals to form diamonds.

Bake baklava for 2½ hours. The pastry will keep its white color, but will be crisp.

While the pastry is baking prepare syrup: Melt sugar in water and lemon juice in a saucepan over medium heat, stirring constantly. Bring to a boil and simmer until it forms a heavy syrup, about 20 to 25 minutes. Remove from heat and keep in a warm place.

Remove pastry from oven. Drain excess butter by tilting the pan. Brush surface of diamonds lightly with some of the drained butter to give luster to the pastry.

Halvadgi,
ou Confiseur du Serail

Pour warm syrup over pastry a little at a time, until all syrup is absorbed. Allow to cool for several hours.

Serve with whipped cream on the side, if desired.

MAKES ABOUT 30 DIAMONDS.
ALLOW 2 PER PERSON.

BAKLAVA WITH CREAM FILLING
Muhallebili Baklava

1 pound Phyllo pastry* sheets
¾ pound sweet butter,
melted

FILLING:
3 cups milk ¼ teaspoon salt
¼ cup sugar ½ cup fine grain farina

SYRUP:
2⅔ cups sugar
2 cups water
2 tablespoons lemon juice

12 pineapple slices, cut in two

Preheat oven to 350 degrees F. after the filling has been prepared.

Divide pastry into 2 equal parts. Lay 1 sheet on a well-buttered 11×16 inch baking pan. Brush surface generously with melted butter. Lay second sheet on top of first and butter. Repeat until half of the pastry sheets have been used.

Cover the unused half of pastry sheets with a kitchen cloth to prevent drying.

Prepare filling: Over medium heat bring milk, sugar, and salt to a boil in a saucepan. Add farina by sprinkling in a little at a time, stirring constantly until the mixture thickens and the farina is well cooked.

Spread the hot farina mixture evenly over the entire surface of pastry sheets. Again build up the remaining half of the pastry sheets, buttering each surface generously, on top of farina. Pour the remaining butter over the top. Cut pastry sheets into 24 equal squares. Bake for 40 to 45 minutes or until light golden.

While the baklava is cooking prepare syrup: Place sugar, water, and lemon juice in a saucepan. Cook over medium heat, stirring constantly, until sugar is dissolved. Bring to a boil and simmer for 15 minutes without stirring. Remove from heat and allow to cool.

Remove baklava from oven. Pour off all excess butter by tilting the pan. Cool for 10 minutes. Brush surface lightly with some of the drained butter to give luster to the pastry. Pour syrup over a little at a time, until all is absorbed. Allow to cool for several hours.

Serve with pineapple slices.

ALLOW 1 TO 2 SQUARES PER PERSON.

BELLE LIPS
Dilber Dudaği

SYRUP:
2 cups sugar
1¾ cups water
1 tablespoon lemon juice

7 tablespoons butter	2 eggs and 1 egg yolk
1¾ cups water	1 tablespoon salad oil
1½ cups flour	1½ cups vegetable shortening
1 teaspoon salt	½ pint heavy cream, whipped

Syrup: Place sugar, 1¾ cups water, and lemon juice in a saucepan. Cook over medium heat, stirring constantly until sugar is dissolved. Bring to a boil and simmer for 10 minutes without stirring. Remove from heat and allow to cool.

Place butter in a saucepan and melt over medium heat. Add 1¾ cups of water and bring to a boil. Reduce heat to low. Add all the flour at once, sprinkle salt over, and continue cooking for 7 minutes, stirring constantly with a wooden spoon. Remove from heat and cool. When thoroughly cooled, add 2 whole eggs and 1 egg yolk, one at a time, beating each into the flour mixture. Then knead well until no lumps remain, about 10 minutes.

Place oil in a small dish and grease fingers and palms to facilitate the handling of the dough. Take a walnut-size piece of dough and shape into a flat round piece. Fold it over to the shape of a pair of lips. Place on wax paper. Repeat until all the dough is used up.

In a frying pan, heat half of the shortening over low heat until lukewarm. Place lips in the pan and wait until they start to swell. Then increase heat to high and fry on each side to light golden. Do not crowd the frying pan, allow enough space to take care of enlarged dough. When 1 or 2 panfuls are done, add the rest of the shortening. Cool the pan after each panful is finished. Place fried lips in cold syrup and leave until next panful is ready. Remove lips from syrup to a serving platter. Allow to cool.

Serve with whipped cream at formal dinners, or with coffee at bridge parties.

MAKES ABOUT 30 PIECES.
ALLOW 2 TO 3 PER PERSON.

CRUMPETS IN SYRUP

Yassı Kadaif

SYRUP:
2 cups sugar
1¾ cups water
1 tablespoon lemon juice

8 crumpets	*4 eggs*
1 cup milk	*1 cup ground almonds*
1 cup vegetable shortening	*½ pint heavy cream, whipped*

Syrup: Place sugar, 1¾ cups water, and lemon juice in a shallow saucepan. Cook over medium heat, stirring constantly until sugar is dissolved. Bring to a boil and simmer for 10 minutes without stirring. Remove from heat and allow to cool.

Place crumpets on a platter and sprinkle with just enough milk to moisten. Do not use too much milk or the crumpets will crumble. Place shortening in frying pan over high heat. Keep a saucepan of boiling water next to the frying pan. While shortening is heating, break the eggs into a bowl and beat lightly—just enough to mix the whites and yolks. Dip each crumpet into the beaten eggs, coating them thoroughly. Fry crumpets 2 minutes on each side to golden brown. Dip each fried crumpet in boiling water, remove quickly, place in cold syrup. When all 8 crumpets are done, place syrup and crumpets on low heat and cook for 12 minutes. Remove from heat and cool for an hour, covered. Remove crumpets to a serving platter, sprinkle generously with ground almonds and serve with whipped cream.

This is a very rich dessert and should be served in cold weather. Good after a fish course.

SERVES 8 PERSONS.

TURKISH DOUGHNUTS
Lokma

SYRUP:
> 2 cups sugar
> 1½ cups water
> 1 tablespoon lemon juice

2 cups flour	1 cup cold water
1 tablespoon butter, melted	1 teaspoon cinnamon,
½ teaspoon salt	optional
¼ ounce yeast, 1 envelope	½ pint heavy cream, whipped,
1⅓ cups lukewarm water	optional
2 cups salad oil	

Syrup: Place sugar, water, and lemon juice in a saucepan. Cook over medium heat, stirring constantly until sugar is dissolved. Bring to a boil and simmer for 10 minutes without stirring. Remove from heat and allow to cool.

Sift flour into a bowl. Add butter and salt. Dissolve yeast in 1⅓ cups lukewarm water. Stir until all lumps disappear. Add this to flour slowly, stirring constantly until mixture is smooth. Place bowl in a warm spot, such as on top of pilot light of a gas stove. Leave there until small holes appear on the surface and the mixture rises, about 20 minutes.

Bring oil to boiling point in a saucepan and reduce heat to medium low. Place a cup of cold water near saucepan. Dip a metal measuring teaspoon into the cup of water, then take ½ teaspoon of the dough mixture and drop it into the hot oil quickly. Fill saucepan, but do not crowd it as the small round balls will puff up. Cook a few seconds and with a perforated kitchen spoon remove puffed balls while they are still white in color. Repeat until all dough is used up.

Then start over and again fry the balls in the same oil until golden brown, turning them constantly with a perforated kitchen spoon so that all sides are evenly browned.

Drop one-quarter of the browned balls into syrup and leave about 10 minutes to absorb syrup. Then remove to serving platter. Repeat until all balls have been soaked in the syrup and removed to platter. Pour remaining syrup over balls and allow to cool.

If desired, sprinkle with cinnamon and serve with whipped cream.

SERVES 12 TO 14 PERSONS.

FARINA NUT HELVA
Irmık Helvası

SYRUP:
> 1 cup sugar
> 1 cup water
> 1 cup milk

> ½ cup butter, melted
> 1 cup large grain farina
> ⅛ cup pignolia nuts or
>   blanched almonds

> 1 teaspoon ground cinnamon
> ½ cup heavy cream, whipped,
>   optional

Syrup: Place sugar in a saucepan with water and milk. Boil over medium heat, stirring constantly for 15 minutes. Remove from heat and allow to cool.

Place butter in heavy saucepan, add farina and nuts. Sauté over low heat stirring constantly with a wooden spoon until nuts turn light brown, about 30 minutes. Be very careful not to burn farina.

Pour the milk syrup gradually into hot farina, stirring until well mixed. Cover and cook over low heat until all the syrup is absorbed. Remove from heat and remove cover. Place a napkin over saucepan and replace cover. Let stand covered ½ hour in a warm place. Stir well and empty onto a serving platter making a mound. Sprinkle the top with cinnamon. Serve warm or cold with whipped cream, if desired.

SERVES 8 TO 10 PERSONS.

HAREM NAVELS
Kadın Göbeği

SYRUP:
2 cups sugar
1¾ cups water
1 tablespoon lemon juice

7 tablespoons butter	1 tablespoon oil
1¾ cups water	1½ cups vegetable shortening
1½ cups flour	¼ cup ground pistachio nuts
1 teaspoon salt	½ pint heavy cream, whipped
2 whole eggs and 1 egg yolk	

Syrup: Place sugar, water, and the lemon juice in a saucepan. Cook over medium heat, stirring constantly until sugar is dissolved. Bring to a boil and simmer for 10 minutes without stirring. Remove from heat and allow to cool.

Place butter in a saucepan and melt over medium heat. Add 1¾ cups water and bring to a boil. Reduce heat to low. Add all the flour at once, sprinkle with salt, and continue cooking for 7 minutes, stirring constantly with a wooden spoon. Remove from heat and cool. When thoroughly cooled, add 2 whole eggs and 1 egg yolk, one at a time, beating each into the flour mixture. Then knead well until no lumps remain, about 10 minutes.

Place oil in a small dish for greasing fingers and palms to facilitate the handling of the dough. Take a piece of dough the size of a walnut and shape into a round flat piece about 1½ to 2 inches in diameter. Oil finger and make a hole in the center. Place on wax paper. Repeat until all the dough is used up.

Heat half of the shortening in a frying pan over low heat until lukewarm. Place the navels in the pan and wait until they start to swell, then increase heat to high and fry on each side to light golden.

Do not crowd the frying pan; allow enough space to take care of enlarged dough. When 1 or 2 panfuls are done, add the rest of the shortening. Cool pan after each panful is finished. Place fried navels in cold syrup and leave until next panful is ready. Remove navels from syrup to a serving platter. Allow to cool. Sprinkle with pistachio nuts and serve with whipped cream.

MAKES 30 TO 34 NAVELS.
ALLOW 2 TO 3 PER PERSON.

Who touches honey licks his fingers.

LEMON DESSERT
Limon Tatlısı

SYRUP:
  2½ cups sugar
  2½ cups water

6 eggs	¼ teaspoon salt
10 tablespoons lemon juice	2 cups frying oil
1 cup sifted flour	¼ cup shredded coconut
1 teaspoon baking soda	½ pint heavy cream, whipped

Syrup: Place sugar and water in saucepan. Cook over medium heat, stirring constantly until sugar is dissolved. Bring to a boil and simmer for 10 minutes without stirring. Remove from heat and allow to cool.

Break eggs into a bowl. Whip with wire whisk or electric mixer for 2 minutes. Add lemon juice and whip for 2 minutes more. Add flour, baking soda, salt, and blend well.

Heat oil in frying pan over high heat. Take a tablespoon of the mixture. Hold spoon vertically and empty into the oil. When pan is filled, reduce heat. Fry each piece until light golden on both sides. Remove from pan with a perforated spoon. Drain off excess oil and drop into cold syrup. Continue until all the mixture is used. Remove dessert pieces to a serving platter after they have absorbed enough syrup to make room for others. Pour remaining syrup over platter. Decorate top with shredded coconut. Serve with whipped cream.

MAKES ABOUT 24 PIECES.
ALLOW 2 PIECES PER PERSON.

REVANI

9 eggs	⅓ cup flour
1 cup sugar	1½ cups fine grain farina
Rind 1 lemon, finely grated	7 tablespoons sweet butter,
Pinch salt	melted

SYRUP:
4 cups sugar
5 cups water
2 tablespoons lemon juice

2 tablespoons ground
   pistachio nuts
4 cups strawberries
½ pint heavy cream, whipped

Preheat oven to 350 degrees F.

Separate eggs into 2 bowls. Add 1 cup sugar and lemon rind to egg yolks and beat well 7 or 8 minutes. Set aside.

Add pinch of salt to egg whites. Beat until stiff, about 7 or 8 minutes.

Mix flour well with farina. Add to egg yolks, a little at a time, stirring with a wooden spoon. Fold in egg whites. Stir until all ingredients are blended thoroughly. Add 6 tablespoons melted butter. Stir again to blend in the butter.

Grease, using remaining butter generously, and flour a 10×2 inch round baking pan.

Empty mixture into the pan. Bake for about 1 hour.

Prepare syrup 15 minutes before cake is ready. Place sugar, water, and lemon juice in saucepan. Cook over medium heat, stirring constantly until sugar is dissolved. Bring to a boil and simmer for 10 minutes without stirring.

Remove cake from oven, pour the boiling syrup over, a little at a time, until all syrup is absorbed. Allow to cool for about 2 hours.

Invert cake onto a round platter by placing the platter over the cake pan and quickly turning it upside down. Cover top with pistachio nuts. Slice cake into thin serving portions. Arrange strawberries around cake, or serve them separately. Serve with whipped cream.

This dessert can be prepared a day in advance. In that case keep in baking pan in the refrigerator until serving time.

MAKES ABOUT 20 TO 24 SLICES.
ALLOW 1 SLICE PER PERSON.

SHREDDED PASTRY DESSERT
Tel Kadayif

1 pound shredded pastry, tel kadayıf[1]	1 cup ground walnuts and 1 cup ground almonds
1½ cups butter, melted	
2 cups ground walnut meats or	

SYRUP:

2½ cups sugar	½ pint heavy cream, whipped
2½ cups water	3 cups strawberries
1 tablespoon lemon juice	

Preheat oven to 350 degrees F.

Separate and discard the thick parts of the shredded pastry. Grease an 11×7×1½ inch baking pan with butter. Spread half of the shredded pastry over pan evenly. Cover with the walnuts. Spread on remaining half of pastry. Pour butter over all.

Bake pastry until light golden, about 40 to 45 minutes.

Prepare syrup while pastry is baking: Place sugar, water, and

---

[1] Tel kadayif is very thin pastry resembling shredded wheat, partially cooked and dried. May be obtained from Near Eastern specialty shops. For a list of such shops see the Appendix.

lemon juice in a saucepan. Cook over medium heat, stirring constantly until sugar is dissolved. Bring to a boil and simmer for 10 minutes without stirring. Keep hot.

Remove pastry from oven. Drain off excess butter. Pour hot syrup over hot pastry. Then cover and allow to cool.

When cold transfer onto a serving platter. Cut into squares of desired size.

Serve with whipped cream and strawberries.

SERVES 12 TO 14 PERSONS.

SPONGE COOKIES A LA TURCA
Sünger Tatlısı

SYRUP:
  2 *cups sugar*
  4 *cups water*
  1 *tablespoon lemon juice*

  6 *egg whites*   2 *tablespoons ground*
  4 *egg yolks*   *pistachio nuts*
  ⅔ *cup rice flour*   2 *cups strawberries*
  ⅔ *cup fine grain farina*   ½ *pint heavy cream, whipped*
  2 *tablespoons oil*

Preheat oven to 350 degrees F.

Syrup: Place sugar, water, and lemon juice in a saucepan. Cook over medium heat, stirring occasionally until sugar is dissolved. Bring to a boil and simmer for 5 minutes without stirring. Remove from heat and keep warm.

Whip egg whites until dry and stiff. Add egg yolks and continue to whip until whites and yolks are well blended.

Mix rice flour well with farina. Add to eggs a little at a time and continue to whip until thoroughly blended.

Grease with oil one 16×18 inch or two 9×12 inch baking pans with 1½ to 2 inch high sides. Place 1 heaping teaspoon of the mixture in the pan. Continue to put spoonfuls of mixture half an inch apart, until all is used. Bake until cookies turn light yellow, about 15 minutes. Remove from oven. Release cookies with a spatula, but keep them in the pan. Pour syrup over them. Turn off the heat and replace pans in oven to absorb syrup. Close oven door and leave about an hour.

Remove pans from oven. Arrange cookies on serving platter and sprinkle pistachio nuts on top.

Serve with strawberries and whipped cream.

MAKES ABOUT 24 COOKIES.
ALLOW 2 PER PERSON.

TWISTED TURBAN
Sarığı Burma

1 pound Phyllo pastry* sheets	½ pound sweet butter
2 packages (6 ounce)	
walnuts, finely ground	

SYRUP:

3 cups sugar	1 tablespoon lemon juice
2½ cups water	½ pint heavy cream, whipped

Preheat oven to 350 degrees F. after the turbans have been prepared.

Place 1 sheet of pastry on kitchen table; spread 1 tablespoon walnuts evenly over the sheet. Use rolling pin about 14 inches long and ½ inch in diameter, or an old wooden curtain rod. Place pin at the shorter end of pastry, as in Figure 1. Roll pastry over pin until the end, Figure 2. Push gently from both ends of rolled pastry forming wrinkles, Figure 3. Pull pin out of pastry gently, Figure 4. Twist wrinkled pastry around like a coiled wire, Figure 5. Repeat until all sheets are used. Place each turban on greased baking pan next to one another, Figure 6.

Heat butter carefully in a saucepan. Do not burn. Pour butter over turbans. Bake for 25 to 30 minutes until light golden.

While the turbans are cooking prepare syrup. Place sugar, water, and lemon juice in saucepan. Cook over medium heat, stirring constantly until sugar is dissolved. Bring to a boil and simmer for 20 minutes without stirring. Remove from heat, keep warm, but not boiling, until turbans are ready.

Remove turban pan from oven. Discard excess butter. Pour warm syrup over the turbans. Allow to cool and to absorb syrup, about 2 hours. Transfer to a serving platter. Serve with whipped cream.

This dessert may be prepared 1 day in advance and kept in the refrigerator until 1 hour before serving time.

MAKES ABOUT 25 TO 29 TURBANS.

SERVE 2 PER PERSON.

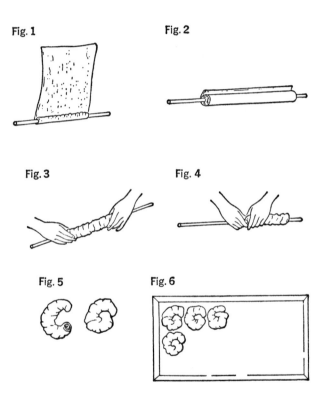

Fig. 1 Fig. 2

Fig. 3 Fig. 4

Fig. 5 Fig. 6

WEDDING COOKIES
Kurabiye

½ pound sweet butter
1 cup sugar
2 cups flour

⅓ pound blanched almonds
1 tablespoon oil

Preheat oven to 350 degrees F.

Cream butter well in a bowl. Add sugar and mix. Add sifted flour. Form into a paste. Spread paste ¼ inch thick on a board. Cut into desired shapes. Press 1 almond on each cooky. Arrange cookies on oil-greased pan. Bake for 10 to 15 minutes.

MAKES ABOUT 20 TO 25 COOKIES,
DEPENDING ON THE SIZE.

YOGURT DESSERT
Yoğurt Tatlısı

1 cup fresh yogurt	*2 cups flour, sifted*
1½ cups confectioners' sugar	*1 tablespoon grated orange*
3 eggs	*or lemon rind*
4 tablespoons butter, melted	*1 teaspoon baking powder*

SYRUP:

2½ cups sugar
3½ cups water
1 tablespoon lemon juice

2 tablespoons pistachio
nuts, ground
1 pint heavy cream, whipped
2 cups strawberries

Preheat oven to 350 degrees F.

Put yogurt in a bowl. Beating with an electric beater, add sugar, eggs, butter, flour, and orange or lemon rind, adding each ingredient a little at a time until a smooth paste is obtained. Add baking powder last and do not overbeat. Pour mixture into a 9×9×2 inch greased baking pan. Bake 40 to 45 minutes.

Prepare syrup 15 minutes before cake is ready. Put sugar, water, and lemon juice in a saucepan. Cook over medium heat, stirring constantly until sugar is dissolved. Bring to a boil and simmer for 10 minutes without stirring. Remove from heat but keep hot.

Cut cake into desired shapes—squares or diamonds. Pour hot syrup over them a little at a time until all syrup is absorbed. Cover with a tray and allow to cool for several hours. This cake can be prepared 1 day in advance and kept in the refrigerator.

Before serving sprinkle with pistachio nuts. Arrange pieces on a serving platter. Serve with whipped cream and strawberries. For preparation of pistachio nuts see Milk Pudding Pistachio Nuts*.

MAKES ABOUT 12 TO 13 PIECES.
ALLOW 1 PIECE PER PERSON.

CREAMED APRICOT BOWL
Kremli Kuru Kayısı

1 pound dried whole apricots	*2 tablespoons lemon juice*
¾ cup sugar	*½ cup blanched finely ground almonds*
1½ cups water	*½ pint heavy cream, whipped*

Soak apricots in cold water overnight. Drain. If soft ones are used, only a few hours of soaking are required.

Place sugar and 1½ cups of water in a saucepan. Bring to a boil, then add apricots. Cook over low heat, uncovered, for about 1 hour, or until apricots are tender and the water is reduced to about ½ cup. Add lemon juice and cook 3 minutes more. Remove from heat. Allow to cool.

Transfer to a glass serving bowl. Smooth the top. Cover with almonds. Spread the cream over the almonds. Serve with Wedding Cookies* or any other desired cookies.

SERVES 8 PERSONS.

STUFFED APRICOTS
Bademli Kuru Kayısı

½ pound dried whole
  apricots
1 cup sugar
¼ cup water
2 tablespoons lemon juice
1 small box (7 ounce)
  vanilla wafers

½ cup chopped blanched
  almonds
½ pint heavy cream, whipped,
  or vanilla ice cream

Soak apricots in cold water overnight. Drain and place in a saucepan with sugar, ¼ cup water, and lemon juice. Cover and cook
over medium heat for 30 minutes, or until sugar becomes heavy
syrup. Remove from heat and allow to cool.

Spread 1 layer of vanilla wafers on a serving platter. Open
apricots without completely separating the two halves. Fill the inside with almonds and close. Place 1 apricot on each wafer. Pour
syrup remaining in the saucepan over the platter.

Serve with whipped cream or ice cream.

ALLOW 2 TO 3 APRICOTS PER PERSON.

MELON DOLMA
Kavun Dolması

1 medium honeydew or
  casaba melon
2 cups seeded and cubed
  mixed fresh fruit in season
  (grapes, cherries,
  strawberries, peaches,
  apricots, pears, plums)

3 tablespoons sugar
1 lime
2 tablespoons rum, sweet
  vermouth, sloe gin, or
  Cointreau
Few fresh mint leaves

Slice through top of the melon. Save top for cover. Remove seeds.
Scoop out melon meat in balls and place in a bowl. Scrape melon
so that inside is skin smooth. Dry the inside with paper.

Mix other fruit with melon balls. Add sugar, juice of half lime, and rum.

Fill melon with this mixture. Cut the other half of the lime into very thin slices. Place over top of filled melon. Decorate with mint leaves. Put top back on.

Wrap melon in aluminum foil and refrigerate 4 to 5 hours before serving.

At serving time, remove foil and cover, so that people may help themselves. Fill a glass bowl with ice and place melon in ice.

Serve with your favorite cookies.

SERVES 6 PERSONS.

PEACHES EREN
Fırında Şeftalı

1 tablespoon butter	*1 cup sugar*
10 large ripe peaches	*½ cup sweet vermouth*
40 whole cloves	*½ pint heavy cream, whipped*

Preheat oven to 350 degrees F.

Grease a large baking pan with butter.

Wash peaches and cut carefully into halves. Remove stones. Place peach halves, skin downward, on the baking pan. Insert 2 cloves in the middle of each half and sprinkle with sugar. Place pan in oven. After the first ½ hour pour vermouth over the peaches. Baste occasionally with juice in the pan. Bake until peaches are tender and the sugar is almost carmelized, about 1½ hours.

Arrange peaches on a serving platter. Pour juice in pan over peaches. Allow to cool.

Serve with whipped cream.

SERVES 8 PERSONS.

PUMPKIN DESSERT
Bal Kabağı Tatlısı

8 pound pumpkin	6 ounces walnuts, ground
2 cups sugar	½ pint heavy cream, whipped
1 cup water	

Pare pumpkin and cut into 1 inch slices. Place in saucepan and sprinkle sugar between layers. Add 1 cup water, cover, and cook over medium heat until tender and all the water is absorbed, about 2 hours. Stir occasionally. Remove from heat, mash, and transfer to a serving platter. Smooth the top and allow to cool. Best results are achieved if refrigerated overnight.

Before serving, spread walnuts over the pumpkin and cover with whipped cream.

SERVES 8 PERSONS.

QUINCE COMPOTE
Ayva Kompostosu

2 cups water	¾ cup sugar
3 large round quinces	½ pint heavy cream, whipped
12 whole cloves	

Place 2 cups of water in a shallow saucepan large enough to hold the halved quinces in 1 layer.

Wash quinces. Cut into halves beginning from stem end. Peel and scoop out core and seeds, making a hollow heart. Tie seeds in a piece of cheesecloth and place in saucepan. Insert 2 cloves into the heart of each half quince. Place halves shallow side up in saucepan.

Add sugar and place saucepan over medium heat. When sugar melts, cover saucepan, decrease heat to very low, and cook until quinces are soft and have turned pink, about 1 hour.

Remove from heat. Take off cover and allow to cool. Place each half in an individual serving bowl and add a little of the juice. Serve with whipped cream.

SERVES 6 PERSONS.

QUINCE MARMALADE
Ayva Marmaladı

4 medium quinces, coarsely grated	5 cups sugar
5 cups water	2 tablespoons lemon juice

Clean the cotton-like dust from the quinces, rubbing by hand, then wash them. Do not peel the skin. Grate coarsely into a bowl.

Bring 5 cups of water to a boil in a saucepan. Add grated quince and boil 10 minutes. Add sugar, stirring constantly until it dissolves. Let marmalade simmer over medium heat uncovered, for about 40 minutes, or until it turns light pinkish in color. Take a little of the juice and drop a few drops with a spoon onto a dish. If the last drop is firm, the marmalade is ready.

Add lemon juice and boil once more. Remove from heat and allow to cool. Pour into jars up to the top, cover tightly, and refrigerate.

MAKES 6 TO 7 CUPS.

ROSE JAM
Gül Reçeli

Enough rose petals to fill a 2 quart saucepan, use old-fashioned pink roses	3 cups sugar
4 cups cold water	2 tablespoons lemon juice

Separate rose petals from the center of the flower and snip off the pointed ends. Wash and place petals in a 4 quart saucepan. Add

4 cups of cold water. Cover and cook on medium heat until petals turn a whitish color, about 15 minutes.

Add sugar and cook uncovered over medium heat until syrup is thick, stirring occasionally. Add lemon juice and let syrup come to a boil. Remove from heat. Empty into an enamel bowl and allow to cool. Later, for future use, pour into small jars up to the top, cover tightly, and refrigerate.

This is a delicious sauce to serve over vanilla ice cream or on toasted buttered cinnamon bread or muffins, with tea or coffee.

If you do not wish to make your own Rose Jam it may be purchased in 1 pound jars from Mediterranean or Near Eastern specialty stores (see Appendix).

MAKES 3 TO 4 CUPS.

12. Turkish Coffee

The English word coffee is derived from the Turkish word Kahve. The coffee tree is a native of Ethiopia and Arabia and even today the best coffee in the world is the Mocha Yemen Arabia. The beverage was introduced into Turkey by the Arabs in the southern extremities of the domain. The tiryakis (addicts) of old only drank Yemen coffee. It was freshly roasted and ground in small amounts, when needed, so as to preserve its flavor. Yemen coffee was imbibed plain, sugar was never added, so as to savor fully its rich and aromatic fragrance.

Coffee was introduced into Europe in the latter half of the sixteenth century by the Ottomans. From Istanbul to Austria and from Vienna to Paris the addiction extended to England.

Coffeehouses, like the discotheques of today, became the meeting place of the avant-garde where Milton and Swift, in their younger years, matured their talents.

The coffeehouse continues to be the meeting place of the traditionalist throughout the Eastern Mediterranean. In the small towns, the coffeehouse spills over to the town square and the singsong of the waiters' *"şekerli bir," "sade iki"* rises above the din of the traffic, as they pass their orders to the cook indoors. *Şekerli* means with sugar, *sade* is plain, and *orta* means medium sweet.

In spite of the advent of the martini, coffee persists as the symbol of friendly exchange. When one stops to call on friends and acquaintances, for business or pleasure, one is always offered a cup of coffee. Serious conversation does not begin before coffee starts the flow of words. And the Turks say that a cup of coffee can seal the bonds of a long friendship.

TURKISH COFFEE

1 demitasse cold water
1 teaspoon pulverized Turkish coffee
1 teaspoon sugar (standard)

Turkish coffee is cooked in a cylindrical pot with a long handle called *jezve**, which is sold in most department stores and shops specializing in Eastern Mediterranean foods (see Appendix). Pulverized coffee can also be obtained from these special food shops. Many shops will also pulverize coffee if the customer requests Turkish coffee.

Place cold water in the *jezve*. Add coffee, sugar, and stir well. Place over low heat and cook to a rising boil, but do not boil. Remove from heat immediately, stir only once. Pour off froth into demitasse. Place back over heat, bring to boil again. Remove immediately, stir once more, and fill the cup.

This is for 1 demitasse. The *jezve* comes in varying sizes. The 4 cup size is preferable. It can be used for 1, 2, 3, or 4 cups, multiplying the ingredients according to the number of cups.

The sugar content of the Turkish coffee may vary according to taste. One teaspoon of sugar is the standard measurement, but it can be just as good with ½ teaspoon or ¼ teaspoon of sugar, or with no sugar at all.

13. Yogurt and Buttermilk

A LAKEFUL OF YOGURT

Yogurt is an indispensable element in the Turkish cuisine. It serves an innumerable variety of purposes. Often served as a sauce, it is a bedtime soporific and many a time it soothes an over-indulged stomach.

It was in Bolu, midway between Ankara and Istanbul, that yogurt's services to the Turkish palate were perfected.

In the days of the Ottoman Empire the chimneys of the Topkapi Palace kitchens were kept smoking continuously by the chefs from Bolu, from whence the best cooks of Turkey hail to this day.

Bolu is a delightful mountain town with a lovely blue lake. One day, Nasrettin Hoca was observed sitting by the lake with a cup of yogurt in his hand. He took a spoonful, put it in the lake, and stirred it the way milk is stirred in order to make yogurt. He was an odd man—foolish and wise at the same time. People were used to his odd behavior and passed him by, not paying much attention to his antics, which he himself forgot as soon as he was done with them. But in this instance, day after day he continued to sit by the lake, stirring its placid waters with his spoonfuls of yogurt. Finally, they asked him what he was doing.

"I am trying to make yogurt," he said.

"Is that possible?" they asked, laughing.

"I know. I know," he answered. "But suppose once in a million it becomes possible. . . . We will have a lakeful of yogurt."

YOGURT

1 quart milk
2 tablespoons yogurt

In a saucepan bring milk to a boil over medium heat. Simmer for
10 to 15 minutes. Set aside until lukewarm. Test by putting your
little finger into the milk. If your finger can stand the heat it
means it is ready.

Pour ½ cup of the milk into a bowl. Mix with 2 tablespoons
commercially prepared yogurt. (Once you have made this recipe,
you may use your own yogurt.) Stir this into milk saucepan. Mix
well. Pour into 1 large bowl or into small bowls. Place bowl on a
tray. Cover top of bowl with wax paper. Wrap the bowl with a thick
towel or blanket piece. Place in a warm spot such as over pilot light
of a gas stove. Do not move until firm. Takes 4 to 6 hours.
When firm, remove wrappings. Allow to cool. Refrigerate.

MAKES 1 QUART.

BUTTERMILK

¼ cup Yogurt*
¾ cup ice cold water
Salt to taste

Place yogurt in a glass. Stir into a smooth paste. Add water a
little at a time, stirring constantly. When all water has been used,
add salt and mix well. This is a refreshing hot weather drink. It
can be kept in the refrigerator until serving time. Multiply the
amount according to the number of servings.

MAKES 1 CUP.
SERVES 1 PERSON.

14. *Menus for Traditional Turkish Dishes*

Turquoise* with sesame crackers
Spring Chicken Papillote*
Mixed peas and carrots, Zucchini Rounds*
Dandelion Greens*
Grapefruit and Orange Pudding* served with Wedding Cookies*
Coffee
Drink: Light white wine

Spinach Eggs*
Stuffed Roast Chicken*
Asparagus and Green Beans à la Turca*
Shepherds' Salad*
Harem Navels* with whipped cream
Coffee
Drink: Light white wine

Wedding Soup* with white Toasted Bread Cubes*
Sultan's Delight*
Artichoke à la Turca*
Baklava* with fresh strawberries and whipped cream
Coffee
Drink: Dry red or rosé wine

Red Lentil Soup*
Baked Bass*
Fried Spinach* and boiled baby carrots
Tomato and Cucumber Salad

Twisted Turban*
Coffee
Drink: Dry white wine

Chicken Walnut*
Gardener's Kebab*
Tomato Pilav* and Okra Stew*
Zucchini Yogurt Salad*
Creamed Apricot Bowl*
Cinnamon cookies
Coffee
Drink: Rosé wine

Spinach Boerek* with Yogurt* on the side
Sole Oriental*
Boiled potatoes and carrots
Cabbage Salad*
Shredded Pastry Dessert* plain or with whipped cream
Coffee
Drink: Dry white wine

Chicken Vermicelli*
Mixed meat dolmas: Eggplant*, Green Pepper*, Tomato*, Zucchini*
    with Yogurt Sauce*
Broad Bean Salad*
Pumpkin Dessert*
Coffee
Drink: Rosé wine

Swordfish on Spits*
Tas Kebab
Vegetable Casserole*
Spinach Root Salad*
Yogurt Dessert* with fresh pineapple slices
Coffee
Drink: Rosé wine

Yogurt Beef Soup*
Yanissary Stew*

Tomato Pilav*
Beet Salad*
Milk Pudding Rose Water*
Coffee
Drink: Red wine

Mixed Hors d'Oeuvres
Fried Mussels*
Cheese Boereks*
Rice Dolmas
Plain white cheese slices
Sardines
Black olives
Hearts of romaine lettuce leaves
Chicken Casserole with Vegetables* with white rice
Harem Navels*
Coffee
Drink: Raki

LUNCH MENUS

Chicken Vermicelli Soup*
Summer Vegetable Pot
Tomato and Cucumber Salad*
Milk Pudding Pistachio Nuts*
Coffee
Drink: Ayran*

Zucchini Imam Bayıldı*
Ground Meat Eggs*
Tomato and Onion Salad*
Farina Nut Helva*
Coffee
Drink: Beer

Root Celery à la Turca*
Cabbage in the Pot*
Assorted dill pickles
Creamed Apricot Bowl*

Coffee
Drink: Beer or Ayran*

Eggplant Pilav*
Baked Bass*
Cauliflower Tarator*
Yogurt Dessert* with fresh slices of pineapple
Coffee
Drink: Sparkling white wine

Jerusalem Artichokes*
Macaroni à la Turca*
Romaine Lettuce Salad*
Milk Pudding Almonds* with ice cream on the side
Coffee
Drink: Sparkling white wine

Hittite Soup*
Eggplant Kebab*
Vermicelli Pilav*
Fried Zucchini Aegean* with Yogurt Sauce I*
Melon Dolma*
Coffee
Drink: Light rosé

Green Beans Istanbul*
Lady Meatballs*
Eggplant Salad*
Noah's Pudding*
Coffee
Drink: Beer or sparkling white wine

Fresh Fava Beans* with Yogurt Sauce I*
Short Ribs in Pot*
Cracked Wheat Pilav*
Peaches Eren*
Coffee
Drink: Beer

Farina Soup
Broiled Mackerel* with Onion Sauce*
Shepherds' Salad*
Harem Navels* with whipped cream
Coffee
Drink: Sparkling white wine

Cheese Boerek*
Cultured Root Celery*
Romaine Lettuce Salad*
Tulumba Tatlısı*
Coffee
Drink: Light rosé

15. *Menus Combining Turkish Dishes with Other Foods*

DINNER MENUS

Red Lentil Soup with Toasted Bread Cubes*
Sirloin steak with your favorite sauce
Oven-roasted potatoes, mixed mushrooms, and pearl onions
Watercress salad
Baklava* with orange slices
Coffee

Shrimp cocktail
Talaş Böreği*
Buttered fresh asparagus, Fried Carrots*
Hearts of lettuce with lemon and oil sauce
Baked Alaska
Coffee

Vegetable Soup
Lamb Knuckles with Chick-peas* with Tomato Pilav*
Boiled peas
Mixed dill pickles
Mixed dry fruit compote
Coffee

Tripe Soup*
Chicken tarragon
French-fried potatoes
Mixed carrots and peas
Tomato and Cucumber Salad*
Caramel custard
Coffee

White Pilav* with sautéed shrimp
Cultured Spinach Roots*
Mashed Potato Salad*
Chocolate soufflé
Coffee

Lobster bisque
Pilav Quail*
Fresh green beans, Eggplant Boereks*
Endive salad
Crème brûlée
Coffee

LUNCHEONS

Melon ball cocktails
Onion Eggs*
Romaine lettuce leaves
Apple pie
Iced tea

Chilled grapefruit halves
Chicken salad with a small dish of Turkish Mashed Potato Salad*
Turkish Rice Pudding*
Coffee

Green Beans Istanbul*
Bouillabaisse
Melon Dolma*
Coffee

Tomato Plaki*
Pork chops with applesauce
Fried Cauliflower*
Iced tea

Cheese Boereks* served with clear chicken broth
Lobster salad
Revani*
Iced tea

Chilled tomato juice
Fried Calf's Liver*
Mashed Potato Salad*
Strawberries with cream
Coffee

Glossary

ASMA YAPRAĞI

Grapevine leaves, used in making rice or meat dolmas. Available in jars in Middle Eastern specialty stores.

AŞÜRE

"Noah's Pudding" is the most appropriate English translation of this dessert. It is composed of numerous dry cereals cooked with sugar and topped with several kinds of nuts.

AYRAN

A light summer drink made with diluted yogurt and salt.

AYVA KOMPOSTOSU

Quince compote.

AYVA MARMALADI

Quince marmalade.

BADEM

Almonds.

BAHÇIVAN KEBABI

This is a meat dish cooked with almost all the ingredients grown in a small household garden.

BAKLA

Fava or horse beans.

BAKLAVA

This is the most famous and universally known Turkish dessert made with Phyllo pastry, filled with walnuts, baked and soaked in syrup.

BALIK

Fish.

BAL KABAĞI KIZARTMASI

Fried pumpkin chips for cocktails.

BAL KABAĞI TATLISI

A special Turkish pumpkin dessert.

BAMYA
  Okra.
BEYAZ PEYNİR EZMESİ
  Mashed white cheese used as a dip or spread.
BEYİN
  Brains.
BEZELYE
  Peas.
BÖREK BOEREK
  Dish made with Phyllo pastry either as a main course or appetizer or
  for cocktails with different fillings.
BORANI
  This is meatless spinach stew cooked with onions and tomato paste.
BÜBER
  Pepper.
BULGUR
  Cracked wheat, cooked and served as rice. Can be obtained from Near
  Eastern specialty stores.
BUZLU BADEM
  Iced almonds.

ÇALI FASULYE
  Green string beans.
CEVİZLİ BEYAZ PEYNİR
  Mashed white cheese with walnuts used as a dip or spread.
CHIPURA
  A pompano-like flat fish.
CİĞER
  Liver.
ÇILBIR
  Name of an egg dish cooked with yogurt.
ÇINAKOK
  A kind of small bluefish.
ÇOBAN SALATASI
  Shepherds' salad.

DIL DOMATESLI
  Flounder baked with tomatoes.
DOLMA
  Literally, dolma is a Turkish word meaning stuffed. In cooking, stuffed
  vegetables are called dolmas. If vegetables are stuffed with rice and
  cooked with oil they are served cold. But if they are stuffed with meat
  they are served hot with different sauces.

DOMATES
Tomatoes.

DOMATESLI PATLICAN KIZARTMASI
Fried eggplants served with tomato sauce.

DÜĞÜN ÇORBASI
Wedding soup, one of the outstanding soups of the Turkish cuisine.

ENGİNAR
Artichoke.

ETLİ KAPUSKA
The name of a special cabbage dish cooked with meat.

FASULYE EZMESİ
Mashed dried kidney bean salad.

FAVA
Mashed dried fava or horse bean salad.

FIRINDA KILIÇ
Baked swordfish.

GÜL REÇELİ
Rose jam, served as a sauce.

GÜL VEYA PORTAKAL ÇİÇEĞİ SUYU
Rose water or orange flower water, available at Mediterranean specialty stores.

GÜVEÇ
Vegetables baked together with meat or poultry in an earthenware casserole and served hot. The vegetables are also cooked without meat or poultry and are served as a side dish.

HAMSİ
Brislings or some similar fish that come from the Black Sea.

HANIM PARMAĞI
Lady's finger, a popular cocktail dish.

HAVUÇ PLAKİSİ
Carrots cooked with olive oil and served cold.

HELVA
Desserts made with farina or flour mixed with nuts and served with cinnamon if desired. This name is also applied to a sweet cooked with sesame seeds and sold in the United States in many supermarkets as "Halvah."

HİNDİ
Turkey, from the family of poultry. The Turks call it the bird from India. The English call it turkey because they thought it came from the East and at that time the East was Ottoman Turkey.

HİNDİBAĞ
Dandelion.
HIYAR
Cucumber.
HÜNKÂR BEĞENDİ
Hünkâr is another name for the Turkish sultan. Hünkâr Beğendi means the sultan liked it. Indeed this is a sophisticated dish of puréed eggplant served with chicken or meat.

İÇ PİLAV
Long grain rice cooked with chicken livers, nuts, currants, and dill.
İMAM BAYILDI
Literally means "The priest (imam) fainted." This is a renowned dish of eggplant, tomatoes, and onions cooked in olive oil and served cold. The story is told of an imam who was a gourmet but tight with his money. His wife, who was very fond of him and paid no attention to his weakness, tried to concoct new dishes to please him. One day she came up with the Imam Bayıldı. After several relished helpings of the new dish, the imam let himself go and fainted. To this day people do not know whether he passed out because he had overeaten, or because he regretted the waste of so much olive oil.
İRMİK
Farina.
ISGARA
Broil.
İSLİM KEBABI
A very tasty dish of meat and eggplant baked in a covered casserole.
ISPANAK
Spinach.
ISPANAK KAVURMASI
Fried spinach leaves served as a side dish.
ISPANAK KÖKÜ
Spinach roots.
İŞKEMBECİ
A small restaurant where only tripe soup and other variety meat dishes are served.
IŞKEMBE ÇORBASI
Tripe soup. A bowl of ışkembe çorbası is an excellent antidote after excessive indulgence.
İZMİR
Name of the largest city on the Aegean coast (ancient Smyrna), home of Smyrna figs and Sultana raisins.

JEZVE
A copper or brass cylindrical pot with a long handle for cooking Turkish coffee.

KABAK
Zucchini.

KADIN BUDU
Literally means lady's thigh. This is a dish of ground meat and rice first formed into oval patties, then dipped into beaten eggs and fried.

KADIN GÖBEĞİ
Literally means lady's navel. It is a rich flour dessert soaked in syrup.

KAĞIT KEBABI
Cubed meat cooked in wax paper.

KAHVE
Turkish word for coffee.

KALKAN
Turbot.

KALYE
It is the name of a special dish prepared with zucchini, onions, tomatoes cooked with butter.

KARNIYARIK
Literally means slashed belly. It is the name of an eggplant dish cooked with ground meat.

KAŞER
A hard Turkish cheese resembling Cheddar.

KAVUN DOLMASI
Melon stuffed with variety of fruits. A good summer dessert.

KEBAB
This word means cooked meat. There are various kinds of kebabs, such as shish kebab broiled over charcoal fire, gardener's kebab cooked in a pot, or kağit kebab wrapped in wax paper and baked in an oven.

KEREVİZ
Celery.

KEREVİZ KÖKÜ
Root celery.

KILIÇ ŞİŞTE
Swordfish broiled over charcoal fire on spits.

KIŞ TÜRLÜSÜ
A winter dish cooked with meat, carrots, celery, potatoes, and leeks.

KIYMA
Ground meat.

KIYMALI BÖREK
Phyllo pastry filled with ground meat and baked.

KIYMALI PİDE
A kind of breadlike muffin prepared with ground meat—makes a delicious dish.

KÖFTE
Anything shaped into meatballs or patties, fried or broiled.

KOKTEYL BÖREĞİ
Phyllo pastry sticks, especially prepared for cocktails.

KURABİYE
Cooky.

KURU FASULYE
Dry beans.

KURU KÖFTE
Fried meatballs.

KUZU BUDU ROSTOSU
Roast leg of lamb.

KUZU KAPAMA
The name of a lamb dish cooked with romaine and Boston lettuce leaves.

KUZU PİRZOLAS
Lamb chops.

LAHANA KAPAMASI
The name of a special cabbage dish cooked with rice and ground meat.

LAKERDA
Canned, salted bonito, makes good hors d'oeuvres on a piece of toast with lemon juice and dill. Available in Near Eastern specialty stores.

LAPA
A specially prepared rice dish.

LEVREK
A kind of bass—one of the superior Bosporus fish.

LİMON TATLISI
A flour dessert with lemon flavoring, easy to make.

LOKMA
A flour dessert fried in oil and soaked in syrup. Lokma literally means one bite. Traditionally it is cooked on the fortieth day after a person's death and distributed to the poor.

LÜFER
Bluefish.

MUHALLEBİ
Milk pudding—there are different kinds, cooked with different flavorings.

MAKARNA
Macaroni.
MARUL SALATASI
Romaine lettuce salad.
MERCİMEK ÇORBASI
Lentil soup.
MEZE
Hors d'oeuvres.
MİDYE PİLAVI
Pilav cooked with mussels.
MİDYE PLAKİSİ
Mussels cooked with olive oil and served cold.
MORİNA
Cod (In Turkey palamut is used for recipes in this book calling for cod; only the caviar from the morina is eaten.)
MÜCVER
Is the name of a special dish of fried zucchini patties, prepared with eggs, flour, parsley, dill, cheese, and scallions. Makes a good side dish.
MUSAKKA
An eggplant dish cooked with ground meat. Also may be made with zucchini or potatoes.

NOHUT EZMESİ
Mashed chick-peas prepared with sesame seed oil, lemon juice, and garlic. The sesame seed oil may be obtained from specialty stores.
NOHUTLU TAVUK
Chicken cooked with tomatoes and chick-peas.

OTURTMA
Is the name of an eggplant dish cooked with meat.

PAÇA
Literally means knuckles. It is the name of a special dish prepared with knuckles and gelatin, set in a mold, and served cold.
PALAMUT
Bonito.
PANCAR SALATASI
Beet salad.
PASTIRMA
Dried beef covered with garlic paste, cut into very thin slices. Available in specialty stores.
PATATES EZMESİ
Mashed potato salad.

PATLICAN
  Eggplant.

PHYLLO PASTRY
  The Turkish name for it is yufka. These are paper-thin sheets of pastry used for making boereks with different fillings. Can be used as appetizers, with cocktails, luncheon dish, or dinner course. Yufka is also used for making several kinds of famous Turkish desserts. Available fresh or frozen in specialty stores.

PİLAV
  A method of cooking long grain rice in chicken or beef broth with butter. Rice was brought into the Middle East from China by the Turks. Hence the Turkish cuisine is distinguished by the great variety in the usage of rice. There are at least fifteen different kinds of pilav, several of which are included in this book. Rice and rice flour are also used in puddings and soups.

PIRASA
  Leeks.

PİRİNÇ
  Rice.

PİYAZ
  Dried white kidney bean salad. Also an onion sauce with parsley used over broiled fish.

PLAKİ
  A method of cooking vegetables or fish with onions, tomatoes, and olive oil and served cold.

PORTAKAL PELTESİ
  Orange pudding.

PUF BÖREĞİ
  A special boerek made with flour and fried in oil.

RAKI
  Turkey's national drink. It is distilled from grapes and flavored with aniseed. When diluted with ice or water it turns cloudy and white. The Turks call it "lion's milk" for when imbibed too much it makes a person "roar like a lion."

REVANİ
  A delectable dessert made with farina, flour, and eggs, soaked in syrup.

SALÇA
  Sauce.

SARIĞI BURMA
  A rich, but flaky dessert with nut filling made from Phyllo pastry.

ŞEHRİYELİ PİLAV
Pilav cooked with vermicelli.

ŞEHRİYELİ TAVUK SUYU
Chicken broth with vermicelli.

SİGARA BÖREĞİ
Boereks shaped like cigarettes.

ŞİŞ KÖFTE
Ground meat broiled over charcoal fire on spits.

SOM BALIĞI
Salmon.

SOVANLI YAHNİ
Beef cooked with onions, tomatoes and vinegar.

SU BÖREĞİ
A boerek specialty made with flour and cheese or ground meat filling, the dough is boiled before baking; crisp on the outside, soft in the inside.

SÜTLAÇ
Rice pudding.

TAHİN OIL
Ground sesame seed oil.

TALAŞ BÖREĞİ
A boerek specialty with cubed meat filling served at formal dinners.

TARAMA
Carp roe, light orange in color with tiny eggs. When mixed according to the recipe given it makes an excellent dip.

TARATOR
A sauce made with ground walnuts or pignolia nuts, oil, and vinegar.

TARATORLU BARBUNYE
Boiled pinto beans served with tarator sauce.

TARHANA
An old fashioned soup mix with an unusual flavor. It was made in the villages, is now produced commercially, and is available in specialty stores.

TAS KEBAB
Cubed meat first cooked alone, then covered with a bowl and cooked with rice and spices.

TATAR BÖREĞİ
Small canoe-shaped boereks with ground meat filling, served with yogurt sauce.

TAVULKU BEĞENDİ
Chicken served with eggplant purée.

TAVUKLU GÜVEÇ
Chicken baked with vegetables.
TEKİR
A kind of small red mullet.
TEL KADAYİF
Very thin pastry resembling shredded wheat, partially cooked and dried.
Available in Near Eastern specialty shops.
TERBİYE
A sauce made with lemon juice, eggs, and broth.
TEREYAĞLI TAZE FASULYE
Green beans cooked with butter and tomatoes and served as a side dish.
TORİK
Large bonito.
TULUMBA TATLISI
A rich flour dessert with almond flavoring.
TÜRLÜ
A variety of vegetables stewed with meat or poultry.

USKUMRU
Mackerel—in the late fall the uskumru travels down the Bosporus and
offers fish gourmets a tasty dish when freshly broiled and garnished
with piyaz sauce. When it returns in the spring it is skinny and it is
caught and dried in the sun. Then it is broiled over charcoal fire and
pounded soft; soaked in vinegar, garnished with dill, it makes an excellent appetizer.
USKUMRU ISGARA
Broiled mackerel.

WHITE CHEESE
This is Turkey's national cheese. It is called "beyaz peynir" in Turkish
and, literally translated, means "white cheese." It is also widely preva-
lent in the Balkans. In the United States it is often referred to as feta.
The Turks use it for breakfast. It is also used as an appetizer with raki.
It is a salted light cheese made of sheep's or cow's milk. Keep it in
water for desalting and softening.
WHOLE WHEAT
It is a special wheat, used for making Noah's Pudding. May be obtained
from Near Eastern specialty shops.

YAHNİ
A method of stewing meat or poultry with onions and tomatoes and
butter.

YALANCI DOLMA

Grapevine leaves stuffed with rice, cooked with olive oil, and served cold.

YAZ TÜRLÜSÜ

A light meat dish cooked with a variety of summer vegetables.

YERELMASI SALATASI

Jerusalem artichoke salad.

YEŞİL BÜBERLİ SALÇA

A salad sauce with green peppers.

YOĞURT

The Turks consider yogurt an inseparable part of their national tradition. It has been known to them as far back in their history as it is remembered. They are still critical of the German scientist who, in the nineteenth century, while visiting Bulgaria, discovered the bacillus that turned milk into yogurt and called it *Lactobacillus bulgaricus.* Its usage is infinite in a Turkish home. It can be eaten plain. It can serve as a basic ingredient for a dessert, or as a sauce, or even as an antidote to food poisoning.

YOĞURT TATLISI

A dessert made from farina and yogurt soaked in syrup. Delicious with cream and berries in season.

YUFKA

Turkish name for Phyllo pastry.

YUMURTA

Eggs.

ZEYBEK

The Turkish equivalent for Robin Hood, often used with reference to the brave people on the Aegean coast of Turkey. They have a dance of their own which is also called zeybek.

ZEYTİNYAĞLI

Vegetables cooked with olive oil and served cold. In the Turkish cuisine dishes cooked with olive oil are served cold.

ZEYTİNYAĞLI DOLMA

This includes a variety of dolmas cooked with rice and olive oil, such as cabbage, green peppers, eggplant, tomato, grapevine leaves, etc.

ZEYTİNYAĞLI ENGİNAR

Artichokes cooked with olive oil.

ZEYTİNYAĞLI KEREVİZ

Root celery cooked with olive oil.

ZEYTİNYAĞLI PIRASA

Leeks cooked with olive oil.

ZEYTİNYAĞLI YERELMASSI

Jerusalem artichokes cooked with olive oil.

SHOPPERS' GUIDE
for
TURKISH FOOD PRODUCTS

Turkish American Trading and Development Corporation is the main importing and distributing firm in the United States for Turkish foods.
Wholesale address   Avni Kaya Erdil
26 Broadway
New York, N.Y. 10004

Retail address   16A Fulton Street
New York, N.Y. 10038

Austin-Nichols and Company are the sole importers of Turkish *raki* for the United States.
Address   Fifty-eighth Street and Fifty-fifth Drive
Maspeth, N.Y. 11378

ALABAMA

Bruno's Food Store
1218 Sixth Avenue South
Birmingham, Ala. 35205

Niarhos Importing Co.
201 South Eighteenth Street
Birmingham, Ala. 35233

Lignos Grocery
160 Government Street
Mobile, Ala. 36602

CALIFORNIA

Sunnyland Bulghur Company
1435 Gearhart Street
Fresno, Calif. 93707

Bezjian's Grocery
4725 Santa Monica Boulevard
Los Angeles, Calif. 90029

Cek Importing Company
2771 West Pico Boulevard
Los Angeles, Calif. 90006

The Turkish Bazaar
6312 West Ninety-second Street
Los Angeles, Calif. 90045

The Istanbul Pastries
247 Third Street
San Francisco, Calif. 94103

Persian Imports
347 Grant Avenue
San Francisco, Calif. 94108

COLORADO

Economy Grocery
1864 Curtis Street
Denver, Colo. 80202

CONNECTICUT

Vittoria Importing Company
35 Lafayette Street
New Britain, Conn. 06051

Dimyan's Market
116 Elm Street
Danbury, Conn. 06810

New York Delicatessen
1207 Chapel Street
New Haven, Conn. 06511

DISTRICT OF COLUMBIA

Aloupis Company
916 Ninth Street N.W.
Washington, D.C. 20001

Skenderis Greek Imports
1612 Twentieth Street N.W.
Washington, D.C. 20009

FLORIDA

Arabic Grocery and Bakery
1615 S.W. Eighth Street
Miami, Fla. 33135

Near East Bakery
878 S.W. Eighth Street
Miami, Fla. 33130

Angel's Market
455 Athens Street
Tarpon Springs, Fla. 33589

GEORGIA

George's Delicatessen
1041 North Highland Avenue N.E.
Atlanta, Ga. 30306

Roxy Delicatessen
1011 Peachtree Street N.E.
Atlanta, Ga. 30309

ILLINOIS

Columbus Food Market
5532–34 West Harrison Street
Chicago, Ill. 60644

New Deal Grocery
2604 West Lawrence
Chicago, Ill. 60625

KENTUCKY

Arimes Market
216 Walton Avenue
Lexington, Ky. 40502

A. Thomas Wholesale Meat Company
309 East Jefferson Street
Louisville, Ky. 40202

LOUISIANA

Central Grocery Company
923 Decatur Street
New Orleans, La. 70116

MAINE

T. Sisters Market
75 Alfred Street
Biddeford, Maine 04005

Model Food Importers & Distributors
89–95 Middle Street
Portland, Maine 04111

Boucouralas Brothers
Common and Middle Streets
Saco, Maine 04072

MARYLAND

Ernest's Grocery, Inc.
501 South Newkirk Street
Baltimore, Md. 21224

Imported Foods, Inc.
409 West Lexington Street
Baltimore, Md. 21201

MASSACHUSETTS

Demoulas Super Markets
321 Main Street
Andover, Mass. 01810

Syrian Grocery Importing Co.
270 Shawmut Avenue
Boston, Mass. 02118

A & A Food Market, Inc.
14 Central Square
Cambridge, Mass. 02139

Demoulas Super Market
288 Chelmsford Street
Chelmsford, Mass. 01824

Demoulas Super Market
25 Lowell Street
Haverhill, Mass. 01831

Demoulas Super Market
700 Essex Street
Lawrence, Mass. 01824

Demoulas Super Market
80 Dummer Street
Lowell, Mass. 01854

Demoulas Super Market
1200 Bridge Street
Lowell, Mass. 01850

Giavis Market, Inc.
351 Market Street
Lowell, Mass. 01854

Demoulas Super Market
164 Haverhill Street
Methuen, Mass. 01844

Demoulas Super Market
350 Winthrop Avenue
North Andover, Mass. 01845

Demoulas Super Market
700 Boston Road
Pinehurst, Mass. 01866

Demoulas Super Market
10 Main Street
Tewksbury, Mass. 01876

Demoulas Super Market
240 Main Street
Wilmington, Mass. 01887

Olympia Market
617 Main Street
Worcester, Mass. 01608

MICHIGAN

Delmar & Company
501–11 Monroe Avenue
Detroit, Mich. 48226

Stemma Confectionery
514 Monroe Avenue
Detroit, Mich. 48226

MONTANA

Hepperles' Store
Plevna, Mont. 59344

NEBRASKA

Leon's Food Mart
Winthrop Road and Ryons
Lincoln, Nebr. 68502

NEW HAMPSHIRE

O. K. Fairbanks Super Market
84 Marlboro Street
Keene, N.H. 03431

Joseph Brothers Market
196 Lake Avenue
Manchester, N.H. 03103

Youngsville Super Market
1536 Candia Road
Manchester, N.H. 03103

Liamos Market
176 West Pearl Street
Nashua, N.H. 03060

Demoulas Super Markets, Inc.
Route 28
Salem, N.H. 03079

NEW JERSEY

Andrew's Delicatessen
305 Sewell Avenue
Asbury Park, N.J. 07712

Crest Delicatessen, Ltd.
607 Central Avenue
East Orange, N.J. 07018

Central Food Stores, Inc.
63 Main Street
Hackensack, N.J. 07601

Gasos Delicatessen
378 Summit Avenue
Jersey City, N.J. 07306

Livingston Plaza Shop-Rite
10 Plaza Place
Livingston, N.J. 07039

South Livingston Shop-Rite
483 South Livingston Avenue
Livingston, N.J. 07039

John's Delicatessen
9 Washington Street
Morristown, N.J. 07960

Tom's Ravioli Company
791 South Orange Avenue
Newark, N.J. 07106

Scotland Road Shop-Rite
321 Scotland Road
Orange, N.J. 07050

Village Shop-Rite
9 South Orange Avenue
South Orange, N.J. 07079

Village Super Market, Inc.
9 South Orange Avenue
South Orange, N.J. 07079

Michael Nafash & Sons
2717 Bergenline Avenue
Union City, N.J. 07087

NEW YORK

H. C. Bohack Company
29–10 Broadway
Astoria, N.Y. 11102

H. C. Bohack Company
47–09 Broadway
Astoria, N.Y. 11103

Kismet Oriental Pastries Company
27–02 Twenty-third Avenue
Astoria, N.Y. 11102

Melkon's
30–74 Thirty-first Street
Astoria, N.Y. 11102

Constantine's Delicatessen
205–10 Forty-eighth Avenue
Bayside, N.Y. 11364

H. C. Bohack Company
156 Henry Street
Brooklyn, N.Y. 11201

H. C. Bohack Company
252 Court Street (Kane)
Brooklyn, N.Y. 11231

H. C. Bohack Company
9119 Third Avenue
Brooklyn, N.Y. 11228

Malko Brothers-Cassatly Company, Inc.
197–99 Atlantic Avenue
Brooklyn, N.Y. 11201

Sahadi Importing Company, Inc.
187 Atlantic Avenue
Brooklyn, N.Y. 11201

Sammy's Imported & Domestic Foods
1348–54 Hertel Avenue
Buffalo, N.Y. 14216

Emir Grocery
135–18 Roosevelt Avenue
Flushing, N.Y. 11354

Italian American Delicatessen
52 West Merrick Road
Freeport, N.Y. 11520

Dairy Fair Delicatessen
31 Station Plaza
Hempstead, N.Y. 11560

K & S Quality Meat Market
79–17 Thirty-seventh Avenue
Jackson Heights, N.Y. 11372

H. C. Bohack Company
84–60 Parsons Boulevard
Jamaica, N.Y. 11432

Alexandroff, Inc.
513 Ninth Avenue
New York, N.Y. 10018

House of Yemen East
370 Third Avenue
New York, N.Y. 10016

K. Kalustyan
123 Lexington Avenue
New York, N.Y. 10016

H. C. Bohack Company
7 Madison Street
New York, N.Y. 10038

H. C. Bohack Company
550 Second Avenue
New York, N.Y. 10016

Karnig Tashjian
380 Third Avenue
New York, N.Y. 10016

Kassos Brothers
570 Ninth Avenue
New York, N.Y. 10036

R. H. Macy and Co.
151 34th Street
Herald Square
New York, N.Y. 10001

Paprikas Weiss Importer
1546 Second Avenue
New York, N.Y. 10028

Poseidon Confectionery
629 Ninth Avenue
New York, N.Y. 10036

Baruirs' Oriental Grocery
40–07 Queens Boulevard
Sunnyside, N.Y. 11104

Thanos Imported Groceries
424 Pearl Street
Syracuse, N.Y. 13203

NORTH CAROLINA

East Trade Grocery
402 East Trade Street
Charlotte, N.C. 28202

Galanides-Raleigh, Inc.
Wicker Drive and Campbell Street
Raleigh, N.C. 27604

OHIO

Ellis Bakery
577 Grant Street
Akron, Ohio 44311

OKLAHOMA

Royal Coffee and Tea Co.
115 South Robinson
Oklahoma City, Oklahoma 73102

PENNSYLVANIA

European Market
520 Court Place
Pittsburgh, Pa. 15219

Stamoolis Brothers Co.
2020 Pennsylvania Avenue
Pittsburgh, Pa. 15222

RHODE ISLAND

Anthony Lazieh
182 Washington Street
Central Falls, R.I. 02863

SOUTH CAROLINA

Piggly Wiggly
445 Meeting Street
Charleston, S.C. 29403

Mitchell's Grocery
137 North Dargan Street
Florence, S.C. 29501

TENNESSEE

The Cheese Market
503A Clinch Avenue S.W.
Knoxville, Tenn. 37902

Barzizza Brothers Inc.
351 South Front Street
Memphis, Tenn. 38103

TEXAS

L. Paletta's
425 North Santa Rosa
San Antonio, Texas 78207

Kandes Liquor & Imports
1202 North Main
Victoria, Texas 77901

VIRGINIA

Nick's Produce & Importing Company
504 East Marshall Street
Richmond, Virginia 23219

The New Yorker Delicatessen
2602 Williamson Road N.W.
Roanoke, Va. 24012

WASHINGTON

Angelo Merlino & Sons
816 Sixth Avenue South
Seattle, Wash. 98134

WEST VIRGINIA

R. A. Medovic
2201 Market Street
Wheeling, W.Va. 26003

WISCONSIN

Topping & Company
736 North Second Street
Milwaukee, Wis. 53203

Index